Teacher Agency

Also Available from Bloomsbury

Reflective Teaching in Schools, Andrew Pollard
Readings for Reflective Teaching in Schools, edited by Andrew Pollard
Reinventing the Curriculum, edited by Mark Priestley and Gert Biesta

Teacher Agency

An Ecological Approach

By Mark Priestley, Gert Biesta
and Sarah Robinson

Bloomsbury Academic
An imprint of Bloomsbury Publishing Plc

B L O O M S B U R Y
LONDON · OXFORD · NEW YORK · NEW DELHI · SYDNEY

Bloomsbury Academic

An imprint of Bloomsbury Publishing Plc

50 Bedford Square	1385 Broadway
London	New York
WC1B 3DP	NY 10018
UK	USA

www.bloomsbury.com

BLOOMSBURY and the Diana logo are trademarks of Bloomsbury Publishing Plc

First published 2015
Reprinted 2017

British Library Cataloguing-in-Publication Data
A catalogue record for this book is available from the British Library.

ISBN: HB: 978-1-4725-3466-8
ePDF: 978-1-4725-2587-1
ePub: 978-1-4725-3288-6

Library of Congress Cataloging-in-Publication Data
Teacher agency : an ecological approach / by Mark Priestley,
Gert Biesta and Sarah Robinson.
pages cm
Includes bibliographical references and index.
ISBN 978-1-4725-3466-8 (hb : alk. paper) – ISBN 978-1-4725-3288-6 (epub) –
ISBN 978-1-4725-2587-1 (epdf) 1. Curriculum change–Scotland.
2. Curriculum planning–Scotland. 3. Teacher participation in curriculum
planning–Scotland. 4. Teaching, Freedom of–Scotland.
5. Classroom environment–Scotland. I. Priestley, Mark (Mark R.)
II. Robinson, Sarah, 1957- III. Title.
LB2806.15.B476 2015
375'.00609411–dc23
2015015374

Typeset by Deanta Global Publishing Services, Chennai, India
Printed and bound in Great Britain

Contents

Acknowledgements

Our warm thanks go to the six fantastic participating teachers and their colleagues, without whom this research and this book would not have materialized. Their continued enthusiasm made this project a delight from start to finish. We also acknowledge the funding from the Economic and Social Research Council (RES-000-22-420) which made this research possible.

Introduction: Teacher Agency
and Curriculum Change

Curriculum for Excellence is much more than a reform of curriculum and assessment. It is predicated on a model of sustained change which sees schools and teachers as co-creators of the curriculum.

(Donaldson 2010, p. 4)

Introduction

There is an emerging tendency in education policy in the United Kingdom and elsewhere to acknowledge the importance of teachers' agency, that is, of their active contribution to shaping their work and its conditions. For example, Scotland's 'Curriculum for Excellence' – which was published in 2004 and formally implemented in the 2010–11 school year and which is the context within which the research reported in this book is set – explicitly sought to move away from a top–down approach to educational improvement towards one in which teachers play a central and crucial role. Indeed, as the quotation above suggests, teacher agency can even be viewed as an integral and essential part of such reforms. The Curriculum Review Programme Board formulated this intention as follows.

> In the past, national curriculum developments have often been supported by central guidelines, cascade models of staff development and the provision of resources to support the implementation of guidance by teachers. Our approach to change is different. It aims to engage teachers in thinking from first principles about their educational aims and values and their classroom practice. The process is based upon evidence of how change can be brought about successfully – through a climate in which reflective practitioners share and develop ideas. (Scottish Executive 2006, p. 4)

Approaches such as these mark a significant shift in the light of several decades of policies that worked to de-professionalize teachers by taking agency away from them and replacing it with prescriptive curricula and limiting and sometimes oppressive regimes of testing, inspection and bureaucratic forms of accountability (see, for example, Gewirtz 2002; Ball 2003; Biesta 2010; Wilkins 2011). The (re)turn to teacher agency not only gives explicit permission to teachers to exert higher degrees of professional judgement and discretion within the contexts in which they work but also sees their agency as a key dimension of teachers' professionalism (see, for example, Heilbronn 2008; Sugrue and Dyrdal-Solbrekke 2011).

But the (re)turn to teacher agency is not without problems. A key question is whether policy intentions are also followed through in practice, that is, whether teachers are indeed offered more space for professional agency. Offering such space is not only a matter of changing the *structures* within which teachers work – something that to a large extent lies within the remit of politicians and policy makers – but also raises questions about the *cultures* that shape the everyday practices of teachers' work – something which not only depends on those who regulate the context within which teachers do their work, but also depends on teachers' own actions and activities, that is, on how they enact such cultures. In addition to structure and culture, there is also the question of individual and collective *capacity*. This is the question of whether teachers – individually and collectively – are still capable of being active agents of their own work, or whether this capacity has been eroded as a result of structures and cultures that sought to restrain rather than to enable teachers' professional agency.

The chapters in this book are an attempt to shed some theoretical and empirical light on these matters. They are based on research conducted in the 'Teacher Agency and Curriculum Change' project, which ran during 2011 and 2012 at the University of Stirling, Scotland, in partnership with a Scottish Local Authority.[1] The immediate occasion for the research was the implementation of Scotland's new 'Curriculum for Excellence', a policy that aimed to change the structure, content and method of Scottish education. 'Curriculum for Excellence' can be seen as an example of modern curricular reform in which teachers are explicitly positioned as agents of change (see Priestley and Biesta 2013). This made it a particularly suitable context for the study of teacher agency. Simply put, the project focused on the ways in which and the extent to which experienced teachers achieve agency in their day-to-day working contexts against the background of the introduction of the new curriculum and on factors that promote or inhibit such agency.

We start this introductory chapter with some observations about what this book is *not* about, in order to delineate the question of teacher agency from other discussions and approaches that focus on the role and position of the teacher. We then provide some information about 'Curriculum for Excellence', the context within which the research was conducted. After this, we provide a description of the design of the research and its main features. We conclude with an overview of the chapters in the book and a preview of our main conclusions.

The particular approach to teacher agency we are offering in this book is termed an *ecological* approach (see also Biesta and Tedder 2007). The main distinctive feature of this approach is that we do not see agency as a capacity of individuals, that is, as something individuals can claim to 'have' or 'possess', but rather see it as something individuals and groups can manage to *achieve* – or not, of course. Agency is therefore to be understood as resulting from the *interplay* of individuals' capacities and environment conditions. This makes it important not just to look at individuals and what they are able or not able to do but also at the cultures, structures and relationships that shape the particular 'ecologies' within which teachers work. It is the *interaction* between capacities and conditions that counts in making sense of teacher agency. This also means that any attempt to enhance teacher agency should not just focus on the capacities of individuals – for example, through programmes of professional learning and development – but should at the very same time pay attention to the factors and dimensions that shape the ecologies of teachers' work.

Focusing on the teacher: What this book is *not* about

Our exploration of teacher agency does not encompass everything there is to say about the role and position of the teacher or everything that has been said or currently is being said. It is therefore also important to make clear what this book is *not* about. Our interest in teacher agency should, for example, be distinguished from recent discourses in which it is argued, in a number of different ways, that teachers 'matter' (e.g. OECD 2005; McKinsey & Co. 2007; Donaldson 2010).

One influential line here, which has its background in school effectiveness and improvement research and which has recently become quite popular among politicians and policy makers, is the belief that the teacher is the most important 'factor' in the educational process (see, for example, Hay McBer 2000; OECD 2005; Sammons and Bakkum 2012 and, for the European policy dimension, Stéger 2014). Even if the teacher is the most important factor, it should not be forgotten, of course, that such a claim is relative to a range of other factors (and a commonly used figure is that only 10–20 per cent of the variance in measured student achievement can be attributed to teachers and teaching; Strauss 2013). But there are a number of reasons why this particular take on the idea that teachers matter should not be conflated with the kind of teacher agency we are interested in.

One reason has to do with the fact that in this way of thinking the teacher is indeed seen as a 'factor' and not as a thinking, judging and acting professional. To think of the teacher as a 'factor' also reveals an underlying conception of education as a 'quasi-causal' process, (on this see Biesta 2015), where teaching is seen as 'input' and student performance as 'output'; rather than that teaching is understood as a complex interactive process of communication, interpretation and joint meaning making where teacher judgement and decision-making are crucial. In addition to this, the suggestion of the teacher as the most important 'factor' in the educational process tends to focus on a rather limited range of educational 'outcomes', most notably achievement in academic subjects, rather than taking into consideration a much broader range of educational dimensions and student achievements. Finally, the upshot of identifying the teacher as the most important 'factor' in the production of certain educational 'outcomes' is a situation where teachers are being blamed – if not punished – if their activities have not managed to make a measurable difference to the achievement of their students. Rather than enhancing and promoting teacher agency, this particular way of approaching the idea that teachers 'matter' thus tends to work in the opposite direction, limiting and confining teachers' space for professional judgement and action.

The idea of teacher agency should also be distinguished from the idea of teacher autonomy, albeit the difference here is a more subtle one. Perhaps we should say, therefore, that the idea of teacher agency should be distinguished from those interpretations of teacher autonomy that would want to see the teacher as the *only* arbiter in all educational matters. The call for (more) teacher autonomy is entirely understandable and justified against the background of policies that have sought to manage education from the top–down, viewing the teacher only as an executor of other people's educational agendas. It is therefore encouraging to see that the balance is beginning to shift away from such an extreme and unhelpful set-up (see, for example, Evers and Kneyber 2015). But the solution is of course not to be found in moving towards a different extreme where another group would claim 'total control' over education. Education always operates within complex sociopolitical configurations, where different stakeholders can legitimately claim their 'stake'. The real challenge is how to balance the interests of different stakeholders such as students, parents, the state, employers and (organizations from) the public sphere. And the key issue is to acknowledge that teachers are stakeholders as well and not just deliverers of other people's agendas, not least because they possess unique professional expertise and experience of the everyday realities of education. The language of teacher agency seeks to position teachers as active agents within this wider complex, where their professional voice and their professional judgement matter.

For similar reasons, the idea of teacher agency should be distinguished from the idea of teacher leadership and the wider discourse on teachers as leaders – a discourse that, as with so many discourses, covers a rather wide spectrum of different views and interpretations (see, for example, Murphy 2005). The most important difference we wish to highlight is the tendency within the discussion on teachers as leaders to highlight *special* roles that teachers take, for example, to lead a project or initiate and/or follow through a particular innovation – a tendency that can also be found in recent literature on teachers as change agents (see, for example, Lukacs 2009). The view here is that teacher leadership is about some teachers leading other teachers. Our focus on teacher agency is more everyday and more inclusive and encompassing, in that we seek to make sense of the ways in which *all* teachers can exert control over their work, that is, exercise professional judgement and discretion. While some teachers may manage to achieve this to a larger degree and in more different contexts and settings than others – and this is part of what we will discuss in detail in the chapters that follow – our interest is in supporting and enhancing the agency of every teacher, not just those who lead or are thought to have a particular capacity for doing so.

One further point to make – to which we will return in more detail in Chapter 1 – is to highlight that our use of the notion of 'agency' should not be understood in sociological terms, that is, in terms of a long-standing discussion within the field of sociology as to whether human action should be understood as the result of the agentic capacities of individuals, structural forces or a combination of the two. This so-called 'agency–structure' debate (see, for a quick introduction, Bunzell 2008) is a discussion within the field of sociology about the nature of sociological explanation, where agency and structure provide two different 'angles' from which the question of the explanation of human (social) action is undertaken (for a useful analysis, see also Hollis 1994). We are interested in agency as a *phenomenon* and more particularly in the question how teachers may achieve agency in their everyday settings and what might help or hinder in this.

The particular setting in which we explored these questions was the implementation of Scotland's 'Curriculum for Excellence'. Before we present the details of the research we conducted, we wish to provide a brief introduction of this particular, and in some respects, remarkable educational innovation so that readers have a sense of the particular context within which the research took place.

Scotland's 'Curriculum for Excellence'

'Curriculum for Excellence' is the national curriculum framework for Scottish schools for children and young people from age three to eighteen. It was developed out of a 2002 consultation exercise – the 'National Debate on Education' – undertaken by the then Scottish Executive on the state of school education (for a more detailed history see Humes 2013). In response to the national debate, ministers established a Curriculum Review Group in November 2003 to identify the purposes of education for the three-to-eighteen age range and to determine key principles for the redesign of the curriculum. This resulted in the publication in November 2004 of the document *A Curriculum for Excellence* (Scottish Executive 2004a).

Perhaps the most distinctive feature of 'Curriculum for Excellence' is the fact that it seeks to organize all educational activities in relation to the promotion of four capacities: the successful learner, the confident individual, the responsible citizen and the effective contributor. The 2004 document lists these four capacities as 'purposes of the curriculum'. On the one hand, the four capacities frame the overall *aspiration* of 'Curriculum for Excellence'. As it was stated in the 2004 document, '(the) aspiration for all children and for every young person is that they should be successful learners, confident individuals, responsible citizens and effective contributors to society and at work' (p. 3). On the other hand, the capacities are presented as intended outcomes of education, in that 'by providing structure, support and direction to young people's learning, the curriculum should enable them to develop these four capacities' (p. 12).

By structuring the organization of education around four capacities understood as purposes, 'Curriculum for Excellence' differs from content-based national curricula, that is, national curricula that consist of a description of everything children and young people should know and be able to do and hence should acquire through their school education. In this regard, 'Curriculum for Excellence' is an example of a new approach to national curriculum development and specification that has emerged in a number of countries around the world in recent years (for a wider analysis and critical discussion of this trend, see Priestley and Biesta 2013).

The 2004 document did not offer an extended justification for its terminology or structure and should be regarded as a macro-level framework, designed to form the basis of subsequent policy development. It was accompanied by the 'Ministerial Response' (Scottish Executive 2004b), which set out future directions for the new curriculum in a more concrete manner, laying out, for example, that the new curriculum would be articulated as 'clear statements of the outcomes which each young person should aspire to achieve' (ibid., p. 4) and hinting that subjects would continue to be the basis of the curriculum. In 2006, the publication of *A Curriculum for Excellence: Progress and Proposals* (Scottish Executive 2006) added more detail, emphasizing the importance of engagement by teachers, the centrality of learning and teaching, and the unification of the curriculum from three to eighteen. This document outlined a series of five sequential levels, establishing the principle that 'expectations will be described in terms of experiences as well as broad significant outcomes' and that these would be 'designed to reflect the Four Capacities' (p. 12). Significantly, it was proposed at this stage that the curriculum would be structured around domains – health and well-being, languages, mathematics, science, social studies, expressive arts, technologies and religious and moral education – as was the case for previous Scottish curricula.

Further guidance has emerged since 2006. This includes the *Building the Curriculum* series, which, for example, has provided additional guidance on the eight curricular domains, the early years curriculum and assessment and a quite detailed description of experiences and outcomes in each of the eight areas (Education Scotland, no date). These descriptions follow a formulaic structure seeking to combine, within simple statements set out in hierarchical levels, both the expected outcomes of learning and the experiences through which the outcomes might be achieved. The implementation of 'Curriculum for Excellence' started in the 2010–11 school year and is overseen by a 'Curriculum for Excellence' Implementation Group. At the time of the writing of this book (autumn 2014), the compulsory curriculum phase of 'Curriculum for Excellence' had been fully implemented, while it was envisaged that full implementation across all levels of the education system would be completed by 2016.

According to its architects, 'Curriculum for Excellence' is 'one of the most ambitious programmes of educational change ever undertaken in Scotland' (Scottish Government 2008, p. 8), building upon earlier programmes of reform, notably 'Assessment is for Learning' (see, for example, Hayward, Priestley and Young 2004; Hutchinson and Hayward 2005). 'Curriculum for Excellence' is often claimed to be distinctive in a number of respects, including its approach to curriculum, the centrality of learning and the learner and the role of teachers.

Curricular structure

'Curriculum for Excellence' is indeed fairly distinctive in terms of its big ideas, particularly where it concerns the adoption of the four capacities as the main orientation point for the planning, development and conduct of education. This is part of a wider framing of the curriculum discussion in terms of values, purposes and principles rather than as an 'aims and objectives' model of curriculum or a content-based approach. In the 2004 *A Curriculum for Excellence* document, an explicit appeal is made, for example, to the words that are inscribed on the mace of the Scottish Parliament – wisdom, justice, compassion and integrity – as well as reference to the importance of respecting 'diverse cultures and beliefs' (Scottish Executive 2004a, p. 19; see also Humes 2013, p. 19; Gillies 2006).

While the language is idiosyncratic to Scotland, the basic approach is more widespread. The capacities, for example, can be seen as part of a wider trend in contemporary curriculum policy to frame education around competencies rather than (just) content (for a fuller discussion see Biesta and Priestley 2013). Such competencies have been alleged to have a strongly instrumental (towards economic and civic goals) slant, being heavily influenced by publications from supra-national organizations such as the Organisation for Economic Co-operation and Development (OECD) (2005) and the European Union (European Council 2006). Some authors have directly criticized the four capacities. For example, Biesta (2008) has been critical of the narrowness of the idea of the 'responsible citizen' capacity, with its focus on social responsibility rather than democratic citizenship, and Watson (2010) has suggested that the capacities have overtones of indoctrination, being 'concerned with setting out not what children are expected to know, but how they should be' (Watson 2010, p. 99).

A second structural feature of 'Curriculum for Excellence' lies in its articulation as outcomes, grouped into linear levels. Again, this is fairly typical of global trends (Young 2009) and moreover continues with the tradition laid down by the predecessor curriculum in Scotland. However, there are two key differences. First, the 'Curriculum for Excellence' outcomes are more loosely framed than previously, being less specific and prescriptive in content, and each level now covers a longer period of a pupil's school career than was formerly the case. Second, the outcomes, now called experiences and outcomes, seek to specify not only the end result – the outcome – of learning but also normally the experience undergone by the pupil in attaining the outcome.

'Curriculum for Excellence' has attracted some criticism for a lack of theoretical rigour in its structure. According to Priestley and Humes (2010), the curriculum combines features from incompatible curricular models, which therefore provide two competing starting points for curriculum development (see also Priestley 2010). The four capacities provide a starting point based around the development of processes and the specification of content to achieve curricular aims. The specification of experiences and outcomes, on the other hand, offers a different starting point that lends itself much more easily to an audit approach to curriculum development and arguably encourages a culture of strategic compliance (also see Priestley, Minty and Eager 2014). The distinction between a rather open curricular framework and an extremely detailed set of outcomes is an important one, as it potentially spells out the difference between a more radical enactment of 'Curriculum for Excellence' as a rather open curriculum framework and a more tokenistic approach that seeks to maintain and justify existing practices under the umbrella of the new curriculum. This is a danger perceived in an analysis of the development of learning outcomes in curricula across Europe (CEDEFOP 2009). According to European Centre for the Development of Vocational Training (CEDEFOP), 'It is worth bearing in mind that detailed targets can become so narrow and specific that the original aims for learning or reform can get lost in the implementation of the detail ("losing sight of the wood for the trees")' (p. 28). They add that, in contrast, 'a more holistic approach to learning outcomes can, in the right circumstances, empower stakeholders to reach new solutions' (p. 42).

Learning

'Curriculum for Excellence' can also be claimed to be distinctive in terms of its approach to learning. This relates to two points: the balance between knowledge and skills and the centrality of the learner. In both respects, 'Curriculum for Excellence' echoes wider trends in curriculum policy to be less focused on knowledge and more on skills and capacities. This is largely justified by proponents as enhancing curricular flexibility to address the demands of a fast-changing world, where workers and citizens will need the skills to quickly acquire new knowledge, as existing knowledge forms become rapidly obsolete. There are two main facets to this curricular shift.

The first is an overt shift from knowledge to skills as the focus of the curriculum (for comment on this worldwide trend, see the 2010 special edition of the European Journal of Education; e.g. Whitty 2010; Yates and Collins 2010; Young and Muller 2010). This is evident in the specification of key competencies, such as 'Curriculum for Excellence's' four capacities. Such a shift has been criticized for oversimplifying and dichotomizing the complex relationship between knowledge and skills. For instance, Young (2009, p. 4) has questioned whether such generic skills can indeed be developed free of contextual knowledge and 'free of the domains in which they are realized'. Related to this is an increasing emphasis on interdisciplinary approaches to organizing the curriculum, something very prominent in the development of 'Curriculum for Excellence' (Education Scotland 2012). Again, such trends have been subject to critique. Young and Muller (2010) have pointed to dangers inherent in a weakening of traditional subject boundaries: an erosion of the distinction between academic knowledge and everyday knowledge; an attendant danger that, in the lack of specification of content, less-experienced teachers will 'fall behind without knowing it, or miss out conceptual steps that may be vital later on' (ibid., p. 23); and a risk that disadvantaged young people will be denied access to powerful knowledge (see also Rata 2012, who warns of the social exclusion inherent in new curricular forms). Nevertheless, many welcome such a focus and caution against alarmism. For example, Whitty (2010, p. 34) points out that 'knowledge is not the same as school subjects and school subjects are not the same thing as academic disciplines'. Moreover, educationalists have defined perfectly rational and rigorous interdisciplinary approaches to defining knowledge that do not downgrade the knowledge in question (for example, Beane 1997).

'Curriculum for Excellence' exemplifies a further common trend in curriculum design, namely the positioning of the learner at the heart of schooling, alongside prominent discourses about personalization and choice (Education Scotland 2012; for an extended discussion of this issue, see: Reeves 2013). Biesta (2010), referring to this trend as the 'learnification' of education, suggests that the focus on learning and the learner reflects an unproblematized acceptance of learning as a good and a failure to address educational questions about the content and purpose of learning, that is, about what is being learnt and what it is being learnt *for*.

This discursive shift is accompanied by a growing incidence in policy documents of references to active learning – 'Curriculum for Excellence' is replete with such references – and the increased popularity of methodologies such as cooperative learning in schools. One issue is that the theoretical underpinnings of such pedagogy are rarely made explicit in 'Curriculum for Excellence'. Policy tends to exhort teachers to utilize active forms of learning, *while* not articulating any form of learning theory, including the social-constructivism upon which they implicitly draw (for an extended discussion of these issues, see: Drew and Mackie 2011).

The role of teachers

As we have already mentioned, intrinsic to 'Curriculum for Excellence' is a renewed vision of teachers as developers of curriculum at a school level, and more widely as agents of change. The Scottish government has taken seriously the changed role of teachers in this process, commissioning, for example, two major reviews of teachers and their work (Donaldson 2010; McCormac 2011). However, assumptions about the role of teachers as agents of change have been shown to be problematic, particularly because policy has tended to focus on raising individual capacity while not addressing the structural and cultural issues that might constrain or enable teacher agency. A particular issue in this regard is the curricular tension built into the conception and implementation of 'Curriculum for Excellence', where an open curricular framework remains embedded in rather strict accountability practices – including use of attainment data and internal inspections – thus constraining the space within which teachers are supposed to develop and exert their professional agency (see, for example, Baumfield et al. 2010).

The question this raises, then, is what helps and hinders teachers in achieving agency in their everyday practice and settings. This was the central question in the 'Teacher Agency and Curriculum Change' project, which we will now introduce in more detail.

The 'Teacher Agency and Curriculum Change' project

This book draws heavily on empirical data generated during a fifteen-month study, the ESRC-funded 'Teacher Agency and Curriculum Change' project (RES-000-22-4208). The main objectives of the project were to:

- Identify biographical and ecological factors that shaped the achievement of teachers' agency as they enacted 'Curriculum for Excellence' within different contexts of the Scottish school system.
- Contribute to the development of educational change theory that accounts for the complex role of teacher agency.
- Inform policy and practice, nationally and internationally, in the related fields of curriculum development and educational change.

The research primarily addressed the following research questions:

1. How is 'Curriculum for Excellence' understood and enacted by teachers in primary and secondary schools?
2. What are the key characteristics of the contexts within which 'Curriculum for Excellence' is enacted?
3. What factors influence the agential responses of teachers to 'Curriculum for Excellence'?
4. What sorts of agency do teachers achieve in the context of 'Curriculum for Excellence'?

The study employed an ethnographic approach and was undertaken within a single education authority in Scotland, in one primary school and two secondary schools. Participants comprised two experienced classroom teachers plus a single senior line manager in each school, all of whom were interviewed at least once, and in most cases three or more times. Data were generated over three distinct phases, following an iterative design where each phase was partially determined by the findings of the previous phase. Data collection involved observation; semi-structured individual and group interviews, including, at the start of the project, a personal and professional history interview; analysis of key policy texts; and teacher network mapping. Project researchers spent several weeks in total in each setting, for example, conducting interviews and leading group sessions. Project data were analysed using a set of codes derived from the teacher agency model depicted in Chapter 1, which allowed us to categorize findings according to the key concepts surrounding agency.

The six main participants played an active role throughout in the study. They met regularly as a group with the research team, were involved in conceptual discussions relating to both agency theory and the research instruments and were kept abreast of emerging findings as the project progressed. They were also involved in a dissemination event, to which senior policy makers and local authority people were invited. Throughout the project, we were concerned to protect the participants from possible harm resulting from their participation in the study. Thus, we have not identified the local authority where the research took place. All schools and the main participating teachers are identified by pseudonyms only. In the case of the schools, we have provided only general contextual information, rather than specific detail that might identify them. Senior managers in each school are identified by role only. Throughout the book, we have avoided making reference to specific teaching subjects. The research adhered to the guidelines for the ethical conduct of research of the British Educational Research Association.

The schools

In Scotland, there are over 2,000 primary schools and over 350 secondary schools with a total enrolment in excess of 600,000 students. Primary schools comprise seven-year cohorts (P1–P7) and secondary schools comprise six (S1–S6). Education in Scotland is compulsory until sixteen years of age (typically the end of year S4, by which time students will have taken their first tier of national qualifications). The three schools in this study, two secondary and one primary, are situated within one local authority. As is common in Scotland, both the secondary schools were recently relocated, under a private finance initiative, to purpose-built, architect-designed buildings with up-to-date technology and facilities.

Lakeside High School is a medium-sized comprehensive school, serving a small town and surrounding villages, with a student roll of around 1,000, covering the full spectrum of secondary cohorts from S1 to S6. The school's catchment area is mixed in socio-economic terms, serving both prosperous villages and more socially disadvantaged communities. Hillview High School is also a six-cohort comprehensive school with a similar student roll of around 1,000. Its catchment has a lower socio-economic profile than that at Lakeside High. Both secondary schools have reaped the benefits of their recent relocation, now enjoying modern and up-to-date technology, theatre, sports and fitness facilities, specialist equipment in laboratories and excellent resources for a range of practical workshops. Townhead Primary is one of the feeder schools for Hillview High School with a roll of approximately 250 students. The building is several decades old and hence does not confer some of the benefits enjoyed by the secondary schools. The school is situated in the middle of a residential area, a mixture of local authority and private housing. The school building is divided into three distinct areas, which physically separate cohorts of pupils and their teachers, making collegial working difficult at times.

The teachers

At each of the schools, two classroom teachers participated in the study. The participants were volunteers, all female, drawn from a pool of experienced and effective teachers identified by school managers. In stating that we wished to involve experienced and effective teachers in the study, we worked from the assumption that if any teachers in the school were able to achieve high degrees of agency in developing the curriculum, it would be people like these. All participants were willing volunteers, expressing an interest in participating in research on the implementation of 'Curriculum for Excellence' and a desire to help understand the process. All of them later stated that participation in the project had made them reflect more deeply about their teaching and the schools' processes of curriculum development.

At Lakeside High School, both the teachers were from a single faculty, social studies. This faculty was highly regarded in the school for being innovative and 'close knit', something affirmed by both teachers as well as by colleagues and managers. Both referred to close professional relationships in the staffroom and a strong concern for the welfare of their students. One teacher, Sara, had around ten years of teaching experience, all at Lakeside High. As a child, her dream had been to become a teacher, and indeed she was the first person in her family to go to university. She expressed profound satisfaction with the organization of the school and with her relationship with most managers and immediate colleagues. She had previously led professional development initiatives for the local authority and is passionate about her subject, hoping that she motivates her students through her own passion to create a positive learning environment. Sara's classroom is lively and she is open about her expectation that her students were there to work and should have fun doing so. Reflecting on her future, she admitted that as she now felt comfortable with her achievements she felt more ambitious about being able to make an impact on the students. She talked about moving into a position with responsibility, possibly as a principal teacher (PT), which would allow her to develop her skills (maybe even at another school), but felt reticent about this.

Her colleague, Susan, articulated similar passions about her subject and about teaching at Lakeside High. She had come into teaching after a career in industry and has since completed a master's course as well as a number of management courses. During her career, she has taken on different roles outside of the classroom, including work with the (then) national agency Learning and Teaching Scotland and the Scottish Qualifications Authority (SQA). She likes a challenge, so when 'Curriculum for Excellence' was first introduced, she decided to take an active role in the development of her subject at a national level. She has been involved in editing and redrafting some of the early iterations. She enjoys experimenting with and designing assessment practices, often innovating in the classroom and discussing curriculum development and assessment with her colleagues. Susan takes pride in 'being ahead of the game', which is reflected in the way she teaches. Her passion for creating and being actively involved with her subject area and being aware of the student's interests were evident in the atmosphere of her classroom.

At Hillview High School, the teachers participating on the project came from two separate faculties. Kate is a teacher in the science, technology, engineering and mathematics (STEM) subjects. She told us that she had always wanted to be a teacher like her father, but he wanted her to have a 'proper' job first. She trained to be an electronics engineer and worked in a private company, where she was involved in organizing and teaching the training programmes for the staff. She was initially quite happy with her career. She was given the opportunity to travel through her work and her pay was much higher than that of her teacher-friends. However, after ten years, she made a decision to leave the company and has now been a teacher for nearly fifteen years and has not regretted the decision to change roles. Her personal interest in sport and health has meant that she has become involved in extracurricular activities within the school. At one point, she was encouraged to apply for a position as a PT and, having been unsuccessful, now realizes that she is quite satisfied with classroom teaching and not having extra responsibility and the extra administrative work. She does, however, like a challenge and is keen to involve herself in new initiatives with the students and other colleagues. Kate has been strongly influenced by the relatively recent introduction of cooperative learning to Scottish schools (since 2000). She does not feel that the development work in 'Curriculum for Excellence' has impacted upon her teaching as she was already working in similar ways.

Her colleague Monica, a teacher in a humanities faculty, also came into teaching later in life. When she left school she took a diploma in arts and design and spent over ten years working in a community arts centre, teaching adults at the centre. During this period, she took a part-time degree. After being made redundant, she decided to study full time while working with children in an after-school care centre. It was this experience that led her to believe she would like to be a primary teacher. However, she was unable to get into the primary training programme and opted for secondary training instead. Finding that she enjoyed teaching immensely, she decided to continue and graduated more than ten years ago. Just two years after getting a position at Hillview High, she was asked to take on the role as acting PT for a short period. She subsequently became interested in students with additional learning needs. Three years before her involvement in the research project, she set up a support class for vulnerable students coming from primary school. Included among these students were Polish immigrants who knew little or no English. At the time of the research project, Monica had again been appointed to a temporary position as PT, which she was reluctant to take, while simultaneously studying for a master's degree. She does not really enjoy the role and finds that there are an enormous number of challenges. She perceives the school's need for more interdisciplinary work and identification of general skills and competences to be in line with the ethos of 'Curriculum for Excellence'.

At Townhead Primary School, two teachers participated in the study. At the beginning of the study, both teachers were P7 teachers, but by the end of the study, one had moved to a P1 class and the second to P6 class. The two teachers had a close professional relationship; Eilidh, the older more-experienced P1 teacher acted as a mentor for Rachael, the younger P6 teacher, who was the least experienced of our participants. Despite this, Eilidh viewed her younger colleague as a positive influence on her, coming with new ideas and having a hands-on grasp of the technology that they were increasingly required to use. Eilidh completed her own schooling without higher qualifications, meaning that she did not possess the prerequisite accreditation to enter teaching. She subsequently entered the profession as a mature teacher and at the time of the research had over thirty years of experience. She does not regard 'Curriculum for Excellence' as something new, as many of the elements are things that she practised many years ago in a different curriculum era when there was a more relaxed attitude towards accountability. She is thus a good example of the sort of teacher whom schools might be expected to look to when developing the new curriculum, but who are in fact often marginalized and seen as 'past it' and a barrier to curricular innovation.[2] Despite the increase in bureaucracy and workload, this teacher regards 'Curriculum for Excellence' as an opportunity to develop teaching and to be creative, but she expressed concerns that there are not enough guidelines and that everyone will end up making their own interpretation of what should be done.

Rachael was a recent entrant to the profession at the time of the research, having graduated just over five years previously; she had taught for the whole of that period at Townhead Primary School. Teaching was a first choice career for her; she does not regret going into teaching and enjoys the challenges presented by working with primary students. It was clear that she was greatly respected by her colleagues as being an innovative teacher, with lots of new ideas. She regards 'Curriculum for Excellence' positively, seeing it as being about making learning meaningful. She relates this back to her own experiences of learning and how when something was meaningful, it motivated her to learn. She has already taken on a leadership role in some of the new 'Curriculum for Excellence' initiatives with other members of staff and feels that she has been successful in doing so. She told us she wanted to remain in teaching but would also like to work at another school and in other positions.

A preview of the chapters: What this book *is* about

In the chapters that follow, we seek to deepen our understanding of what teacher agency is, why it is important for meaningful educational practice and what might help and what might hinder good teacher agency. We do this in the following ways: through theoretical development and reflection, through review and critical discussion of existing literature and through the presentation of our empirical research.

We begin, in Chapter 1, with a discussion of the literature on agency and, more specifically, teacher agency in order to present the theoretical approach taken in this book, which, as mentioned, we refer to as an ecological approach in which agency is not seen as a capacity of individuals but as an achievement that is the outcome of the interaction of individual capacity with environing conditions. The model we use to conceptualize and analyse the achievement of agency makes a distinction between three dimensions of agency: influences from the past (the iterational dimension); orientations towards the future (the projective dimension); and engagement with the here and now (the practical–evaluative dimension).

We use this model in Chapters 2, 3, 4 and 5, where we present findings from our empirical research in each chapter combined with an overview of relevant literature. In Chapter 2, we focus on teachers' beliefs and aspirations, asking what these beliefs look like, where they come from and which role they play in the achievement of agency, paying attention both to how beliefs and aspirations support the achievement of agency and how they limit and restrain such achievement. In Chapter 3, we move to the wider vocabularies and discourses teachers use to think about and engage with their practices. Again, we ask what these vocabularies and discourses look like, where they come from and how they contribute to the achievement of agency, and again we pay attention to the ways in which such vocabularies and discourses help in the achievement of agency and the ways in which they limit or hinder such achievement. In Chapter 4, we shift the attention to the role of relationships, trying to map the impact of social structures and cultures on the achievement of agency. Here we show, through a comparison of two of our case-study schools, that teachers with very similar beliefs and aspirations and largely similar vocabularies and discourses still end up with very different opportunities for the achievement of agency – opportunities that are significantly influenced by the wider relational and social structures within which they work. If Chapters 2, 3 and 4 focus mainly on aspects that are internal to the context of the school, Chapter 5 looks at the wider culture of performativity to show how this culture impacts on the achievement of teacher agency and the ways in which and the extent to which teachers are able to resist their actions to be completely defined by this culture.

In Chapter 6, we bring the main insights from our research together. We look at the individual, cultural and structural dimensions of teacher agency and summarize the main findings from our theoretical and empirical explorations. In the chapter, we focus on three questions: What is teacher agency? Where does teacher agency come from? and What does teacher agency make possible? Here, we make a strong case for the promotion of teacher agency as a response to policies that, for too long, have tried to disempower and de-professionalize teachers. In Chapter 7, we try to give more concrete answers to the question how teacher agency can be enhanced and promoted, indicating what can be done at the macro level of policy formation, the meso level of policy interpretation and the micro level of policy enactment.

Understanding Teacher Agency

Introduction

In this chapter, we explore the nature of agency (and teacher agency), providing a systematic and in-depth conceptualization of a term that is often applied loosely and uncritically. There can be no doubt that agency is a slippery and much contested term, even to the extent that some people may wonder why we need such a concept in educational and social research in the first place or why we would need to have a notion of *teacher* agency. The contested nature of the concept of agency has particularly been evident in the long-standing structure–agency debate in sociology (see, for example, Giddens 1984; Archer 1988). Yet, as Emirbayer and Mische suggest,

> in the struggle to demonstrate the interpenetration of agency and structure, many theorists have failed to distinguish agency as an analytical category in its own right. (Emirbayer and Mische 1998, p. 963)

The slipperiness of the notion of 'agency' can be clearly seen in the common tendency to conflate agency and action. For many, agency is viewed as a *variable* used in explaining or understanding social action. In such approaches, agency is often set against structure, where the key question is whether structure or agency is more important in determining or shaping social action (see Hollis 1994). A regular corollary of such a conceptualization of agency is a tendency to view agency as an *innate capacity* of the human; agency in such a view is seen as something that people possess, so that people can be seen as being more or less agentic as individuals. An alternative conceptualization of agency is to see it as an *emergent phenomenon* – as something that is achieved by individuals, through the interplay of personal capacities and the resources, affordances and constraints of the environment by means of which individuals act. This latter, ecological conceptualization of agency emphasizes the importance of both individual capacity and contextual dimensions in shaping agency and, moreover, views the achievement of agency as a temporal process (see also Emirbayer and Mische 1998).

The distinction between *agency as variable*, *agency as capacity* and *agency as phenomenon* is an important distinction that is often overlooked in the literature, resulting in much misunderstanding and miscommunication. Yet it is crucial for grasping what we seek to achieve in this book. In this chapter, we provide the theoretical framing for our research, with the ultimate goal of showing why agency is an important concept that has the potential for casting a new light on the professional conditions that frame teachers' work. Moreover, we discuss how a particular conception of agency – which we will refer to as an *ecological approach* – is especially useful in this respect. A key concern in this chapter is to clearly differentiate between this and other conceptions of agency. In this chapter, we therefore address the following. We first introduce the ecological conceptualization of agency as an emergent phenomenon. In doing so, we explicitly differentiate our approach from other conceptualizations, particularly those that view agency as a personal capacity or as a variable in the explanation of social action. Moreover, we illustrate how many definitions of agency, for example, as freedom to act or as the 'capacity for autonomous action … [independent] of the determining constraints of social structure' (Calhoun, cited by Biesta and Tedder 2006, p. 5), can be problematic if not fully thought through. We then discuss the theoretical dimensions of the ecological understanding of agency in more detail. In doing so, we show how this approach is both relational – highlighting how humans operate *by means of* their social and material environments – and temporal – as agency is rooted in past experience, orientated to the future and located in the contingencies of the present. Next, we look at the notion of teacher agency – agency that occurs specifically in relation to the professional working practices of teachers. This is an area that is currently under-theorized and we offer in this book a theoretically informed view to address this gap. Against this background, we present the model that informs the research in this book.

Conceptualizing agency

Agency has been extensively discussed within a large canon of literature going back many years. There are interpretations of agency with roots in a range of different academic disciplines, including sociology, philosophy, economics and anthropology. Also, agency has been theorized according to differing intellectual traditions, including postmodern, post-structural, sociocultural, identity and life-course perspectives (for a discussion of these approaches to agency in relation to professional practice, see Eteläpelto et al. 2013). Discussions about agency are often conducted in terms of the structure–agency debate. Fuchs (2001), for example, has shown that there is a tendency in social theory and research to either focus on an over-socialized, macro view of agency – thus ignoring the local and specific – or to concentrate on overly individualized notions of agency – thus ignoring questions of structure, context and resources. Archer (1988) calls these tendencies, respectively, *downwards conflation* – where agency is subjugated by social forces – and *upwards conflation* – where society is little more than an epiphenomenon of individual efforts. In the latter part of the twentieth century, a number of sociologists made systematic attempts to find a middle ground in this discussion or indeed to reframe the debate altogether. These include Bourdieu's (1977) notion of *habitus*, Giddens's (1984) theory of *structuration*, Archer's (1995) *realist social theory* and *relational theories of agency* inspired by, for example, the actor-network theory (see Dépelteau 2008).

Leaving aside for now the question as to whether these debates enhance our understanding of these issues, it is clear that they illustrate the complexity of agency as a topic for analysis and study. This complexity, along with an associated slipperiness in the usage of the term agency, is manifest in much of the literature. A key problem here is the lack of a clear conceptualization of agency in much of the literature. Emirbayer and Mische (1998) – in their seminal article *What is Agency?* – offer the following observation, which is worth reproducing in full.

> The concept of agency has become a source of increasing strain and confusion in social thought. Variants of action theory, normative theory, and political-institutional analysis have defended, attacked, buried, and resuscitated the concept in often contradictory and overlapping ways. At the centre of the debate, the term agency itself has maintained an elusive, albeit resonant, vagueness; it has all too seldom inspired systematic analysis, despite the long list of terms with which it has been associated: selfhood, motivation, will, purposiveness, intentionality, choice, initiative, freedom and creativity. Moreover, in the struggle to demonstrate the interpenetration of agency and structure, many theorists have failed to distinguish agency as an analytical category in its own right – with distinctive theoretical dimensions and temporally variable social manifestations. (Emirbayer and Mische 1998, pp. 962–63)

It is thus evident that any account of agency should start with a thorough and clear conceptualization of the term. In short, then, what is agency? It is worth starting with some of the more commonplace definitions of the term agency. In simple terms, agency can be described as the ability or potential to act. Less prosaically, it has been described as the 'capacity for autonomous action ... [independent] of the determining constraints of social structure' (Calhoun, cited by Biesta and Tedder 2006, p. 5) or as the capacity of actors to 'critically shape their responses to problematic situations' (as noted by Biesta and Tedder 2006, p. 11). Agency can also be viewed as autonomy and causal efficacy (Archer 2000). Taylor (cited by Edwards 2005, p. 169) provides a definition that has a similar emphasis, seeing agency as 'the capacity to identify the goals at which one is directing one's action and to evaluate whether one had been successful'. Lipponen and Kumpulainen (2011, p. 813) point to a tendency in much writing to see agency as the 'power to transform ... (and) ... resistance to and transformation of dominant power relations'.

The above definitions seek to capture the nature of agency, but all are potentially problematic, because they may be taken to suggest an overly individualistic view of agency as human capacity, seeing agency as something that people possess to varying degrees as a result of their personal attributes. They can be taken to read that the agentic individual is agentic solely because of his or her personal abilities or agentic capacity, even where that agency cannot be exercised. This is the main reason why in our research we pursue a different approach, one where agency is seen as emerging from the *interaction* of individual 'capacity' with environing 'conditions'. Our perspective on agency has its roots in the philosophy of action, particularly as it has been developed in pragmatism, particularly John Dewey's 'transactional realism' (Biesta and Burbules 2003) and George Herbert Mead's 'symbolic interactionism' (Blumer 1969; see also Biesta 1998). Rather than seeing agency as residing in individuals as a property or capacity, this *ecological* view of agency sees agency as an emergent phenomenon of the ecological conditions through which it is enacted.

> This concept of agency highlights that actors always act *by means* of their environment rather than simply in their environment [so that] the achievement of agency will always result from the *interplay of individual efforts, available resources and contextual and structural factors as they come together in particular and, in a sense, always unique situations.* (Biesta and Tedder 2007, p. 137; emphasis added)

Agency, in other words, is not something that people can *have* or *possess*; it is rather to be understood as something that people *do* or *achieve* (Biesta and Tedder 2006). It denotes a 'quality' of the *engagement* of actors with temporal–relational contexts-for-action, not a quality of the actors themselves. Viewing agency in such terms thus helps to understand not only how humans are able to be reflexive and creative, acting counter to societal constraints, but also how individuals are enabled and constrained by their social and material environments. While agency is inherent in human action, agency and action are conceptually distinct and should not be conflated with each other (see also Emirbayer and Mische 1998). The main distinctive factor is that agency involves *intentionality*, the capacity to formulate possibilities for action, active consideration of such possibilities and the exercise of choice. But it also includes the causative properties of contextual factors – social and material structures and cultural forms that influence human behaviour – which is why, as mentioned, a full understanding of agency must consider how individual capacity interplays with contextual factors. In the next section, we develop these arguments in more detail through a theorization of how capacity and context interact to form agency. The work of Emirbayer and Mische (1998) provides the main reference point for this.

Theorizing agency: An ecological approach

Building on pragmatism, Emirbayer and Mische (1998) have theorized agency with the dual aim of robustly conceptualizing agency and overcoming the theoretical one-sidedness of existing theories of agency, which, in their view, tend to focus either on routine or on purpose or on judgement. They make a case for a theory of agency that encompasses the dynamic interplay between these three dimensions and that takes into consideration 'how this interplay varies within different structural contexts of action' (ibid., p. 963). For this reason, they suggest that the achievement of agency should be understood as a configuration of influences from the past, orientations towards the future and engagement with the present. They refer to these three dimensions as the *iterational*, the *projective* and the *practical-evaluative* dimension, respectively. In concrete actions, all three dimensions play a role – the influences from the past, the orientation towards the future and the engagement with the here and now – but the degree to which they contribute in concrete situations varies. This is why Emirbayer and Mische speak of a '*chordal triad* of agency within which all three dimensions resonate as separate but not always harmonious tones' (ibid., p. 972, emph. in original). Thus, they define agency as '*the temporally constructed engagement by actors of different structural environments – the temporal-relational contexts of action – which, through the interplay of habit, imagination, and judgement, both reproduces and transforms those structures in interactive response to the problems posed by changing historical situations*' (ibid., p. 970, emph. in original). From this, they suggest that agency should be understood as a 'temporally embedded process of social engagement, informed by the past (in its habitual aspect), oriented toward the future (as a capacity to imagine alternative possibilities) and "acted out" in the present (as a capacity to contextualize past habits and future projects with the contingencies of the moment)' (ibid., p. 963).

Emirbayer's and Mische's ideas are helpful because first of all they show that agency doesn't come from nowhere but builds upon past achievements, understandings and patterns of action. This is expressed in the *iterational* element of agency that has to do with '*the selective reactivation by actors of past patterns of thought and action, routinely incorporated in practical activity, thereby giving stability and order to social universes and helping to sustain identities, interactions, and institutions over time*' (ibid., p. 971; emph. in original). A key word here is 'selective'. According to Emirbayer and Mische, 'the agentic reactivation of schemes inculcated through past experience tends to correspond to (and thus reproduces) societal patterns' (ibid., p. 977) – but this level of routinization does not have to be the case. Actors do not always act from habit, following routinized patterns of behaviour, but are able to recognize, appropriate and refashion past patterns of behaviours and experience as they seek to *manoeuvre among repertoires* in dealing with present dilemmas and engage in *expectation maintenance* in their orientations towards the future. A key implication here is that actors able to draw upon a rich repertoire of experience might be expected to be able to develop more expansive orientations to the future and draw upon a greater range of responses to the dilemmas and problems of the present context, than might be the case with less experience.

Emirbayer and Mische's approach is also helpful because it acknowledges that agency is in some way 'motivated', that is, it is linked to the intention to bring about a future that is different from the present and the past. This is encapsulated in the *projective* element of agency that encompasses '*the imaginative generation by actors of possible future trajectories of action, in which received structures of thought and action may be creatively reconfigured in relation to actors' hopes, fears, and desires for the future*' (ibid., p. 971; emph. in original). Such a process of continual imaginative reconstruction of the future involves 'draw(ing) upon past experiences in order to clarify motives, goals and intentions, to locate possible future constraints, and to identify morally and practically appropriate courses of action' (ibid., p. 989). An implication here is that people who are able to form expansive projections about their future trajectories might be expected to achieve greater levels of agency than those whose aspirations are more limited.

Although agency is involved with the past and the future, it can only ever be 'acted out' in the present, which is precisely what is expressed in the *practical-evaluative* dimension, which entails '*the capacity of actors to make practical and normative judgements among alternative possible trajectories of action, in response to the emerging demands, dilemmas, and ambiguities of presently evolving situations*' (ibid., p. 971, emph. in original). Judgements are both practical – shaped by the affordances and constraints of the context – and evaluative – for example, judgements of risk in any given situation.

Emirbayer's and Mische's approach also emphasizes the importance of *context and structure* in that agency is seen as the 'temporally constructed engagement with different structural environments' (ibid., p. 970). The combination of context and time highlights that it is not only important to understand agency in terms of the individual's life course, but it is at the very same time also important to understand transformations of contexts-for-action over time. According to Emirbayer and Mische, such contexts are primarily to be understood as *social* contexts in that agency is 'always a dialogical process by and through which actors immersed in temporal passage engage with others within collectively organized contexts of action' (ibid., p. 974). However, we would argue that such contexts are also *material*, in that agency is partly shaped by the availability of physical resources and the nature of physical constraints.

Agency can therefore be characterized as an emergent phenomenon, something that occurs or is achieved within continually shifting contexts over time and with orientations towards past, future and present, which differ within each and every instance of agency achieved. There are a number of implications suggested by this approach to agency, which we explore empirically throughout the book. For example, a key implication is that if agency is achieved rather than being solely about the capacity of actors, then the importance of context should be taken more seriously by public policy makers and leaders in public organizations, as such contexts may serve to disable individuals with otherwise high agentic capacity. A further corollary of this lies in the conclusion that, if agency today is shaped by experiences from the past, then we can conclude that today's contexts will impact upon future agency. Such conclusions have clear implications for those designing public policy today, particularly when the goal is to raise capacity, for example, the ability of teachers to develop a new national curriculum. A second implication lies in an observation by Emirbayer and Mische that what might pass for agency is not necessarily so. For example, agency may be involved in the reproduction of social patterns through active resistance to change, when to the casual observer what seems to be occurring is habitual behaviour by the actors concerned. Conversely, 'actors who feel creative and deliberative while in the flow of unproblematic trajectories' (ibid., p. 1008) may not be achieving high levels of agency, as they simply go with the flow. These and other issues will be revisited in the chapters that follow. Before we do so, we first need to say a few things about agency as it relates to a specific occupational group, namely teachers, in order then to present the model we have used to analyse teacher agency in our research.

Understanding teacher agency

While agency *per se* has been extensively theorized (if not well conceptualized), teacher agency – that is, agency theorized specifically in respect of the activities of teachers in schools – has not received the attention it deserves. There has been little explicit research or theory development (Vongalis-Macrow 2007) about this 'vague' concept (Pyhältö, Pietarinen and Soini 2012) and existing change models tend to both underplay and misconstrue the role of teacher agency in educational innovation (Leander and Osborne 2008). In this section, we briefly examine literature that focuses on teacher agency. We start with a caveat: while we can claim that there is a lack of literature explicitly focusing on teacher agency that is not to say that agency has not been utilized as a concept in the literature covering the professional work of teachers. Often the use of the term agency is implicit, linked to discussions of professionalism (e.g. Brown and McIntyre 1993; Goodson 2003; Sachs 2003), accountability (e.g. Hargreaves 1993; Smyth and Shacklock 1998; Sahlberg 2010) or educational change (e.g. Hoban 2002; Fullan 2003). Sometimes, agency appears as a more explicit concept (e.g. Helsby 1999). However, we maintain that rarely is agency actively conceptualized and/ or theorized in such literature.

For the purpose of this chapter, we confine our review to literature with an explicit focus on teacher agency: literature that one might reasonably expect to offer some form of conceptualization or theorization of teacher agency to the debate. Reviewing this literature confirms the contention by Vongalis-Macrow (2007) that there is little literature on the topic. Since Vongalis-Macrow wrote this in 2007, there has been an increase in writing on teacher agency, but this is not significant. Leaving aside our own contributions to the debate (Priestley et al. 2012; Priestley, Biesta and Robinson 2012; Priestley, Robinson and Biesta 2012; Priestley, Biesta and Robinson 2013; Biesta, Priestley, and Robinson 2015), which follow the track outlined in this chapter, the following issues emerge in the literature on teacher agency.

First, teacher agency is often conceived as a slogan to support school-based reform. Thus, one regularly hears teachers referred to as 'agents of change' (Fullan 2003) in relation to the implementation of policy. In our view, this provides a one-dimensional, and even misleading, view of agency, linking it to innovation or in some cases creativity, but ultimately suggesting that to be agentic is to follow lines laid down by others. This is redolent of the observation by Emirbayer and Mische (1998, p. 1008) that 'actors who feel creative and deliberative while in the flow of unproblematic trajectories' are not necessarily achieving agency. Such notions rarely acknowledge that agency may be achieved by teachers as they *oppose or subvert* policy, often for good educational reasons (Sannino 2010), and that resistance is not always inherently conservative, routinized behaviour but can be an active, agentic process (for an interesting discussion of different forms of teacher mediation of policy, see Osborn at al. 1997).

A second issue relates to whether such literature adequately conceptualizes agency. Sannino (2010), in her account of agency as resistance, certainly conceptualizes resistance but does not offer a similar detailed conceptualization of agency, other than to suggest different variants of agency such as resistance and self-initiative. Similarly, Riveros, Newton and Burgess (2012, p. 208) argue that 'current formulations of professional learning communities need a more robust explanatory framework regarding the role of teachers' agency in school practices and school dynamics'. The authors add that 'a coherent conception of agency for professional learning communities must acknowledge the situated character of human beings in their context of practice' (ibid., p. 209). In line with other researchers, they do not, however, offer a detailed conceptualization of what they mean by agency.

Other authors offer a limited conceptualization of teacher agency, but in an underdeveloped manner. Vongalis-MaCrow (2007), as previously noted, commented on the lack of substantive theorization of teacher agency, but does not offer a detailed account herself. In a paper mainly focusing on the ways in which teachers navigate the changing globalized contexts within which they work, she provides a brief deconstruction of the concept of agency, drawing upon the work of Archer and suggesting that agency comprises three interconnected aspects: obligations, authority and autonomy. In common with much of the literature, this does not provide a clear conception of what agency is but rather seeks to theorize how it is constituted. Ketelaar et al. (2012) likewise offer a limited treatment of the concept of agency in their paper on educational innovation. Their definition of agency appears to adhere to an ecological model, as they talk about teachers experiencing agency, and state that 'agency is … shaped by both the teacher and the school context' (p. 275). However, they do not offer an extended conceptualization of agency nor do they theorize agency in a developed way. Similarly, Vaughn (2013) discusses the 'construct of teacher agency' (p. 121), suggesting that it involves vision and teaching 'against the grain' (ibid.) but does not develop the conception in any detail.

Other writers have made more systematic attempts to conceptualize and theorize agency. For instance, Lasky (2005), in her sociocultural treatment of teacher agency, offers an extended discussion, defining agency as both individual capacity (for example, beliefs, identity, knowledge and emotional well-being) and social influences (such as language, policy, norms and social structures). According to Lasky, 'individual agency to change a context is possible in the ways people act to affect their immediate settings through using resources that are culturally, socially and historically developed' (ibid., p. 900). This construction of agency seems to chime with the ecological approach, offering potential to both define and theorize agency as a concept and showing how agency is possible for teachers through their relational and temporal connections. Pyhältö, Pietarinen and Soini (2012, 2014) also offer a more-extended-than-usual approach to conceptualizing teacher agency, taking a sociocultural perspective. These authors suggest that:

> Teachers' professional agency is considered a capacity that prepares the way for the intentional and responsible management of new learning, both at an individual and community level. This concept includes using others intentionally as a resource for learning and, equally, serving as a support for them. … Accordingly, teachers' professional agency is not a fixed disposition of an individual teacher, but is highly relational and thus embedded in professional interactions between teachers, pupils and their parents, as well as with other members of the school community. (2014, p. 307)

Lipponen and Kumpulainen (2011), following Biesta and Tedder (2006), offer an explicit ecological conception of agency in their writing about teachers, 'thinking about agency in terms of achievement' – as 'not a fixed quality or disposition' but rather as 'something that people do in social practice' (Lipponen and Kumpulainen 2011, p. 813). Finally, some authors have identified different 'types' of agency, which appear to use the term in ways that transcend its original meanings in sociological literature. For example, Edwards (2005) has posited the notion of relational agency – a concept also underpinning the work of Pyhältö, Pietarinen and Soini (2012, 2014) – which she defines as 'a capacity to offer support and to ask for support from others' (Edwards 2005, p. 168), an ability, in other words, to draw upon social capital, which implies both the notion of agency as the personal capacity to draw upon social capital (relational resources) and the extent to which such resources exist in the first place.

A framework for understanding teacher agency

This short review of literature illustrates that there is a large space for new ways of understanding and theorizing agency in relation to the work of teachers. The ecological conception of agency-as-achievement (Biesta and Tedder 2007), developed in more detail in the three-dimensional, temporal–relational perspective on agency offered by Emirbayer and Mische (1998), offers considerable potential to extend current thinking about teacher agency, making it possible to generate rich understandings of how agency is achieved by concrete individuals in concrete situations and of the different factors that promote or inhibit the achievement of agency. Based on the assumption of agency as a situated achievement, and informed by Emirbayer's and Mische's suggestion that the achievement of agency is the outcome of the interplay of iterational, practical–evaluative and projective dimensions, we develop, in this section of the chapter, an approach to understanding the agency of teachers, a professional group working in quite distinctive professional contexts. This approach, which we refer to within the book as *the ecological approach to teacher agency*, constitutes both a *methodological* and a *theoretical* framework for empirical inquiry relating to the ways in which teachers achieve agency in their professional contexts. It has been utilized to guide data collection and assist in data analysis. Within each dimension, we have identified a number of further aspects that are likely to shape the achievement on agency. This is an analytical separation (Archer 1988; Emirbayer and Mische 1998), which seeks to examine the interplay between the different components that shape agency, while accepting that neat separation is not always possible empirically. Thus, for example, this approach can allow us to determine when past patterns of behaviour are more significant in shaping agency than the lived conditions of the present or whether practical constraints are more facilitating or inhibiting in the present domain than evaluative considerations (for example, judgements about likely levels of risk).

The diagram below represents the key dimensions of the teacher agency model, illustrating the ways in which we analytically separate out key elements of each dimension. With regard to the iterational dimension, we distinguish between the influence of the more general life histories of teachers and their more specific professional histories (which include both their own education as a teacher and the accumulated experience of being a teacher). With regard to the projective dimension, we distinguish between short-term and long(er)-term orientations of action. And with regard to the practical–evaluative dimension, we make a distinction between cultural, material and structural aspects. Cultural aspects have to do with ways of speaking and thinking, of values, beliefs and aspirations, and encompass both inner and outer dialogue. Material aspects have to do with the resources that promote or hinder agency and the wider physical environment in and through which agency is achieved. Structural aspects have to do with the social structures and relational resources that contribute to the achievement of agency.

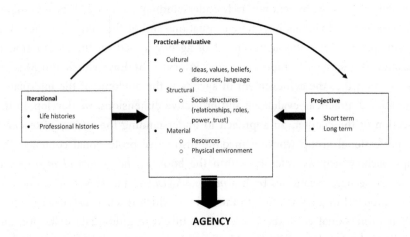

The model thus highlights that the achievement of agency is always informed by past experience – and in the particular case of teacher agency, this concerns both professional and personal experience. The model also highlights that the achievement of agency is always orientated towards the future in some combination of short(er)-term and long(er)-term objectives, values and aspirations. And it emphasizes that agency is always enacted in a concrete situation; it is both constrained and supported by discursive, material and relational resources available to actors.

The iterational, practical–evaluative and projective aspects of teachers' work

The above discussion is abstract, and it is necessary to relate it in more concrete terms to the practical worlds of teachers, drawing on some hypothetical situations and illustrating how the model will be used to frame the discussion in the forthcoming chapters of the book.

The iterational dimension of teachers' work

While we would dissent from those voices that frame teacher agency as personal capacity, we would not disagree with the notion that such capacity is important in enabling agency to emerge. Agency, if seen as the capacity to act, will indeed be enriched if people have a broad repertoire of responses upon which they may draw. In respect of teachers, we would point to a number of iterational aspects that contribute to teacher agency. These include personal capacity (skills and knowledge), beliefs (professional and personal) and values. What these have in common is their rooting in past experiences. Clearly, for the teachers of tomorrow, it is important to attend to the nature of what will become those past experiences in the present, which is where the importance of teacher education lies. Such education (both initial education and continuing professional development) should focus on capacity building – and if the focus is to be on developing agents of change and professional developers of the curriculum, then programmes of professional development should focus on developing this capacity, to interrupt habitual ways of thinking about schooling and to encourage an innovative and questioning mindset. Arguably, this should include a thorough engagement with educational purposes and with the principles of curriculum development.

Professional education forms only a small part of the formation of teachers' professional experience. Day-to-day experience in schools – dialogue with colleagues, exposure to school culture and other professional engagement would seem to be significant too. It might be argued that teachers working in less innovative schools are less likely to experience a wide repertoire of responses to problematic situations than colleagues in schools where innovation is encouraged and supported. In turn, professional experience is perhaps less significant than personal experience in shaping teacher agency. Moreover, such experience largely lies beyond the control of policy makers. However, it is interesting to reflect upon the sorts of experiences that might contribute to the development of the sorts of qualities and capacities required by teachers as they become agents of change. Teachers' own schooling must be significant in the development of the capacity to question and innovate. Professional experience outwith education is another significant and interesting pointer to the sorts of agency achieved by teachers. For instance, recent research (Priestley et al. 2012) suggests that teachers with significant experience of working in other professions might have a wider repertoire for manoeuvre when faced with the challenges and ambiguities of the teacher's day-to-day work.

The projective dimension of teachers' work

The projective dimension of teacher agency concerns their aspirations in respect of their work – both long term and short term. Such aspirations may be entirely positive, relating to the development and welfare of students (Lasky 2005) and lead to agency that is protective of students' interests. Such agency may support policy intentions, or it may run counter to them (Osborn et al. 1997; Ladwig 2010). In both cases, it can be driven by sincerely held, often long-term, aspirations rooted strongly in teachers' values and beliefs. Or aspirations may be more narrowly instrumental, for example, maintaining a 'normal desirable state' in the classroom (Brown and McIntyre 1993) or 'playing the game' (Gleeson and Gunter 2001). This game can take the form of fabrication of the school's image – careful impression management and discourses of excellence (Keddie, Mills and Pendergast 2011) and the concealing of 'dirty laundry' (Cowie, Taylor and Croxford 2007), as well as more serious corruption and cheating (Ball 2003; Sahlberg 2010). The forms of agency evident in these latter cases are clearly quite different to those in the former example and motivated by quite different aspirations.

Whatever the form these aspirations take, and whatever the motivation for them, we suggest that they are invariably largely rooted in teachers' prior experiences. Thus we must not underestimate the importance of strongly held beliefs about subject identity, for example, or teachers' motivations to do their best for their students, as these are important in shaping the form aspirations will take. Teachers' prior professional experiences will help form such experiences. Thus, for example, a previous experience of a negative school inspection may make teachers risk averse in their work, and hence agency is circumscribed. Many writers have pointed to the ways in which teacher agency is eroded by heavy-duty accountability mechanisms and the culture of performativity that they encourage (e.g. Smyth and Shacklock 1998; Helsby 1999; Sahlberg 2011), and it is our view that the type of teacher agency emerging in schools today has been significantly shaped by the past two decades of managerialism in education.

The practical–evaluative dimension of teachers' work

The above discussion leads naturally into the practical–evaluative dimension of teachers' work. This relates to the day-to-day working environment within which teachers work. Teaching has been characterized as a profession rife with ambiguity (e.g. Helsby 1999), laden with emotional politics (Hargreaves 1998), context dependent and contestable in terms of its aims. Teachers make daily decisions that are difficult, involving compromise and at times conflict with their aspirations, feeling coerced by what they might see as arbitrary and unnecessary intrusions into their work. Moreover, they do so often on the basis of insufficient time to reflect and to engage in professional dialogue with colleagues. Thus, the practical–evaluative dimension forms a major influence on agency, powerfully shaping (and often distorting) decision making and action, offering both possibilities for agency (for example, by making available resources) and inhibiting it (for example, by creating perceptions of unacceptable risk). For the purposes of this chapter, we offer the following two themes to illustrate the sorts of factors that act as part of the practical–evaluative dimension of teacher agency. These will be explored empirically in later chapters; for now, we simply offer them as possible areas for inquiry into teacher agency.

The first concerns conflicting pressures in teachers' work. In Scotland, for example, Reeves (2008) has documented tensions between a new curriculum that opens up possibilities for teacher agency and a quality improvement initiative (based around inspections, self-evaluation and attainment) that has been shown to corrode it (Helsby 1999; see also Priestley, Robinson and Biesta 2012). The second theme relates to relationships in schools. In Scotland, for example, many secondary schools are organized hierarchically, with strong vertical structures but more limited horizontal relationships. Research (e.g. Coburn and Russell 2008) suggests that schools that develop effective structures to encourage such relationships cope more effectively with new policy, enabling teachers to engage dialogically with and make sense of new policy. Coburn and Russell point to two aspects of such relationships: (1) tie strength (engendering trust); and (2) tie span – relationships that extend beyond the school, breaking cycles of inward looking practice and allowing access to external, expert knowledge. The point here is that while teachers may come to a situation equipped with substantial capacity (e.g. skills and knowledge) and strong educational aspirations, innovation may simply prove to be too difficult, or too risky to enact.

Concluding comments

In this chapter, we have outlined how we conceptualize and theorize agency and how this shapes our approach to understanding the factors that are likely to promote or inhibit teacher agency. We have argued that teacher agency should not be understood as an individual capacity – as something that individuals have or don't have – but as something that is achieved in and through concrete contexts-for-action. We have also argued that the achievement of agency is the outcome of the interplay of iterational, practical–evaluative and projective dimensions and that within these dimensions further potentially relevant aspects can be distinguished. The iterational and projective dimensions highlight how the achievement of agency is influenced both by past experience (in the widest sense of the word, including formal education and training and informal professional and personal experience) and by the aims and ends that inform educational action, both those that are relevant in the particular context and wider personal and professional values, aims and ambitions. Agency is, however, always achieved in concrete and specific situations, and this is what the focus of the practical–evaluative dimension is. This dimension of the achievement of agency highlights, on the one hand, the practical – that is, what is practically possible and feasible in this concrete situation – and, on the other hand, the evaluative – that is the way in which the actor evaluates both the 'issues' at hand and the possibilities for action in the concrete situation. The achievement of agency in a particular concrete situation is not only dependent on the actor but also on the availability of resources that can be deployed in the situation. We have distinguished between cultural, material and structural resources in order to highlight the importance of: (1) ways of thinking, understanding and talking about the issues and the situation – and this concerns both 'inner' dialogue (one's own thinking) and 'outer' dialogue (one's conversations with others in the situation); (2) the material aspects of the situation (the built environment, the physical resources, etcetera); and (3) social relationships (both the way in which particular relationships can support the achievement of agency and the way in which such relationships can hinder this achievement).

In all this, it remains important to highlight the idea of agency as an achievement rather than an (individual) capacity. While the capacities and capabilities of individuals are important and might be seen as a necessary condition for the achievement of agency, it is never a sufficient condition, as agency always has to be achieved in concrete situations. This means that the achievement of agency also depends on existing cultures of thinking, working and doing (see also James and Biesta 2007; Biesta 2011), and on wider structural issues. To promote teacher agency is therefore not only a matter of teacher education and professional development in order to increase teachers' capacity and capability but also requires attention to cultures and structures. Without attention to the latter two levels as well, it is unlikely that the call for teachers to become agents of change will effect a real transformation of educational processes and practices.

In the next four chapters, we deploy the approach to teacher agency outlined in this chapter in the presentation, analysis and interpretation of data from our research.

Teacher Beliefs and Aspirations

Introduction

In this chapter, we focus on the role and significance of teacher beliefs, which, the literature suggests, play an important role in teacher agency. Teacher beliefs have in recent years received a significant amount of attention from scholars in the field (e.g. Nespor 1987; Pajares 1992; Meirink et al. 2009), generating a large body of literature. This work suggests that beliefs are instrumental in shaping teachers' practice and that such beliefs may be relatively immune to efforts from teacher educators and policy makers to change them. The latter point is particularly relevant in the context of attempts to reform education, such as in the case of the introduction of new curriculum frameworks like 'Curriculum for Excellence'. It resonates with the observation made by Cuban that 'schools change reforms as much as reforms change schools' (Cuban 1998, p. 453) and is echoed in the comment made by Nespor that

> teachers' perceptions of and orientations to the knowledge they are presented with may be shaped by belief systems beyond the immediate influence of teacher education. (Nespor 1987, p. 326)

For us, the above issues are closely intertwined with teacher agency, and yet the literature on teacher beliefs does not explicitly relate the concepts of teacher beliefs and teacher agency. This constitutes a major lacuna, as the beliefs that teachers hold play a major role in providing their actions with sense and direction. This is why, in this chapter, we probe deeper into teacher beliefs.

As with all dimensions of our ecological approach to agency, teacher beliefs 'play out' in the here and now, that is, in the concrete settings in which teachers act. This has to do with the practical–evaluative dimension of agency where beliefs play a role in the ways in which teachers conceive of the concrete situations in which they act and the 'issues' that they encounter in those situations, as well as in the way in which they value and evaluate such situations. The beliefs that teachers have not only play a role in how they understand the situation they are in but also give their actions a sense of direction – which has to do with the projective dimension of agency. Here, beliefs emerge in the form of what, in this chapter, we will refer to as *aspirations*. In addition to how beliefs *function*, there is the question of where teachers' beliefs come from. This concerns the iterational dimension of agency. Viewed in this way, there are three questions to ask about the role of beliefs in teacher agency. First is the more descriptive question as to which beliefs that teachers actually hold. This includes both the beliefs about the here and now – such as teachers' beliefs about the nature of education or their beliefs about children and of their abilities or a lack thereof – and teachers' intentions and aspirations for what they seek to achieve in the future through their actions. Second is the more analytical question as to where the beliefs that teachers hold come from. And third is the question as to what teachers do with their beliefs and aspirations, that is, how these beliefs and aspirations play a role in the achievement of agency. Throughout this chapter, we will seek to provide answers to each of these questions.

This chapter primarily deals with teacher beliefs and does so at an individual level. In the next chapter, we develop the discussion further by exploring the wider individual and collective discourses of which these beliefs are part, including professional and policy discourses. Below, we first provide a brief overview of some of the key literature in the field of teacher beliefs. We then embark on a discussion of our empirical study, where we describe and discuss beliefs articulated by teachers participating in our research. We present and discuss the data thematically under three headings: *beliefs about children and young people*; *beliefs about teaching*; and *beliefs about educational purpose*.

In analysing the data, we were struck by the similarity of beliefs articulated across this small group of teachers, despite their location in different sectors of education and in different schools. These teachers largely shared a professional discourse that seemed to frame many of their beliefs about students and their roles as teachers, as well as their views on the purposes of education in quite similar ways. When analysed at the level of *content* – that is, focusing on what the beliefs are 'about' – we see beliefs that appear to be fairly restricted in scope, more geared to short-term goals and predominantly articulated via the language of recent policy documentation. It is only when such beliefs are placed within the wider context of the vocabularies and discourses that teachers use – a task we will turn to in the next chapter – that they gain more depth and nuance. This raises important questions about the nature and scope of the discursive resources teachers have available to them and how this impacts on their achievement of agency or a lack thereof. We offer a strong caveat about this before embarking on our discussion, as some of the ensuing discussion may seem to portray the teachers in a negative light. This is not our intention, and we would emphasize at the outset that we were impressed throughout the project with the professionalism, competence and dedication of all of the teachers who participated in the research. Moreover, we re-emphasize – as depicted within our theoretical model – that agency is not simply a matter of individual capacity (and belief is merely a subset of this). As an ecological construct, it is also subject to structural, cultural and material influences. Teacher professional discourses are to a large extent as they are because of the teachers' positioning within their professional environments, and their agency (or lack of) is heavily influenced by factors that are often beyond their immediate control.

Teacher beliefs: An overview of the literature

As we noted above, there is a wide body of literature relating to teacher beliefs. This literature has comprehensively conceptualized the construct of teacher beliefs (e.g. Nespor 1987; Pajares 1992; Rubie-Davies, Flint and McDonald 2012), demonstrating how, for example, teachers are able to hold contradictory beliefs simultaneously (e.g. Yerrick, Park and Nugent 1997; Wallace and Kang 2004; Belo et al. 2014); how beliefs might impede or otherwise mediate engagement with educational reform policy (e.g. van der Schaaf, Stocking and Verloop 2008; Ertmer and Ottenbreit-Leftwich 2010; Milner et al. 2012); and how in-service professional development impacts upon teacher beliefs (e.g. van Driel, Beijard and Verloop 2001; Avalos 2011; Borg 2011).

However, the literature has a number of limitations. First, there is still little research on how teacher beliefs change over time (Belo et al. 2014). Second, as we noted, few studies explicitly relate teacher beliefs to teacher agency (for recent exceptions see: Wallace and Priestley 2011; Priestley et al. 2012; Biesta, Priestley and Robinson 2015). Third, a lot of the literature is predicated on the notion of schools in deficit and is firmly hitched to educational change agendas. For example, Ertmer and Ottenbreit-Leftwich (2010, p. 256) suggest that 'teachers' mindsets must change' in order to accommodate the introduction of information technology into classrooms. The strong association of teacher beliefs with educational change in much of the literature is strongly evident in the foci and themes that feature in the literature. These include the following.

- There are a great many publications dealing with teacher beliefs in respect of language teaching, often linked explicitly to worldwide moves to shift pedagogy from grammar translation methods to communicative language teaching (e.g. Borg 2003, 2011; Nishino 2012).
- Many publications relate to science teaching and are explicitly concerned with shifting classroom practices from transmission approaches, predicated upon epistemological beliefs about science as a relatively fixed body of content, to more 'modern' constructivist approaches and inquiry-based learning (e.g. Yerrick, Park and Nugent 1997; Keys and Bryan 2001; Wallace and Kang 2004; Belo et al. 2014).
- Many studies concern the introduction of new technology and the implementation of technology-based learning, often in the face of what are seen as negative beliefs by teachers (e.g. Ertmer and Ottenbreit-Leftwich 2010; Song and Looi 2012).
- And there are numerous studies that relate to a more generic reform of pedagogy, where teacher beliefs are often seen as being at odds with mandated innovation. A notable example is assessment reform – for example, assessment for learning, formative assessment, portfolio assessment – which has recently been the subject of large-scale policy initiatives (e.g. van der Schaaf, Stocking and Verloop 2008; Brown, Harris and Harnett 2012).

We summarize here some of the themes that characterize this literature.

Defining teacher beliefs

It is first worth examining how the literature defines teacher beliefs. Pajares (1992, citing Clark) suggested that beliefs 'tend to be eclectic aggregations of cause–effect propositions from many sources, rules of thumb, generalizations drawn from personal experience, beliefs, values, biases, and prejudices' (p. 314). He suggests that it is difficult to differentiate clearly between knowledge and beliefs, the latter being a 'messy construct' (ibid., p. 307).

Nespor (1987) suggests that beliefs facilitate the retrieval and reconstitution of memory processes, thus being instrumental in task definition and cognitive strategy selection, and facilitating manoeuvre between repertoires. He views teacher beliefs as affective, narrative in nature and relying on correspondences with evaluations from the past. According to Nespor, beliefs are episodic, often deriving from powerful experiences or critical incidents in the individual's past.

Nespor identifies six dimensions or features of beliefs (as opposed to knowledge which he differentiates from beliefs). These are: (1) *existential presumption* (belief about the existence or non-existence of entities, such as, for example, the idea that students are lazy); (2) *alternativity* (beliefs are representations of alternative world views, whether achieved or not); (3) *affective/evaluative aspects* (beliefs tend to be rooted more strongly in affective rather than cognitive processes than is the case with knowledge); (4) *episodic storage* (beliefs derive their power from their rootedness in strongly experienced episodes in people's pasts); (5) *non-consensuality* (beliefs are more readily disputable than knowledge); and (6) *unboundedness* (beliefs form 'loosely bounded systems and highly variable and uncertain linkages to events, situations and knowledge systems' – Nespor 1987, p. 321). This framing is useful in defining the parameters of belief and in attempting an analytical differentiation of knowledge and beliefs.

Teacher beliefs can be identified as a subset of wider belief systems held by individuals. Often, these are difficult to disentangle, although much literature seeks to do so, and indeed Pajares (1992, p. 326) warns that 'seeing educational beliefs as detached from and unconnected to a broader belief system, for example, is ill advised and probably unproductive'.

Categorizing teacher beliefs

Various authors have sought to specify different sub-categories of teacher belief. For example, some authors have distinguished between traditional belief sets and progressive belief sets. The former *orientation* (Belo et al. 2014) has been variously characterized as being performative, qualification led, content driven, subject oriented and teacher regulated. The latter has been framed as being driven by personal development, as learning or student centred, as constructivist and participative and as promoting mastery (e.g. Wallace and Kang 2004; Meirink et al. 2009; Ertmer and Ottenbreit-Leftwich 2010; Belo et al. 2014). Belo and colleagues (2014) point to the unhelpfulness of dichotomizing beliefs between these two poles, suggesting that teachers can hold contradictory beliefs that fall into both camps. Thus, there may be tension between conflicting professional beliefs (Wallace and Kang 2004); there may be tension between personal belief and professional beliefs (Wallace and Priestley 2011) or there may be dissonance between core and peripheral beliefs (van der Schaaf, Stocking and Verloop 2008; Nishino 2012).

Other authors have sought to categorize beliefs according to the object of belief. Pajares (1992) suggests that unless beliefs are seen to be '*beliefs about*'

(p. 316, emph. in original) something, they remain 'diffuse and ungainly, too difficult to operationalize, too context free' (ibid.). Pajares suggests that teacher beliefs can be broken down into beliefs about teacher confidence (efficacy beliefs); about the nature of knowledge (epistemological beliefs); student performance beliefs (including beliefs about student attributes); and pedagogical beliefs (which may include subject-specific beliefs about the best way to teach). Broadly, these are beliefs about self, students and the subject taught (see ibid., p. 308). Similarly, Devine, Fahie and McGillicuddy (2013) put forward a typology of beliefs about 'self, context, knowledge, pedagogy and students' (p. 104). Fang (1996) suggests that teacher beliefs can be differentiated as beliefs about students and beliefs about the subject (including pedagogy). Van der Schaaf, Stokking and Verloop (2008) posit three types of beliefs: behavioural beliefs (expected effects of practices); subjective norms (such as expected support from others); and control beliefs (expected factors that will impact upon practices).

Beliefs and context

Another important strand of the literature, and one that is key to understanding how agency is shaped by different aspects of its ecology, is the relationship between beliefs and context. It is generally accepted that beliefs and practices do not necessarily correspond. Pajares (1992) points to the importance of understanding how dissonance between beliefs and structural/cultural contexts shapes practice. Nishino (2012) suggests that contextual factors prevent correspondence between beliefs and practices. Rubie-Davies, Flint and McDonald (2012) assert that teacher beliefs are always likely to be moderated by contextual factors. These are important themes in respect of the ecological approach to teacher agency and will be explored later in this chapter in relation to our empirical data. Nevertheless, existing research suggests that teacher beliefs strongly influence teacher behaviour (e.g. Nespor 1987; van Driel, Beijard, and Verloop 2001; Yerrick, Park, and Nugent 1997), as the former 'may guide' the latter 'either deliberately or spontaneously' (van der Schaaf, Stocking and Verloop 2008, p. 1692).

Thus, beliefs form an important dimension of teacher agency, and it is important to also acknowledge that teacher mediation of policy is to a large extent shaped according to teachers' beliefs. Osborn et al. (1997) suggest various forms of mediation, in response to mandated reform, which have their roots to some extent in teacher beliefs. For example, they coin the term *protective mediation* to describe action where teachers believe strongly that it is their role to protect students from what they see as the damaging effects of new policy. They utilize the term *conspiratorial mediation* to describe action that is concerned with undermining reform. Such literature suggests that even within restrictive environments created by prescriptive policies such as England's 'National Curriculum', teachers are able to find ways to mediate the curriculum, filtering 'change through their own values, which are in turn influenced by gender, social class, previous experience in the classroom, professional training and other historical and biographical factors' (Osborn et al. 1997, p. 57). According to Bowe, Ball and Gold (1992), such trends are especially evident in high-capacity departments. An interesting question for us in conducting this study is whether teachers with strong professional beliefs are able to achieve agency more readily than others whose beliefs are less well defined – in other words, do strong professional beliefs enable teachers to act otherwise in the face of strong social pressures when their working environments restrict agency or to manoeuvre between repertoires when they are faced with impossible dilemmas in their work.

The formation of teacher beliefs

Further issues to consider in this section are how teacher beliefs are formed and whether once formed they are mutable. There is a widespread view in much of the literature that teacher beliefs are formed early in a teacher's career. Indeed, many authors suggest that the majority of teachers' beliefs are formed through their early life experiences (particularly their own schooling) before they undertake pre-service teacher education (Pajares 1992; Nishino 2012). This literature lends credence to Elliot Eisner's (1994) maxim that teachers' professional socialization begins at the age of five.

Pajares (1992) argues that this is a problem in respect of reforming the educational system.

> Most students who choose education as a career have had a positive identification with teaching, and this leads to continuity of conventional practice and reaffirmation, rather than challenge, of the past. It does not occur to most preservice teachers, for example, that one of their future functions might be, should be, as agents for societal change. Students become teachers unable, and subconsciously unwilling, to affect a system in need of reform. (p. 323)

This is, of course, an issue of agency. Teachers whose belief sets are fixed by early experiences may lack an ability to manoeuvre between a broad range of repertoires in their practice and may thus be unable to act flexibly and agentically in the face of problematic dilemmas in their professional lives.

A related issue lies in whether beliefs may be subject to change over time due to professional experience and professional development activity. There is some disagreement in the literature as to the mutability of teacher beliefs: many writers follow Pajares in taking the view that 'beliefs are formed early and tend to self-perpetuate, persevering even against contradictions caused by reason, time, schooling, or experience' (p. 324) and that belief shift is not common in adulthood (e.g. Belo et al. 2014). Some suggest that teachers with a student-centred orientation are more likely to embrace new ideas and change their beliefs (e.g. Meirink 2009). Others are more optimistic that powerful forms of professional development can shift teachers' beliefs (e.g. Borg 2011). It is likely that Meirink et al. (2009) are correct in their belief that there is a shortage of research in this area and that we do not yet have a clear picture.

A final point relates to the nature of teacher beliefs, which may be tacit and inarticulate (van der Schaaf, Stocking and Verloop 2008; Belo et al. 2014). According to van der Schaaf, Stokking and Verloop (2008), reflexivity about beliefs is an important aspect of teachers' agency because 'only by becoming aware of their beliefs, can teachers further develop their repertoire' (p. 1691), presumably through recognition of, and attention to, dissonance between competing belief sets.

Exploring teacher beliefs

The existing literature on teacher beliefs indicates that they play an important role in teachers' actions and hence in the achievement of agency. As we have mentioned in the introduction, teacher beliefs always 'play out' in the present, that is, in the concrete situations in which teachers act. Such beliefs are rooted in the past, in that they have developed from previous experiences – both personal/biographical and professional. In addition, beliefs – in the form of aspirations, intentions, expectations and goals, give actions in the here and now a strong (sense of) direction – which concerns the projective dimension of agency. We have organized the discussion of our findings about teachers' beliefs under three headings: *beliefs about children and young people*; *beliefs about teaching*; and *beliefs about educational purpose*. In what follows, we discuss these beliefs with reference to our three questions: (1) What are the beliefs that teachers hold? (2) Where do these beliefs come from? (3) And how do they play a role in the achievement of agency (or lack thereof)?

Beliefs relating to children and young people

The data clearly convey the strong sense of teachers' professional responsibility towards their students. The teachers reported working long hours, including work taken home. The secondary teachers talked of using their free time in school to focus on students' needs and issues, a knock-on consequence being that planning and other curricular work had to be done out of school working hours. All the teachers believed that the relationships they developed with their students were critical to establishing what they would generally refer to as a framework for learning. The significance of what was often referred to as a safe and caring learning environment for everyone who came into their classrooms was articulated strongly. In general, these were teachers who wished to do their best for their students and who frequently talked in terms of maximizing student potential. We will come back to this construct in due course when we discuss the beliefs of the teachers relating to purposes of education, but make a note of it at this point in relation to the positive professional orientation of the teachers towards students.

Nevertheless, these generally positive aspects were tempered by what might be seen as a deficit view of children. This view was exhibited, tacitly at least, through use of a particular language by majority of the teachers participating in our research, suggesting the presence of strong professional discourses about children that in turn seem to limit teacher agency in particular ways in respect of curriculum development. A strong discourse by teachers of 'existential presumption' (Nespor 1987) lay in the repeated use of terms like 'able', 'bright' and 'poor' to describe their students. Examples of this sort of language can be found in the following excerpts.

The more able pupils still want classroom teaching from the front. They want to have things written down. They want to be taught in the old established way of teaching and that is what they want because they see that as their route to get to further education. The less able pupils prefer the less structure but they are in actual fact the ones who are less able to manage their own learning. [Susan]

You have got a really gifted able child and you have got a pupil who can barely read and write at a secondary level, they are still in primary two, three reading, writing ability. [Sara]

In my opinion that is the right thing especially for people who are not the brightest. They need life skills. They need skills to be able to help them in areas that they are maybe not so great at. [Rachael]

These quotations are interesting on a number of levels. For example, they strongly suggest that many teachers continue to see education primarily in terms of its qualification function (Biesta 2010), with a concomitant emphasis on getting through the syllabus. In the light of such perception of the teacher's job, our data suggest that some teachers see the inclusion of 'less able' children in their classes as unhelpful. Such language suggests that many teachers continue to see ability as a unitary and fixed concept, despite the recent prevalence in educational discourse of notions of multiple intelligence and learning styles, for example.

Interestingly, these latter beliefs were also strongly evident in our transcripts, suggesting that a contested and often confused terrain of competing discourses underpins teachers' practices. For instance, teachers talked a great deal about personalization and choice, such as in the following example.

> If you understand that you have individuals in your classroom and not a homogenous group, then you can respond differently and have different strategies and different goals that are appropriate to whichever person is in front of you at that time. [Susan]

Another theme that seems to lie in some tension to the espoused notions of ability described above relates to teachers' views about pupils becoming more responsible for their own learning – a trend termed 'responsibilization' by Davies (2006). Such discourses underpin 'Curriculum for Excellence', and this language was used regularly by our participants, including in ways that contradict other beliefs about children. Two teachers spoke about the shift from knowledge to skills in the new curriculum, suggesting that their role was now to develop

> independent learners. Confident about being given a task and using the right skills in order to do it the best way they can. [Rachael]

Another teacher explained it similarly.

> You are teaching a lot of the skills that we want the children to have, the independence, working on their own, choosing what they are doing, deciding which way. [Eilidh]

Still another teacher put it far more explicitly, giving some revealing insights into her views about the relative responsibility afforded to teachers and pupils.

> Could you imagine a teacher turning round to the kids and saying, 'right I am just going to fail you all because I could not be bothered doing the marking'. But

that is effectively what they are doing by saying, 'can I not just drop out'. So it is infuriating when you make the decision that 'right, I am going to need to do this' but the kids just seem to back off. It does get your blood boiling a little bit. ... But then you think in that case, 'how much influence could I actually have' because what if they are deciding that and then they have not got a parent at their back saying, 'no, computer off, homework'. So I do not know. There is [sic] some kids I will never get through to. [Sara]

One teacher, who expressed strong support throughout her interviews for 'Curriculum for Excellence' and the notion of students taking responsibility for their own learning, suggested that this idea was problematic because of the capabilities of the students themselves.

> No, they do not actually understand what responsibility for their own learning is. And they are not capable of managing it. [Susan]

The above quotes are illustrative of tensions in teachers' beliefs about children and young people and their abilities and capabilities. They partly see their role as a directive and active one – to fix perceived deficits in students that have their roots in social backgrounds and general levels of ability. And yet, at a rhetorical level at least, and in potential tension with this directive role, these teachers subscribe to the discourses of the new curriculum, particularly with regard to responsibilization. There is a sense here that there is a grey area in the issue of whose responsibility it is to ensure that learning takes place. Thus, students with 'poor' ability or students who do not take 'responsibility' for their own learning provide a justification for the teacher to abdicate some professional responsibility, blaming students as 'mad, bad or stupid' (Watzlawick, Wickland and Fisch, in Salomon 1992, p. 45). Or conversely, such traits provide a justification for the teacher to intervene to take charge and assume responsibility and, on occasion, even to protect students from what might be considered as faults in the education system.

An example of this latter tendency is found in one teacher's recourse to what has been termed 'protective mediation' (Osborn et al. 1997), a way of acting where teachers – agentically – seek to protect their students from aspects of policies and practices that they consider unhelpful or harmful. She mentioned that she sometimes gave tests without telling pupils that they were being tested. Upon being questioned about this practice, she stated that she believed that excessive testing placed harmful demands upon students; thus, while she felt obliged (by the system) to administer tests, she also sought to protect students from their worst excesses. Such action suggests a high degree of agency; this teacher clearly sees alternative courses of action, and her decisions in this matter are clearly driven by her beliefs about education and young people. The direction taken in such cases is likely to be highly dependent on how teachers see their own role in the process. This is examined in the next section. We will return to teacher responsibility later in the chapter as this, along with the beliefs that underpin it, has profound implications for the agency achieved by teachers.

Beliefs about the role of the teacher

As with their beliefs about students, our participants displayed a largely homogeneous range of views about their roles as teachers. Most notable was a commonly acknowledged view that the role has changed – from that of a deliverer of knowledge to that of a facilitator of learning and from a subject specialist to a teacher of children. We found this slightly surprising, given the previously discussed views of the teachers towards children's ability. It also seems to fly in the face of the prevalent and commonly expressed view that teachers – especially secondary teachers – are sceptical about both the pedagogical approaches advocated within 'Curriculum for Excellence' and its apparent shift towards inter-disciplinarity (for example, for an argument against a downgrading of subject knowledge, see: Ford 2011; also, for an analysis of the place of knowledge in 'Curriculum for Excellence', see: Priestley and Sinnema 2014). Indeed, only one participant strongly referred to the importance of subject knowledge, lamenting what she saw as the detrimental effects of vocationalism on the academic content of her subject. Again, as previously noted, such tensions are probably indicative of the complex origins of teachers' vocabularies and discourses, partly shaped by the concrete context in which they work and the policy that is shaping this context and partly being the outcome of their own educational and professional biography – an issue we return to in Chapter 3.

All of the participants talked about their changed role as facilitators of learning and, as we will show in more detail in Chapter 3, some teachers were more comfortable with this perceived shift than others. There was some evidence, as found in previous research, that the teachers were able 'to assimilate the messages of reform institutes without changing fundamental views of ... teaching' (Yerrick, Park, and Nugent 1997, p. 155) and to find ways 'to view potentially contrary messages in ways that accentuate their own beliefs' (p. 154). Thus, in some cases, this role was seen in an overtly student-centred and divergent manner:

I studied a bit of the background to [its] philosophy and realized how that is actually teaching them social skills as well. In a good way. And teaching them not just to assume things about people, or make assumptions about life. And really quite difficult critical thinking skills as well. It was difficult to teach that. You are not teaching it actually. You are a facilitator. [Monica]

In others, there seemed to be a more instrumental and directive approach, one suggesting convergence and following the demands of the syllabus:

The teacher's role is as a facilitator [laughs] to encourage and enable the learner. To have access to the stimulus you need to encourage them to make the right choices. Or to learn in a particular style. To jump through hoops and pass exams because, at the end of the day, that is how it is measured. [Susan]

A major focus of the new curriculum is to introduce more interdisciplinary work. In principle, this was applauded by many of the teachers, although the understanding of what that meant in practice caused concern, particularly in the secondary schools. This belies the sorts of views expressed by Ford (2011). One of the senior managers – at Lakeside High School – expressed his belief that interdisciplinary work was the way forward for the school. He went as far as to say that this kind of work made a 'good school', linking interdisciplinary work to student choice and to personalized learning.

This is what makes a good school; people should really have known that already about the importance of working across different faculties. The importance of giving personalization and choice at the right time and giving guidance at the right time and so on. [senior manager]

He believed that it was his responsibility to cultivate trust and confidence in his staff. He expected them to be willing to take risks and to try out new ideas. Such autonomy – the notion that teachers are to be agents of change within the new curriculum – elicited some interesting thoughts from some of the teachers. All of the participants expressed anxiety at the prospect of this. Two teachers, in particular, espoused views that are probably indicative of wider currents of thinking among Scottish teachers: deference to authority, a lack of willingness to take responsibility for issues seen to the remit of those further up the chain and nervousness about being 'required' to be autonomous in their work. One teacher, who in lots of ways was seen to achieve agency in her work, stated that:

You just do a good job. You try your best. You do not muck around. You do not do things you should not do or challenge superiors in a way unless it's obviously something genuine. [Sara]

Another expressed strong anxieties about curriculum development.

> Somebody goes on a course and they come back, we had girls on a course who came back and said 'this is just unbelievable what they are saying about it', 'you have got to take one statement in and unpack that whole thing and then put that into lots of other little statements and then work out how you are going to achieve delivering that or how you are going to do this'. And you just think, it is a job. I can't give more of my time, my time personally. I feel, I am in from 9 to 3 teaching the children and from 3 till, I know I am 3 till 6, and more, trying to prepare for the next day without having to then say 'when am I going to do all this?'. It is not feasibly possible. And every school, every council and every teacher are all trying to do this instead of somebody somewhere coming up with it. The E's and O's[1] were meant to be there to declutter your programme but what you are wanting you to do now is to take that statement and then start building from it. [Eilidh]

Interestingly, despite this apparent reluctance to rock the boat, and/or to become more actively engaged in developing the curriculum in school, all of the teachers readily criticized a range of issues that they saw as impacting negatively on their ability to do their jobs. These included the impact of accountability (which will be further developed in Chapter 5), particularly what they saw as the overemphasis on attainment noted in the previous section (which was seen as being in tension with 'Curriculum for Excellence'), and a perceived tendency for teachers' voices to be ignored in favour of the views of people with little or no immediate connection with schools and workload issues. Many such complaints were framed by the fact that these teachers clearly took pride in their work. At first glance, it is puzzling how professionals can apparently abdicate responsibility for aspects of their work and then complain that they are not being listened to. In the next section, we examine this issue in the light of how these teachers view the purposes of education.

Beliefs about educational purpose

The teachers in our research demonstrated broadly similar beliefs about educational purpose. These tended to coalesce around a small number of key themes. Two key themes are socialization and the development of key skills or competencies. According to one teacher:

> Well the main thing you would come straight away is for learning. But not just academic learning. You are building them as individuals to know how to relate

to others, how to socialize, interact. To get them prepared for the wider world. ...
The socialization part for me is really important. ... Schools can provide kids
with things that they might not get at home, some kids obviously. The chance to
work with other people in a supportive environment. The chance to be part of a
team. Not necessarily the actual explicit curriculum, what is going on behind the
scenes. It is a place for kids to find themselves. [Sara]

Another teacher expressed similar views.

With the 'Curriculum for Excellence' ... they are focusing more on skills. And it
is skills for learning, skills for work, skills for life that you are focusing on more.
So when you are doing a topic, you are not always thinking about the knowledge
that they are going to get from it. Coz is that knowledge ever going to be used?
It is nice to learn things, facts but that cannot be transferred. That is not going
to help them when they leave school [laughs]. Whereas the skills that help them
learn those things or do a certain activity in a certain way is what will help them
in the future. [Rachael]

Several issues jump out from these transcripts, which broadly reflect views
encountered in interviews with all of the teachers and senior managers. First,
these views provide what we might term a rather instrumental or functionalist
engagement with the question of educational purpose, that is, seeing it more
in terms of particular aims rather than with regard to the bigger question what
education is *for* (see Biesta 2010). While socialization and skills development
can be seen as long-term aspirations for the curriculum – in this regard,
they are not concrete 'learning outcomes' that can be achieved at the end of
a single lesson – they are nonetheless concrete in their orientation. It might
also be argued that such aims are somewhat convergent in nature, especially
those relating to socialization. These seem to be about the development of
predetermined capacities and dispositions which are more about equipping
students to function effectively in a society 'as it is', rather than providing them
with the skills to handle uncertainty and to be agents of change in their own turn
as they contribute to the development of a society that 'might be'.

Second, if one digs deeper into the discourses of skills development and
socialization expressed by these teachers, one is struck by what is missing. The
teachers tended to articulate aims that are rather open in nature: phrases such
as 'reaching their potential' and 'finding themselves' are common in the data.
There is talk of developing teamwork skills and thinking skills but no systematic
evidence in the data of sense making[2] to further unpack what these mean and
little articulation of the fine detail. Often the aim of education is somewhat

tautological: the aim of education is learning, but there is little clear picture of what is being learnt, or why. Surprisingly, especially in the secondary schools, and as previously mentioned, there is little sense in our data of education being about the acquisition of knowledge. Similarly, and perhaps equally surprising, there is also little about qualification or accreditation as a purpose of education. This is mentioned by some participants, but most often in negative terms (as a competing pressure) and rarely as an explicit purpose of education despite the high profile given to attainment data in Scottish schools. Also conspicuous by its absence is an explicit discourse about wider educational values. At no point did any of our respondents talk, for example, about social justice or democratic values, albeit, as we will show in Chapter 3, within their wider views about education there was awareness of the wider social purpose of education. Yet many beliefs seemed to centre around notions of personal responsibility and participation as core goals of citizenship, for which schools should prepare students (for an extended discussion of these concepts in a North American context, see: Westheimer and Kahne 2004; for an application of these ideas in the Scottish context, see: Biesta 2013a).

Two further issues are worthy of mention in relation to educational purposes. The first concerns whether teacher aspirations are long term or short term in nature. Addressing the first question, it is apparent that much of the professional dialogue about educational purpose is not in fact long term. Where it is, and as noted above, there tends to be a fairly strong instrumental slant to it. Our data suggest that a large proportion of teacher aspirations in respect of their teaching are relatively short term in nature, and that a good deal of day-to-day planning and activity is performed with this in mind. This concurs with earlier research (Brown and McIntyre 1993) which strongly suggested that teacher decision-making is driven by a perceived need to maintain a 'normal desirable state' in the classroom. The following excerpts provide a flavour of this, suggesting that much teacher action is shaped by short-term aspirations to tick curricular boxes, deliver enjoyable lessons, keep students engaged and interested and keep classes quiet and well behaved.

> Very organised, loads of tasks, very 'Curriculum for Excellence' hitting. Health and well-being, literacy and numeracy and [subject deleted], blah, blah, blah. All the things. And very much about working in a group. [Susan]

> I think my priority is always engaging the kids and producing lessons that they like and enjoy and can relate to. And that is always my focus. And like I said in the background, floating in the edges, I'm aware of 'Curriculum for Excellence'

and that it does introduce changes. There is going to be having to think about it moments in the future. But right now I don't feel like it's having that big an impact on a daily basis. ... I want the kids to come in and enjoy my class and enjoy what we do. And that's always my priority. It's always the question I ask at the end of every lesson at the end of every day, 'am I doing a good job, are they enjoying it, are they not enjoying it?' That's always my priority. [Sara]

I do like going and finding different things to do just to make it more interesting for me and for the children. And just coming with the times. [Rachael]

For me it is the fun that they have. If they learn, you see them develop, regardless of how slow or fast it is. But they enjoy it. But also that I am enjoying it. The days that I know I have not enjoyed, I know that I am sometimes a bit more narky and maybe they are not enjoying it so much. When they do something, when they are smiling, particularly primary ones. [Eilidh]

This focus on process and the comparative lack of explicit engagement with purpose and values strongly suggests a disconnection between purpose and method, which may well impact on the quality of education that emerges as a result of teacher engagement with 'Curriculum for Excellence'. This latter danger is neatly encapsulated by this anguished extract from one interview.

And then you also wonder about the pupil experience. We had a visit from the inspector last week and he was following one of my sixth year pupils. And the [unclear words] this was the only class we did any work in. In another class they were making a poster. This is someone in sixth year, doing advanced higher something and they were making a poster. Now I am not saying making a poster is not a useful thing to do but it seems like the pupils are very, very fed up with making posters. It is like everyone has got the idea that 'Curriculum for Excellence' is about making a poster about what you have learned. [Monica]

We will return to the issue of purpose in the final section of the chapter, but it is first worth briefly dwelling upon a second issue. This relates to the language used by teachers in framing the projective. One thing that is evident from our conversations with the teachers is the influence of policy language on the ways in which they frame their practices. This is evident in the terminology used by the teachers, even where (as, for example, in the case described above of students taking responsibility for their learning) there were clearly large differences in how different teachers interpreted the terms used. One question this raises is what the professional discourses of teachers actually look like and to what extent these are being influenced by policy language, policy concepts and policy demands. This may, after all, reduce the opportunities for the achievement of agency by limiting the teachers' potential for envisaging different futures and by denying them the language with which to engage critically with policy. We return in detail to this issue in Chapter 3. Furthermore, in apparent lack of opportunities for systematic sense making of the core concepts of 'Curriculum for Excellence', teachers' understandings of the concepts often remain superficial and vague. A number of teachers expressed overt doubts on this matter.

> The actual 'Curriculum for Excellence' philosophy, if that is the right use of the word, where it is all about the children, it is all about preparing them for all of these things but then they come up with something that is very airy fairy. [Eilidh]

> The theories sound great and then what we are getting on bits of paper just seems like, 'oh we have to change this and do this'. And I do not know, it is overly complicated but then there is a mixture between outlines and then not enough detail. ... Most people I have spoken to feel the same as I do, that they are fumbling about trying things. [Monica]

This latter issue raises interesting questions about the ways in which schools are structured, and the opportunities that teachers have to engage in generative dialogue (Imants 2002) with one another. We return to a detailed discussion of teacher networks and relationships in Chapter 4.

Discussion and conclusions

The foregoing analysis raises some important issues about the ways in which teachers engage with new curricular policy and about their agency. Teacher agency is highly dependent upon the personal qualities that teachers bring to their work. Such capacity, which forms the major part of the iterational dimension of their agency, includes professional knowledge and skills, and in many senses, there is little doubt that the experienced teachers in our project are highly advanced in these respects. However, the iterational dimension also includes the beliefs and values that the teachers bring to their work. Our analysis reveals that such beliefs and values are not held in a vacuum but are themselves the result of the range of influences, demands and pressures that structure the settings – the particular ecologies – within which teachers think and act. Part of the problem seems to lie in the often mixed and contradictory discourses encountered in schools and in teachers' often superficial understandings of such discourses. This will be discussed in more detail in the next chapter.

Many of the discourses of modern schooling actually appear to be a mish-mash of competing and vague ideas – personalization, choice, learning, subjects, etc. – and where opportunities for systematic sense making in schools are limited, teachers can easily be left confused about their role. These confusions were clearly evident in many of the personal and professional beliefs we encountered during the research. Arguably, much of the blame for this situation lies in externally imposed systems that alter the dynamics of schooling, leading to incremental change without the development of a clear philosophy of education to underpin the changes in question (see also Chapter 5) and a professional collegiality that enables its development. It is notable that even in the secondary school where we witnessed a clearer sense of purpose, higher levels of professional confidence and purposeful relational structures to enabling collegial working (this will be discussed further in Chapter 5), we found little evidence of long-term thinking about the purposes of education. This perhaps says more about the cultures of schooling than the structures, reinforcing Michael Fullan's (2003) dictum that change requires reculturing as well as restructuring.

This leads us onto questions of purpose and value – part of the projective dimension of agency. Our data suggest that at the level of beliefs many teachers struggle to locate their work within deep consideration of the purposes of education. Teachers are driven by goals in their work, but such goals often seem to be short term in nature, focusing on process rather than long-term effects. It is only when we look in detail at the underlying vocabularies and discourses that teachers use to make sense of the environments in which they act – which we will do in the next chapter – that wider concerns and longer-term views and expectations about schooling become visible. Yet, in the context of the everyday practice, such views not only remain largely invisible but, as a result, may also have less impact, if any. A narrow, implicit framing of purpose has, we believe, implications for the ways in which teachers achieve agency. The comparative lack of a clear vision about what education is for seems to seriously limit the possibilities for action to develop a good education. Purposes that are narrowly framed inevitably narrow consideration of what is possible and frame subsequent action accordingly.

Salomon (1992) offers insights about this in terms of the professional responsibility of teachers, drawing a distinction between efficiency and effectiveness. Our data suggest that the teachers in our project were highly efficient in getting the job done, despite inevitable difficulties encountered in terms of social, cultural and material constraints on their work. These teachers had a large repertoire of technical responses to enable their lessons to run smoothly. They were effective in achieving certain short-term goals, for example, introducing new forms of pedagogy that were deemed suitable for 'Curriculum for Excellence'. One might also argue that there was a long-term effectiveness in socializing young people, particularly in terms of the schools running smoothly in the long term. However, the data suggest a fairly narrow engagement with consideration of the 'effects' of education – 'desirable residues to be manifested later on' (p. 44).

Salomon argues that such approaches represent a derogation of teacher responsibility. He posits three types of teacher responsibility:

- a proper carrying out of the role as a teacher (necessary as to whether a teacher is transmitting content or orchestrating activity);
- responsibility for learning processes and outcomes;
- serious consideration of method and content in the light of normative and moral criteria – that is, consideration of long-term educational purposes and values. This responsibility is about 'giving serious consideration to the desirable and less desirable long-term effects of the constantly improvised learning environment' (ibid., p. 46).

It is clear from our data that the first responsibility was taken seriously by the teachers in our project. The second is more of a grey area, given the discourses about shifting responsibility to students. Nevertheless, our data suggest that the teachers tended to take this responsibility very seriously as well, despite the aforementioned ambiguity. The third area of responsibility seems to be more problematic. The relative absence of explicit long-term beliefs about the purposes of education appears to be a major deficit in the schools where our research was undertaken. Moreover, this is an issue of teacher agency. We would argue that such narrowness of vision and purpose limits and delineates teacher agency in particular ways, narrowly defining what is possible within the terrain opened up by 'Curriculum for Excellence'.

The data presented in this chapter, which obviously only refer to three particular, although nonetheless interesting, cases, do indicate that teachers' beliefs matter to the extent to which, and the degree in which, teachers are able to achieve agency within the particular educational ecologies in which they work. What our particular approach to the issue of teacher agency helps to make visible is what role teachers' beliefs play, both with regard to the ways in which such beliefs provide a 'window' on the here and now (the practical–evaluative dimension of agency) and the ways in which such beliefs give direction towards the future (the projective dimension). Perhaps the most important finding in the particular cases we have presented here – one that becomes highly visible when one investigates individual teachers' belief – is the absence of a robust professional discourse about teaching. Instead, we have seen the prevalence of beliefs that are strongly orientated towards the here and now and that are also strongly influenced by current and recent policy rather than by more encompassing orientations about the wider purpose and meaning of schooling. The relative absence of a robust professional discourse that teachers can bring to the situations in which they work, and a relatively weak set of orientations towards the future, thus seem to limit the possibilities teachers have to utilize their beliefs in achieving agency within contexts that are to a significant degree – albeit not entirely – constructed by systems of accountability, which seem to prioritize and value certain modes of action over others. These are, of course, questions to do with school culture and the wider societal discourses that frame the work of schools. In the next chapter, we further develop this analysis, by considering teachers' personal and professional vocabularies and discourses and the ways in which these contribute to the achievement of agency.

If, in conclusion, we return to the three questions that have informed our analysis – (1) What are the teachers' beliefs? (2) Where do they come from? (3) And how do they impact on the achievement of agency (or lack thereof)? – we have, in this chapter, provided a detailed account of the beliefs the teachers in our project held about children, about teachers and about the purposes of education. While many of the beliefs expressed may not sound unfamiliar to those working in contemporary education, it is perhaps remarkable that many beliefs seem to echo current policies and trends. We could say, therefore, that such policies and trends seem to be quite successful in shaping teachers' beliefs, although, as we will show in the next chapter, with some teachers the impact of policy on beliefs, language and discourse is much stronger than on others. The extent to which policy discourse has been internalized thus raises questions about the degree to which teachers may have resources to act differently, should they judge that this might be important. This does not mean that the teachers in our project did not act in agentic ways, but the structure and character of their beliefs raise important questions about the extent to which they had resources for seeing things differently.

To put it differently, our research reveals the ways in which, and the extent to which, teachers tend to adjust to the prevailing framework of 'Curriculum for Excellence' because of the limited resources for engaging with it in a more critical manner, and also with limited aspirations that would allow them to explore different directions. This is, of course, not just a matter of beliefs – as we will discuss in later chapters – but also of the context within which, and the conditions under which, teachers work. Our analysis suggests that, although the beliefs that teachers have are 'in line' with, and are actually the result of, the policy environment in which they work, they may provide little 'help' for teachers to engage with this environment in a critical manner. With regard to the second question – where the beliefs that these teachers hold come from? – we can conclude that the existing policy and practice environment appears to have exerted a significant influence on the teachers' beliefs. It is only when we place these beliefs within the wider context of teachers' vocabularies and discourses and the particular ecologies within which such vocabularies and discourses are formed and utilized that we can begin to see more nuance, including differences between individual teachers that, when just viewed at the level of beliefs, may remain largely invisible.

While one conclusion to draw from this is to suggest that teacher beliefs are more malleable than some researchers may assume, we should also not forget the 'drivers' of the particular contexts in which these teachers worked, which, as we will show in more detail in later chapters, did significantly constrain the teachers' scope for independent action and judgement. While this does not diminish the importance of teachers' beliefs for their achievement of agency, the particular 'case' we have presented here predominantly provides insights into how beliefs may limit teacher agency, which does, as mentioned, highlight the importance of a more independent set of professional beliefs. This moves the discussion from questions about individual beliefs to the wider discourses within which teachers work and form their beliefs. This is the focus on the next chapter.

Teacher Vocabularies and Discourses

Introduction

In the previous chapter, we have looked in detail at the particular beliefs teachers bring to their work. Such beliefs are important in two respects: they provide a focus for engaging with the present – the practical–evaluative dimension of teacher agency – and they provide a sense of direction towards the future – the projective dimension. If in the previous chapter we zoomed *in* on beliefs, in this chapter we zoom *out* and look at the wider vocabularies and discourses teachers utilize to talk about, give meaning to and think about their actions and about the practices they act in. Such vocabularies and discourses are of crucial importance because they can, in a very fundamental sense, be seen as the 'material' teachers think *with*. It is quite easy to say that some people can't think, or that they can't think properly, but what is often forgotten in such judgements is that thinking is not some kind of abstract operation but is always concrete and always happens 'in' and 'through' language. This means, to put it simply, that the quality of thought and reasoning crucially depends on the quality of the vocabularies and discourses one thinks with – and this is why teachers' vocabularies and discourses matter, both for the ways in which they see and reflect on their practice and for the ways in which such seeing and thinking help or hinder the achievement of agency.

In this chapter, we therefore explore in more detail the vocabularies and discourses the teachers in our project used. We are not just focusing on questions of content – that is, on *what* teachers say – but also, and more importantly for this chapter, on what we might call the form of what teachers say – that is, on the question of *how* things are said. In a quite straightforward sense, we will, in this chapter, therefore focus on how teachers *talk* – how they talk about their job, their actions, their professional life, their personal experiences, their ways of making sense of the situation they encounter and so on – as we believe that such talk provides insights into the vocabularies and discourses that play a role in teachers' thinking and doing.

As in the previous chapter, our analysis is guided by three questions: one question is what these vocabularies and discourses look like; the second is where they might come from and the third is how they are relevant for the achievement of agency (or lack thereof). As it is the detail of the talk that matters in this chapter, we quote more extensively from the interviews than in the previous chapter because it is only when we look at the detail of the talk that we can begin to see how the talk 'flows' and 'functions', so to speak, how the teachers 'operate' with the concepts, ideas, beliefs and values they have, and where this leads them in making sense of the situations in which they act. Whereas in the previous chapter, we provided a thematic analysis of our findings, in this chapter, we focus on individual teachers and their vocabularies and discourses.

The interest in teachers' vocabularies and discourses has for a long time been studied under the rubric of knowledge, most notably teachers' professional knowledge. This interest can be traced back to Shulman's distinction between different kinds of teacher knowledge – content knowledge, general knowledge, curriculum knowledge, pedagogical content knowledge, knowledge of learners and their characteristic, knowledge of educational contexts, knowledge of educational ends, purposes and values and their philosophical and historical grounds (see Shulman 1986, p. 8) – or Schwab's interest in the role of practical reasoning and judgement in teaching (see Schwab 2013[1970]; Biesta 2013b); work that itself is embedded within wider discourses about knowledge and judgement in a wide range of professional practices (see, for example, Schön 1983, 1987; Eraut 1994). Within the research on teacher knowledge, a distinction can be found between a more 'narrow' approach that focuses on teachers' propositional or theoretical knowledge – nowadays often connected to scientifically validated evidence about 'what works' (see Biesta 2007b, for an overview and critical discussion), and a more 'encompassing' approach in which teachers' knowledge is not only knowledge *for* teachers generated elsewhere but also the knowledge *of* teachers (for the distinction see Fenstermacher 1994). This is the 'stock of knowledge' gained from a range of sources and experiences, including the ongoing engagement with the practice of teaching itself (for an overview see Verloop, van Driel and Meijer 2001; see also Ben-Peretz 2011).

Whereas some research has tried to move away from the personal and the experiential towards the construction of a common or shared 'knowledge base' for teaching (for example, Verloop, van Driel and Meijer 2001), other research has explicitly stayed with teachers' 'personal practical knowledge' (Connelly and Clandinin 1988) in order to deepen our understanding of the complexities and significance of such embodied practical knowledge. This work has taken a particular interest in the narrative dimensions of such knowledge (see ibid.; also Goodson et al. 2010). It is here that there is a connection with what we seek to do in this chapter, where our focus is not on teacher knowledge in the narrow sense of the word – that is, their propositional knowledge *about* education – and also not just on the cognitive dimensions of their discourse but rather on the wider ways of speaking they utilize to talk about and make sense of their practice. Knowledge is part of this – both official/propositional knowledge and the experiential knowledge of themselves and their colleagues – but values and beliefs play a role in this too, and at the most 'mundane' level, it simply is about how teachers *talk* about education.

Our focus in reconstructing such talk is on the questions how, in what way and to what extent such talk helps or hinders the achievement of agency. In this regard, we see the teachers' talk – their vocabularies and discourses – as an important *resource* for the achievement of agency. In what follows, we not only seek to make visible what this resource looks like but also how it functions and, more specifically, how it functions in relation to the particular context of our research: the implementation of 'Curriculum for Excellence'. While we will focus on individual teachers and their vocabularies and discourses, it is of course important to bear in mind that such vocabularies and discourses are not invented by teachers but are the outcome of the complex interaction between personal sense making and wider vocabularies and discourses that emanate from a wide range of different sources, including policy, research and public opinion (see, for example, Nichols and Griffith 2009).

As we will show in this chapter, some of these discourses are powerful because they are part of the official structures within teachers' work – for example, the impact of a focus on student achievement; an issue to which we will return in Chapter 6. Other discourses are powerful because they are fashionable within educational circles, such as, for example, the 'new language of learning' (Biesta 2007a, 2010). In this discourse, pupils and students have been redefined as learners, teaching has become the facilitation of learning and schools have been redesignated as learning environments and places for learning. The language of learning has been quickly co-opted in many educational circles and has put pressure on an older and in a sense more explicitly normative language of education, one in which the point of schooling is not defined in terms of facilitating students' learning but where there is a clear engagement with the question of purpose, that is, the question of what the learning is supposed to be *for*.

In the sections that follow, we will show how the discursive resources with which teachers talk and think are both the outcome of their own personal and professional experience and such wider discourses. We will also show that some discourses seem to support the ways in which the teachers make sense of their practice, while others seem to interfere with and distort what they feel matters and should matter in education.

Talking about education (1)

One crucial question in relation to the theme of this chapter is what teachers actually talk about when they talk about education. How, in other words, do they see the 'project' of education and what do they think that the particular task of the school is? Not surprisingly, some teachers have a more articulate way to talk about this than others. When we first look at the primary teachers in our project, we see a clear tendency to think of education in relation to future life and living. One of the primary teachers, in response to our question about what education is for, said that it was 'for growing and living, for life.'

> If we didn't have learning then you wouldn't be able to have the skills in order to survive in anything that starts from the basic skills you learn just as a baby … gradually growing up. And then it is obviously more advanced skills. [Rachael]

She did not think, though, that children would perceive it in this way as well.

> People would not think it is education although, because learning is education. Children, I do not think would see the link. If they were doing something they would not think that they are necessarily having education. They think of education as anything that happened in school, like written things. [Rachael]

For this teacher, there is, therefore, on the one hand a clear distinction between learning as something that can happen all the time and everywhere – 'There is never a point when there is no learning happening' – and what the school is for, although it is interesting that in her way of talking, 'learning' is also what is key in the school. In response to the question what school is for, she said:

> Well, the main thing you would come straight away is for learning. But not just academic learning. You are building them as individuals to know how to relate

to others, how to socialise, interact. To get them prepared for the wider world. [Rachael]

This wider world is particularly conceived in terms of the world of work, which, for this teacher, is an important element of the life for which schools should prepare children.

> And I probably just link it to [work] because you see life as well if you do not work then you are not going to be living much of a life cause you are not going to be making any money. So a lot of it is linked to the work. [Rachael]

What is noticeable in the discourse of this teacher is that she appears to have adopted the idea that 'Curriculum for Excellence' marks a shift in thinking and doing from a focus on knowledge to a focus on skills. 'Skills is the big push,' in her view, which she sees as quite different from the five to fourteen curriculum that 'was all about knowledge.' She sees this as a welcome shift, as 'Curriculum for Excellence' allows her to focus more on education that prepares children for life. What is interesting about the way in which she talks about it is not only the strong distinction she sees between education focused on knowledge and education focused on life but also that she is quite negative about the former (thus buying into a rather common misperception that skills do not require knowledge or that having knowledge or being knowledgeable is devoid of any skills; on this see Gill and Thomson 2012).

> Is it nice to learn things, facts, but that cannot be transferred. That is not going to help them when they leave school. … Whereas the skills that help them learn those things or do a certain activity in a certain way is what will help them in the future. [Rachael]

During the six years that she has been a teacher, she does see this as an important shift in her thinking and in her practice.

> I supposed I have gradually changed in that way that, well I suppose 'cause it is quite all about knowledge. You are not really thinking as much about the skills. … 'Cause you are busy wanting your end product from them. But really the process should take a lot longer cause you should be teaching them the elements to put all together to make this final. So yeh, I do think it has changed. [Rachael]

The emphasis 'Curriculum for Excellence' places on skills is also what the other primary teacher we spoke with mentions as a key aspect of how it has 'landed' in their school. This partly has to do with the discourse of 'Curriculum for Excellence' itself, though the second teacher we spoke to in this school also mentioned that in their school they had decided 'on about twelve skills we felt as a school that if we can do these then our children will leave [Townhead Primary] better people.'

> We chose them linking up skills for work, skills for life, skills for learning. We took these as the topics and worked out, if you wanted to learn, what skills are important. Yes every skill is. I know we will do other ones, incidentally as we go along, but we felt we had to start somewhere. [Eilidh]

If the first teacher not only perceived 'Curriculum for Excellence' in terms of a shift from knowledge to skills but also saw this as a desirable shift, the second teacher saw this far less as an opposition. In her view, 'As an educator you do need to teach the knowledge as well as the skills.' More generally her talk about education and being a teacher contained much more detail and perhaps we could also say nuance – something that may have to do with the fact that she had been in education for a much longer period of time. Here is, for example, how she spoke about her task of being a teacher.

> I think … if I look at it I think it changes between primary one and primary seven. I think in primary one initially it is very much a nurturing and the rules of behaviour within a school have to … you have to pull them back in some ways. It can't be free. An awful lot of them live outside, in their own society where they do what they want, when they want, how they want. And it is just to try and get them back into the fact that, 'no that is not it, we have our rules in here and you have to become a valued member of this school' but in order to do that there has to be respect shown and given. So whereas by primary seven hopefully a lot of that has been instilled but you have got the few, and it is a few, who are pulling against society even at ten, eleven years old. Fighting against it. It is them, it is a control thing and bringing them back and trying to. … But as an educator you do need to teach the knowledge as well as the skills. So as much as it is about teaching the skills so they can go out there has to be certain amounts of knowledge. It is clichés, the relevance of it all. But I think if you do show them that if you couldn't read, you can't go into the bus station and read the times of the trains, how are you going to find the times of the trains? You can't use your computer. It is about trying to show them that 'yes you might find it boring when I am doing this all about timetables, but actually here is the reason for it'. And I think we are beginning to do that a lot more. [Eilidh]

Whereas both teachers connect the point of education with future participation in society, including the world of work, the 'story of education' of the second teacher is a more detailed and nuanced one. That balance is important in this story is also reflected in the way in which this teacher compares her own experiences at school with the current situation.

> The only thing that I can remember from school, and it is such a long time ago from primary, would be the very definite mornings for maths and language work, and the afternoons for the fun activities. I think that what we have got now is far better. I think we integrate much more and the children who maybe won't succeed at the maths and language side of it will succeed in many other areas of the curriculum. I personally wasn't classed as a bright pupil because my English skills were not wonderful in primary. But we didn't do the gym which I excelled in. We didn't do a lot of arty type things. But it was all very much on writing, reading and initially, once I moved up obviously … but secondary school, I just remember it being extremely academic based. Sit down, get on with it, and if you could then you succeeded and if you didn't you went into some other form of employment. I suppose even in my day, moving out to another form of employment was still possible whereas nowadays it is much more difficult. [Eilidh]

Here we see how her own views on education are partly a reflection of her own experience in school – and she clearly sees the benefits of a more integrated approach as in her own educational biography she obviously suffered from a lack thereof during her own time at school.

While it is difficult to pin down why the two discourses of these teachers differ, one important factor lies in the fact that they are from a different professional generation, in that the first teacher had only been teaching for six years whereas the second had been 'in the system' for nearly thirty years already – referring to herself as a 'crabbit old teacher'. There are, in more technical language, two aspects that need to be taken into consideration here, one which we might call an 'age effect' – that is, the impact of having been around for a longer period of time – and the other a 'generation effect', where the second teacher may have been exposed to very different views about education and very different education practices. The 'age effect' is clearly visible in the following remark where she emphasizes that older ideas seem to be coming back.

> I have seen, in teaching, the child centred, the integrated day, the whole class teaching, five to fourteen and then back round to this more child centred, integration on everything again. They always do say that you come round in circles. And that is where I am now, thinking actually what I am doing now in primary one, because I started off in a primary one, a lot of similarities. [Eilidh]

Yet she is also aware that she has become more experienced and more confident over time.

> I think I have become better. I think … when I think back to some of the lessons
> I maybe did when I first started and I think 'oh gosh, I didn't do that did I?' and I
> know we all learn by mistakes and sometimes it is no bad thing because then you
> can talk about it and discuss it, even with the children. But I think because you
> have made these mistakes you become a better teacher. I go to do something and
> then I don't have to think too much about it because I think 'that is not going
> to work, change it'. Whereas maybe twenty years ago I would have tried it and it
> didn't work so the next time I have not. [Eilidh]

Taking the impact of age/experience and generation together, we can see that
the second teacher has access to a discourse that gives her a 'bigger picture',
which allows her to put things in perspective. In this regard, we can say that
the first teacher is more dependent on the policy discourse of 'Curriculum
for Excellence', at least partly because she had not yet had the opportunity to
experience and work through a series of policy and practice shifts and thus has
had less opportunity to develop her discursive 'resources'. What is clear from
the discussion above is that such resources – more concretely, the way they talk
about and understand education, the school and their role as a teacher – provide
an important window on the situation they are in: a window both to perceive
and to evaluate what is going on (and what is absent or missing).

Such discourses are, however, not just personal/biographical and professional
but are also related to the particular responsibilities one has as a teacher. They
are, in other words, also a function of the particular ecological conditions of
teachers' work. This is clearly visible in some of the ways in which the head teacher
of the school spoke about her work, the school and education more generally.
On the one hand, her discourse is obviously influenced by the particular set of
responsibilities that come with the role, and thus they reflect some of the outside
expectations and pressures quite well. This is first of all visible in how she sees
her role within the school.

> So I am responsible for absolutely everything. I am responsible for health and
> safety. I am responsible for the educational development of the pupils. I am
> responsible for all the legislative requirements that they have to implement
> to make sure that health and safety is [*sic*] in place. Additional support needs
> legislation is being followed. All the child protection stuff, assessments, risk
> assessments, educational excursions assessments, the whole quality assurance
> agenda, the provision of the curriculum, parental complaints, personnel issues,
> everything. [head teacher]

But it is also clear in some of the descriptions about priorities and processes,
such as the following quote.

It is a difficulty in terms of time management as you can imagine! So we have a quality assurance calendar which [laughs] is usually up here. So these are the different things that we try to do in the course of the year. So in terms of managing my time to make sure I do not just become totally administrative, what I try to do is when I have tracking attainment meetings with the teachers, which I will do termly, if there are issues that come up at these meetings in relation to underperformance, then I prioritise my time, the deputy head teacher's time. And we go in and provide focused support for pupils. So since August to now, the priority for us has been primary three, primary four and primary five. [head teacher]

Yet there is another side to her discourse, which is visible in her views about good education where, as she put it, 'it really just all hinges in terms of the catchment area'.

It is a very mixed catchment area. ... I totally believe in the principles [in a policy document], which is about trying to break the cycle of deprivation within [the local authority]. And to ensure that pupils have the opportunity to maximise their potential. And to give them as much of a holistic approach, experience as possible so that they have the opportunity to experience success and to motivate and galvanise. And just break this whole cycle of deprivation. That is what I believe. [head teacher]

While attainment matters in relation to such wider views about the point and purpose of education, it is clear that attainment is not an aim in itself, but in her view of education, it serves a wider purpose. There is, in other words, a different 'story' about education that has a strong motivating force. Interestingly, in this case, it is connected to this teacher's own educational biography. When asked whether she believes that the school can indeed break the cycle of deprivation, she responded in the following way.

Well I came from, myself, an area that is considered to be a deprived area in [name of town]. I came from [name of area]. And my mother was a home help. My father was an electrician. They were very hard-working people. And I suppose I was quite fortunate in as much as I was an only child. So I never actually lacked anything. But the driving force for me was always that they had high values about education. Education was always seen as the way of getting a good job. 'And if you stick in at school you will get a good job'. And I always wanted to please and I wanted to make them proud of me so I worked hard. But I wanted this good job because I wanted to have a nice house and I wanted to have nice holidays. And this had all been indoctrinated in a way. 'You need to do this. You need to get a good job. You do not want to be working as a home help

or doing what I have had to do, working in a factory. You need to work hard'.
[head teacher]

These biographical experiences provide a strong educational 'story' that clearly
impacts on how she looks at the present.

> But if we replay that situation to this context just now, I am not sure that I would
> have been able to go to university because I would have had to make choices
> about big debts because they would not have been able to fund me. I know from
> my own personal experience that it costs a lot of money to educate a child at
> university. And it can go on for a long time. And I do not know how I would have
> been able to access that. I do not know enough about the system. I just know that
> for my daughter we did not get any help and we had to fund it all ourselves. And
> my mum and dad certainly could not have done that. So I suppose there must
> be ways round that. But it would mean that you end university having a huge
> amount of debt. And my mother and father do not like debt. So they might have
> been pushing me in other directions. More about trying to get a job with the
> qualifications that you get when you leave school. [head teacher]

It is therefore not surprising that she believes 'that education can make a
difference – otherwise I do not think I would want to be doing the job that I
am doing'. Within this discourse, there is a strong emphasis on skills and on
values – 'Good positive values. Our school motto is respect'. While she sees
the focus on skills as 'one of the big changes' brought about by 'Curriculum for
Excellence', she emphasizes that in her school 'we have always taken the trouble
to provide opportunities for pupils to develop the kind of skills and attributes
required by "Curriculum for Excellence"', so in this regard, she does not think 'it
is going to make a huge difference.'

Her perception that 'Curriculum for Excellence' is not so much a break
with the past, as it fits with what has been central to education for her anyway,
may also have played a role in the way in which she describes how she and her
colleagues have approached its implementation – if that's the right word in this
case. Talking about the four capacities, she stressed the sheer impossibility of
developing practice from such general principles.

> It was not manageable. How do you plan a curriculum around all of that? You
> cannot. How do you assess all of that? You cannot. So we have decided to take
> ownership of it all. And we have decided as a staff, in the absence of any clear
> guidance on what is it that you want. If you are promoting skills for life, skills
> for learning and skills for work, give us the template. What is it that you really
> really want us to do in relation to these skills? In the absence of that we have put

together our own little template of what we think is manageable. And what we think the children should be able to achieve by the end of primary seven. So we have all contributed to that, we have all discussed it and we have all agreed to it. And that is how we will measure and monitor the progress. Now whether that is right or wrong I do not know. But nobody else has actually helped us with that. So I am just doing my own thing. [head teacher]

Here, we find an example of a rather agentic engagement with 'Curriculum for Excellence', coming out of a clear conviction that this is what the framework seeks to bring about.

It does provide a much more flexible framework because we are allowed to take more ownership of the curriculum. So we are not being given structured 'you must have this amount of allocation for maths and English'. So that is very good. [head teacher]

There is also clear evidence of what we have called above a 'generation effect'.

But in some ways it is taking us back to how things were before five to fourteen when you were planning with this web idea. And you were trying to make everything relate your maths and all of the curricular areas had to relate to a theme. So in a way Curriculum for Excellence is taking us back to that route because it is meant to be child centred. And it is meant to be the interest of the children that drives everything. [head teacher]

Our data do allow us to conclude that there is evidence here of an agentic *engagement* with 'Curriculum for Excellence'. How this works out in practice is still another matter, largely beyond the scope of our observations, albeit that we can see that within the school there seems to be a more collective sense of direction and a collective 'story' where it concerns the implementation of 'Curriculum for Excellence' – a story very much focusing on skills and on providing opportunities for the particular population of the school. This shows something about how individual discourses are related to the professional culture in the school. At the level of structure, the data give the impression that much of this is managed in relation to achievements and outcomes, which partly has to do with the requirements from the environment within which the school operates but also with the way in which the school – or at least some of the teachers within the school – see this focus as a way towards achieving their wider ambitions.

Looking at these three teachers, we can thus see some noticeable differences in discourses, where some are more detailed, refined and developed than others. There is a clear age effect here – the teachers who have been in the system longer have had more time to develop their discourse and have clearly done so – and also a clear generation effect in that the teachers who have been around longer have access to different experiences, from their own education, their teacher education and the different policy 'waves' that have influenced their practice over time. The biographical dimension is particularly interesting and shows how particular experiences in their own educational biography – the iterational dimension – provide a strong 'drive' towards the future – the projective dimension – and makes a clear difference in the here and now – the practical–evaluative dimension. The availability of a more elaborate discourse seems to allow for a more 'relaxed' perspective on current developments as it allows the teachers to put things in perspective. In this regard, the discourse of the teacher who has been around for a much shorter period of time seems to be more closely influenced by current policy and is more 'one-dimensional', so we might say, and thus provides less opportunities for navigating the complexities of the here and now – which is not to suggest, of course, that over time this discourse may also not grow, expand, deepen and become more complex and refined. While there appears to be, therefore, a relationship between the qualities of the discourse the teachers have available and the agency they are able to achieve – the degree to which they are able to navigate the here and now is less defined by external requirements and demands and more by their own professional views and values – the question what such agentic action achieves, that is, whether the agency is 'good' agency is not immediately answerable. This has a lot to do with the fact that what counts as 'good' agency depends significantly on the criteria one applies and hence on what one sees as good or successful education. The ways these teachers talk about education clearly shows a difference between the demands from the 'outside' and some of their own views about what matters.

Talking about education (2)

The way in which our research was designed – interviewing and observing teachers in three different schools: one primary and two secondary schools – makes it possible to see to what extent the discourses that teachers utilize in their work are personal/professional and to what extent they are related to the particular ecologies in which they work, that is, the cultures and structures that shape their context for action. While we did notice differences, there are also many similarities when we focus on the ways in which the teachers from secondary schools spoke about education.

The conversations we had with one senior manager at Hillview High provided a very clear example of what we have termed above the 'generation effect', which has to do with the fact that the way in which this teacher spoke about education had its origins in the past. In the way she spoke about education, the comparison between the past and the present was frequently depicted as a loss, thus indicating that things as they are nowadays were not as good as they were in the past. For example, when talking about the tendency in education to measure and assess everything, she provided the following observation.

> We have lost the capacity to explore. To feel our way because for whatever reason we have become less secure, less happy with that because perhaps other people are less happy with it. But for me real learning is about going into the unknown and feeling your way and seeing what you discover and making sense of it. And finding things that you certainly do not know before you start out with. But to me, too many people are not doing that [laughs]. [senior manager]

She actually saw this development itself as a difference between generations.

> For some people in recent years, education has become much more of a job. Teaching has become much more of a job that needs to be done between your employed hours. There is much less of the Scottish approach to education that I came into education embracing and that I have never really lost sight of. And people of my generation in teaching, most would consider that you are educating the whole person. That you are coming from a position of teacher first, subject teacher second. [senior manager]

Her own teacher education – which she did in the 1970s – played a formative role in this and, once more, provides an outlook where recent developments are seen as a decline from how things were in the past.

> Perhaps it says something about our own university education. It certainly does in my case, I know that. That we did not see ourselves first and foremost as having to just deliver our own subject curriculum. We wanted to be part of a family in a school. We wanted to be part of a community and all that goes with that including the negative side of developing a community. And I do not see that in the same numbers as I did when I was a young teacher. [senior manager]

While she welcomes many more recent developments and initiatives, she is concerned about what teachers are doing with them and are able to do with them.

> They are all fantastic initiatives. But no single one of them on their own is enough. They are all part of a teacher's toolkit if you like. But I am worried about that concept of toolkit. It is that, that for me has made many staff think along the lines of being a practitioner simply thinking of themselves as a jobbing teacher. [senior manager]

From this angle, she is also concerned about the recent ways in which professional development of teachers is depicted and approached.

> There is an expectation now that three or four years and if you have done all these courses you will immediately be promoted and will be in to a management role. I do not care how able you are, if you have not learned your craft after three years, you are going to find your judgement seriously challenged on a day-to-day basis. And in my early years teaching, teaching was always a long slow process in terms of your movement through the ranks, as it were. It was conventionally seven years as a teacher. And six or seven years and then you became an APT[1] and you learned the ropes from someone else. And then you became a principal teacher and you learned the ropes from someone else. That hierarchy, that sense of learning from other people, I do not see as pronounced as it was in the past. [senior manager]

For this teacher, then, teaching is not about the application of a toolkit but is a craft that needs to be developed and refined through experience – a process that obviously takes time.

There is one further aspect of the discourse of this teacher that we wish to mention, as it is quite different from what most other teachers spoke about and is also distinctively different from what policy seems to emphasize, that is, focusing on measurable outcomes. This teacher's discourse about education highlights that education is a difficult process and necessarily has to be difficult.

> The best learning happens after pain. It is about an intellectual pain. It is about recognising that this is not easy. And sometimes you have got to have the conversation that says, 'I am very sorry about this but that is not good enough. What you are doing is just not going to cut the mustard. And we do have to look. I will help you to come to terms with what that is but it is just not up to scratch. This is what needs to be done. Here is where we are. Why are you doing this'. You have to somehow or other encourage somebody to genuinely get to their soul. Without it everything is sitting on the surface. … Now my methods of teaching in a classroom have always been to try to encourage young people to come into touch with that soul, if you like. And without it really there is no real learning. … But it is painful. [senior manager]

For this teacher, this also has a lot to do with her agency, not least because to challenge and encourage students to stay with what is difficult requires conviction and a degree of courage. There is a clear decision point in relation to this.

> So you decide, do you challenge that and take all the fallout that goes with that. Or do you go over the surface of it and just accept it. There are some people who will accept it. And there are some people who will say, 'My integrity stops me from being able to continue with that.' [senior manager]

She is aware that being principled about what matters in education makes the job less easy – 'in a way I give myself a lot of extra grief' is how she described it. And again she sees this more principled stance disappearing – again a loss in comparison to the past.

> But the voice inside me, my educational voice, my experienced voice that tells me I have got to address this means I take on the difficulty. And stirring up the puddle tends to mean it gets clearer in the end. But I do not know whether we live in a time now where many people are of that same opinion. And that people are looking for an easy life. I hear it here with people, 'how long have I got to go before I am home'. Now distance does lend enchantment. I do not think we, in the past, felt that kind of degree of pressure. There was more of an interest in people staying at the end of the day, sitting in the staff room talking about educational matters in an informal fashion. Now since McCrone,[2] people are thinking in terms of quantifying their time for their CPD. They are quantifying their time for their preparation. There has been a sea change that has been imposed from other sources that has now really embedded us in an education culture that is not a good one. [senior manager]

While this teacher's discourse was quite elaborate and specific, other teachers, as we have also discussed in the previous chapter, had a way of talking about education that was much closer to the policy discourse of learning and of skills. When asked, for example, what education is for, one of the other teachers responded in a way quite similar to what we have seen from one of the primary teachers.

> It is to learn. To help children to learn. But I wouldn't always agree that you are only learning in school. I think people are learning all the time. ... I think education is all about learning from each other as well as guiding children to learn new things. ... I think probably when you come into teaching at first you think you teach a subject and that is it. Then I quickly realised that I am actually having to teach social skills here. I am having to teach children how to learn.

How to use skills to help them learn. And I think I was probably quite naive when I came into teaching. I thought they would know to put a title at the top of the page, and the date, and that sort of thing. But it is all these little things as well that you are teaching them. Teaching them how to be organised. Teaching them how to have relationships, to have manners, to think. ... [Monica]

If this answer to the question what education is *for* stayed quite close to the language of learning and of skills, another teacher in the same school articulated this differently.

Preparing the pupils for whatever they want to do and giving them choices and opportunities to do things that otherwise they would not do if they were not in education. To try and give them a broader outlook on life and different people and different ways of living and different things that they could do in the future. [Kate]

When asked whether education was about transmitting particular pieces of knowledge so that students can pass exams, the teacher was quick to respond with a 'No I do not think so', although she did acknowledge that it is 'what we are measured on', and that it is important for pupils in that 'if they have decided that they want to go a certain route, so say they decide they want to be a doctor, then obviously they do need to pass certain exams so it becomes much more about that'.

While this second teacher had a slightly more detailed discourse about education, much of what we discussed with her in the interviews had to do with concrete examples and issues she had encountered, about which she provided much detail but which did not really gave the impression that there was a wider professional discourse informing her action and reflection. Although there was a lot of talk, it was, in other words, not much evidence of an overarching discourse that provided her with a frame to see, evaluate and judge. This is not to suggest that there was no evidence of agency – when asked she was quite adamant that she felt she had the freedom to put her ideas into practice – but the emphasis in her talk was on the practical–evaluative dimension, that is, on concrete issues in the here and now.

One further point to mention is that the two latter teachers both had come to teaching later in their life, as we detail in Chapter 1. We are mentioning this because having a career outside of education before becoming a teacher is the exception more than the rule. In this regard, it is interesting that in the group of teachers who took part in the project – who were teachers identified by their managers as being quite agentic – we find three teachers who have not followed the more standard career that takes teachers from school, to a degree, to teacher education and back into school. Perhaps this also explains why, for example, compared to the first teacher we discussed from this school, their discourse about education was more limited and probably more influenced by current and recent policy than was the case with the first teacher. This is not meant as a judgement about their discourse but as an observation, and again it may well be that over time these teachers will 'build' their professional discourse based on increased experience of working in education.

One of the teachers we interviewed in the other school, Lakeside, also had a career before she entered the teaching profession. Susan's discourse about education is an interesting mix of: a more fashionable/contemporary language that sees education as being about 'encouraging the learner,' 'personalization and choice,' the teacher as 'a facilitator,' 'skills for living, skills for life,' setting students on the road 'to fulfil their potential,' and observations and ways of conceiving of education that are quite critical of how some of these ideas play out in 'Curriculum for Excellence' and how education more generally seems to have drifted away from what matters to her.

> Education has got less and less to do with the individual pupils. And it values individuality less and less. And it appears to me to have become more bureaucratic and top heavy. And when there is so little money available for education and the budgets are being cut, they are being cut in the wrong place. It is actually bodies in the classroom that is needed. Not at management and higher levels. And it is encouraging pupils to learn. And the people who encourage the learner are the ordinary teachers, the ones who enjoy doing what they do and inspire. And that is the role of a teacher, to inspire them to want to learn more. Not necessarily about the subject you are teaching but just to inspire them to learn anything. [Susan]

While on the one hand, she sees education as a very individual journey, and whereas she recognizes that this is a key idea in 'Curriculum for Excellence', she does not see a significant gap between theory and practice.

> Personalisation and choice! That sounds brilliant but in actual fact that is not going to be what it is. It is going to be personalisation of choice of the teacher teaching the subject. Not the pupil. [Susan]

She has similar doubts about the idea that students should be responsible for their own learning because she believes that 'they do not actually understand what responsibility for their own learning is, and they are not capable of managing it'. She describes the predicament in relation to this as follows:

And the more able pupils still want classroom teaching from the front. They want to have things written down. They want to be taught in the old established way of teaching. And that is what they want because they see that as their route to get to further education. The less able pupils prefer the less structure, but they are in actual fact the ones who are less able to manage their own learning. Yet that is where the focus is. [Susan]

Also, while she is aware of the influence of testing on the practice of education, she makes a clear distinction between what's being tested and what matters for her, though she does encounter situations where she is 'in the minority' as someone 'actually who was teaching broadly, not just to the exam.' 'The reality,' as she said, 'is we are judged by the end result of exams.' But this implies that significant achievements that fall outside of the scope of what is being examined are not really acknowledged, which is obviously a source of frustration for her.

> I had a brilliant experience with a pupil through four, five, six years; of somebody who is not achieving A grades and whatever. But you have seen them grow to be lovely human beings. … But that is not valued. That is not measurable in a league table. But the point where they have got to from when they come to you at age eleven or twelve, to the point when they leave at sixteen, seventeen or eighteen. There can be a huge development that is not measurable on an education statistical table. … But that is such an important part of growing up. [Susan]

While she feels herself restricted by the emphasis on exams and measurement, this doesn't stop her from achieving what she sets out to achieve which, 'on the whole', she believes she can. In this regard, one restriction she experiences is time – there is not enough time to do everything she would want to do. Another interesting restriction she mentions 'is actually the pupils themselves and their attitude to learning in that they can be quite put off learning by previous experience'. She explains her own ability to navigate these complexities in terms of her personality. '(It) is because of who I am. It is because I grab opportunities and run with them'. This is a pattern she doesn't always see in other teachers. Some teachers, according to her, 'are not willing to take risks' and the main reason for this lies in 'reliance on exam results and the need to provide evidence – and the evidence of a written piece of work is seen as of more value than something that might be a wall display or PowerPoint presentation'. In her view, this has affected teachers' confidence: 'Our confidence has been eroded.'

So with this teacher, we have someone who has a mixed discourse, but one that effectively allows her to have a critical perspective on 'Curriculum for Excellence' in that she is able to indicate where the curriculum really matches up with her own views about what matters educationally and where there are tensions. There are therefore discursive resources that allow her to take a stance towards the prevailing policy – to judge what makes sense and what does not. While she does explain her agency predominantly as a personality trait – the kind of person she is – this does not preclude the fact that she has a way to talk about education that not only gives her a drive and sense of direction (the projective dimension) but also allows her to evaluate situations she encounters (the evaluative dimension) and to act on the basis of these evaluations (the practical–evaluative dimension). What is less visible, at least in the data available, is what the origins of her educational discourse were (the iterational dimension).

One of the other teachers we interviewed in this school provided some more insights in what had shaped her educational outlook, perhaps less so in terms of her educational discourse, but definitely in terms of what it means to do a job well, something which she connected to the working-class background in which she grew up. Here is how she provided an insight in these experiences.

> Yes, but my parents were and still are the kind that … both my parents growing up working class. My dad was and still is a lorry driver, my mum was a dinner lady and she is now a receptionist. And they were just very much you work hard, you do what your teachers tell you. And that was it. 'I am stuck with my homework', 'right, let's sit down and go over it' and they would help. But they were not pushy. They were there and they supported and encouraged but they never said, 'right, we want you to get five highers and we want you to go to University'. … And then when I said, 'I want to go to Uni'. 'Right, fine, okay. We will help you'. Chose my Uni, went to Uni. 'Want to be a teacher'. 'Right, fine'. It was more just 'you work hard, you do as you are told, you give your best'. And because both myself and my brother went down different routes in life and they were always just of the opinion, 'we will support you in whatever way you go'. [Sara]

Not only did this provide her with a set of strong values that gave her own work direction (the projective dimension), it also provided an orientation for her teaching. As for her own perspective, she summarized it as follows:

> You just do a good job. You try your best. You do not muck around. You do not do things you should not do or challenge superiors in a way unless it's obviously something genuine. [Sara]

To which she then added:

> And that is what I try and get across to the kids. You work hard and you do what you are told and you act on the advice you are given. You do not try and cheat

or shortcut or squirm your way out of things. If you are struggling, you ask for help. [Sara]

This discourse is actually quite important for her, in that it shapes what she finds important in teaching, both in terms of what she seeks to achieve (the projective dimension) and in terms of how she views and values the situations she encounters (the practical–evaluative dimension).

> As I say, there are some kids in our classes that are looking for a shortcut. And 'can I not drop this, can I not. …' And you are just like 'no. It's a pressure point. You are going to just have to make your peace with that and realise okay for about the next month or two I am going to have to just really really work. But then at the end of that month or two you have got your summer holidays. There is the reward. You get time off and you can do whatever you like'. [Sara]

That this outlook does provide her with a perspective to judge what she encounters in the present is clear in the following quote.

> But yes there are kids that don't have that mentality. And it is annoying sometimes because it is like the more and more they switch off or detach, the more and more stressed you get. And you think, 'Wait a minute, I am not the one doing the exam.' [Sara]

That providing students with structure and a steady 'push' are important in her conception of education is also evident in the following passage, where she also recounts how, in the longer term, the students are able to see the benefits of this approach. When asked whether she thought she was able to enact these views in the classroom, she said:

> I try to. I really do try. And I think that there are kids that can see I have managed to influence them in a positive way because I try to just say to the kids, 'you know how I always get slagged off for being the organised one and the tidy and all of that'. And I am just like, 'but you have got one whole year's worth of work to wade through for your exam. And the worst thing ever would be if this was like you had a bit of that topic in that folder and a bit of that, and it was all over the shop. So if you start off in an organised way come revision time, everything is there. You are not going to have to have that battle'. And I say to them, 'I know I am the crazy stationery lady. Like how you get crazy cat ladies, I am the crazy stationery lady' [laughs] but there have actually been kids who have said to me, if I had not shown them how to do that, they would have just been an absolute nightmare. But even things as well like when they are doing NABs[3] or their prelims[4] and I am saying to them, 'just because this is not going to the SQA, do not just opt for your minimum. Show off, do the best that you can'. [Sara]

We have evidence here, then, of an articulate educational discourse, a way of talking and thinking that gives a strong sense of direction to the educational practice of this teacher. What is interesting, however, is that there is a clear difference between the places where she feels able to enact this discourse and the places where she feels limited in doing so – which again sheds some light on the ecological conditions of the achievement of agency. Where she does feel there is a space for acting on the basis of her ideas is in her own classroom. When we suggested that we felt that she was 'fairly autonomous' in her own classroom, she immediately responded by saying 'oh yes, in my own classroom, absolutely – yes, definitely'.

> And even in the department in terms of [our subject area], yes. And I work with people in my department who think the same way. Like we were talking about [a colleague] last time. So yes it is dead easy there. And on another angle, in the faculty, I am lucky enough to work in a faculty where the leadership has not gone the opposite way and where everything is controlled. [Sara]

So from the 'bottom up' it looks like she acts in situations where it is possible to achieve agency, where it is possible to enact a conception of education that clearly matters to her. But this is not all she has to say about it, because when asked about the presence or absence of synergy between her own views and the beliefs and vision of the school, she is more hesitant. The first response to our question here was a 'Mmhmm' and after an 'okay' from us a 'yes' and a laugh.

> There is [sic] different levels of tension. There is one level even within the faculty, I am trying to be very diplomatic here, I will look at certain things and I will think, 'that is really important. That ought to be done properly and it is not being done properly'. And in my head I will think how I would do it. But obviously I am powerless. [Sara]

That in this context she feels that she *is* powerless indicates that the achievement of agency is not just a matter of capacity or having a clear discourse and a clear sense of direction and of what matters; it is always achieved – or not – in concrete ecological conditions. And whereas at classroom and, to some extent, at faculty level, these conditions seem such that it is possible to achieve agency, within the wider context of the school, this obviously becomes more challenging.

Just as we raised the question of whether having managerial responsibilities has an impact on discourse and vision within the primary school context, this is also a question relevant in the secondary context. One of the senior managers we spoke from Lakeside felt that where it really matters there is actually little difference between being a teacher and being a senior manager because in both cases the key 'issue' for him is relationships.

> As a teacher of [subject] for many years, how I do my job as a depute is how I did my job as a teacher and as a principal teacher in that you build relationships with people. And people worked hard for you because of that, because they did not want to let you down. ... So the model that I operate as a depute is pretty much the same as the model I operated as a principal teacher, not only with the staff that I work with but also with the pupils that I had in my care as well. That you show them that you care. ... And if they trust you and if they go with you, they will learn a lot and they will achieve a lot. And at the same time they will have fun. At the same time they will grow as people as well. [senior manager]

That the theme of relationships is part of a quite elaborate discourse about what matters in education can be seen from the following quote.

> It is the only way that it has got a chance of being successful is if that is one of the foundations of how it works. I always talked about, I do not know where I did this, but I remember doing something with some staff in the past about how being in a school and being a teacher is like being a house whereby your curricular knowledge and what you know and what you do is the bit above the ground that you can see that is the house. But the relationships aspect of it is the foundation. So you can know everything in the world but if you have not got that foundation underneath there it is eventually going to fall apart. And I really believe that. And that is why I am the depute and was the sort of teacher that I was because that is more important than anything else. Even if you are not the most knowledgeable teacher of your subject, it does not matter because you are going to be inspiring people to learn more anyway. Not always from you but from their own skills and developing their own skills and finding things out. So I think that is the way to do it. And the relationships aspect is not just about staff. It is about people as well. That is how the culture of the school has developed where the pupils trust the staff as to when they say they are going to do something, they do something. And it is the same person. If you walk into my office on a Monday morning or a Thursday afternoon or a Friday teatime or whenever it is, you are going to get the same person. You are not going to get a different person in the morning because you are feeling lousy about something. You make the effort to be the same for everyone all the time. And they know exactly how they stand with you. And that is what we very much try and get across to staff. And we see work consistency a lot in the school about how you deal with things. How you deal with issues, how you deal with pupils. And it is really really important. [senior manager]

This account of what matters in education is not only quite elaborate and detailed but from the interview data it becomes clear that this permeates much if not all of what this manager does, both in his role as depute and in his previous role as a teacher. In this regard, we might say that the discourse is not only detailed but also 'strong,' in that it provides a clear orientation (the projective dimension) and a clear criterion for judgement of the here and now (the practical–evaluative dimension).

There are indications in the data that this discourse, with its core belief in the power of relationships, goes a long way back and has been a constant in his career and also something that has proven to be meaningful.

> And I have been now teaching for thirty three, this is my thirty fourth year teaching. And I know a lot about how things work. And I know a lot about how I think schools work and so on. But I am not the cleverest person in the school. And I am not the most innovative. And I am not the person who has got the best ideas in the school. Why should I, just because someone has only been teaching five years, say to someone 'well no we are not going to do it that way because I have been doing this a long time and that is not going to work'. And how you encourage people to grow as professionals as you give them responsibility. If they make a mess of it and it does not work, well that is okay. 'You tried, it did not work, we will try something different next time'. As long as no-one is hurt at the end of the day it might be the best thing that you ever try. And if you do not try you are not going to know. So again it is about having trust in the people who are doing it. And by allowing people to do that sort of thing, them saying 'well I had that idea, I was allowed to run with it. Even though it did not work, I was still allowed to try it'. So that has a huge impact on how staff feel about their place within the school as well. [senior manager]

The strength of belief and vision is not just an individual thing but is also part of the explicit vision of the school, which has to do with 'people feeling valued, both staff and pupils, and encouraging pupils and staff to be able to achieve their potential at all times'. This also plays a role in the way in which his views about what schools are for are articulated, which again contains a clear emphasis on what we might call the human factor.

> The easy answer is to have them as well prepared for the life that they will meet the day they leave school. And I often say that to pupils that everything we do here is focused on how you will be the day that you leave. Everything we do, whether it is in terms of qualifications or how you deal with problems. How you deal with individuals or whatever. Everything we do in school is focused on

that one day when you leave, when you go and you decide what it is you want to do. That you are as well prepared as you possibly can be as a human being, as a qualified person or whatever. [senior manager]

In terms of how to do this, there is a clear view expressed that there as well it is about relationships.

It is not about what you teach, it is about how you teach basically. And it is about how you build relationships. We have a school that is like that and have had a school that has been like that for quite a long time. [senior manager]

We further develop the issue of relationships in Chapter 4. The presence of a 'strong' discourse about what matters in education plus the fact that this discourse has become part of the vision, culture and practice of the school has led to a situation where 'Curriculum for Excellence' was less an intervention aiming to alter the direction of the school but more a natural extension of the direction in which the school was heading anyway.

'Curriculum for Excellence' has emphasised that if you are looking at the good practice that is highlighted in a 'Curriculum for Excellence' and how the school should be operated, that is how all schools should be operating anyway. What they are saying, 'this is what makes a good school', people should really have known that already about the importance of working across different faculties. The importance of giving personalisation and choice at the right time and giving guidance at the right time and so on. So schools that were operating well and were successful on many levels were doing already what 'Curriculum for Excellence' is highlighting that they should be doing now. And we were doing that, maybe not 100 per cent of the time but we were aware that what makes a good school are these building blocks. And then after that the pupils and the staff run with it. And it just becomes a better place. [senior manager]

A final point to make here is that because of the strength of vision and a sense that the school was already heading in the direction in which 'Curriculum for Excellence' sought to go, the experiences and outcomes were much more perceived as a negative intervention, something that staff found 'limiting' because it tried to specify in (too) much detail what should have followed naturally from pursuing the underlying philosophy of 'Curriculum for Excellence'. In this light, the experiences and outcomes are seen as 'almost a national curriculum by another name', and not as something enabling.

Discussion and conclusions

In this chapter, we have sought to explore the discursive resources that play a role in teachers' achievement of agency. We have tried to characterize the different ways in which the teachers in our project spoke about their practice; we have tried to find out where such talk comes from; and we have tried to shed light on the ways in which their talk – their vocabularies and discourses – plays a role in the achievement of agency. A couple of things stand out. One is that all teachers do have something to say about education, but that some discourses are (far) more elaborate and detailed than others and that the discourses also display different 'strengths' of conviction. In each case, we have seen how the teachers' discourse allowed them to have views about the current situation – the practical–evaluative dimension in which agency is achieved – so in this sense, the chapter does show how discursive resources matter for the achievement of agency. In some cases, there was little difference between the teacher's discourse and the prevailing situation, while in other cases the difference was significant, allowing teachers not only to be critical of what was going on but also giving them an alternative outlook that, within the confines of the situation they are in and carry responsibility for, allowed them to act differently, closer to their own values and convictions. While this does show that discursive resources play an important role in the achievement of agency, the question that remains unanswered is whether such agency can be characterized as 'good'. This, as we have already mentioned in the introduction, ultimately depends on one's views about what education ought to be like. Most teachers who did express a difference between their own views and what they saw was happening in their schools, also as a result of the implementation of 'Curriculum for Excellence', had difficulty with the instrumentalization of education and with a narrow focus on attainment, and where possible – within the scope of their own agency, so we might say – they did try to counter this.

Zooming in on the vocabularies and discourses made it also possible to see in more detail where such vocabularies and discourses come from. There was a clear biographical dimension, not only in how teachers viewed education but also with regard to their educational values. There was also clear evidence of age effects – the influence of experience – and generation effects – the influence of having had experience of very different contexts, practices and ideas, than what currently is prevalent. Where vocabularies and discourses were more 'formed' as a result of such influences, there was evidence of a stronger orientation towards the future (the projective dimension of agency), which did appear to make a difference in how teachers acted in the here and now. With regard to the 'quality' of the discourse, we also saw examples where a more nuanced and developed and elaborate discourse allowed teachers to have a more nuanced view about the situations they found themselves in – in some cases, we characterized this as a more 'relaxed' view that was able to distinguish policy fashions from longer-term trends and the things that really matter. What was interesting with one of the teachers in the secondary school was that the degree in which she saw herself able to achieve agency significantly depended on context – she felt more able within the environment of her own classroom and felt less able ('powerless') within the wider context of the school. Finally, we also found evidence of the influence of policy discourse – not least the discourse of 'Curriculum for Excellence' itself – and wider trends, including many traces of the 'language of learning.'

In summary, we can say that discursive resources do matter for the achievement of agency. As with beliefs, the wider vocabularies and discourses teachers have available provide an important 'window' on the here and now – and thus play an important role in the practical–evaluative dimensions of agency – and also provide an important reference point towards the future – the projective dimension. Although the vocabularies and discourses are first of all 'of' individual teachers, it is also clear that such vocabularies and discourses are not uniquely individual but are shared, both because they emanate from shared histories and because they function in shared practices. How relationships play a role in such practices and how they help or hinder the achievement of agency are the questions to which we turn in the next chapter.

The Importance of Relationships

Introduction

In the previous two chapters, we have focused on what we might call the cultural resources or more specifically the *cultural forms* (Archer 1988) or *cultural structures* (Emirbayer and Goodwin 1994) teachers utilize in their work: the beliefs they hold and the vocabularies and discourses in and through which they articulate their beliefs and underlying values and concerns. In this chapter, we examine another key dimension of the model presented in Chapter 1, namely the social and professional relationships experienced by teachers and the wider networks within which their work takes place. This is the domain of *social structures*. Social and cultural structures are empirically intertwined – 'never to be reified as separate, concrete entities, much less hierarchized as if one of them ... were always more causally significant than the other' (ibid., p. 1444). Nevertheless, as we have already argued, it is possible, and indeed desirable, to separate them analytically, to '*examine their interplay*' (Archer 1988, p. 80, emph. in original) and untie the 'constitutive elements' (ibid.). Teachers' relationships – with other professionals as well as with people in the wider communities in which they work – have the potential to impact significantly on their professional agency.

> At a time when schools are not well supported, while under tremendous pressures to do more and do it better, these collaborative cultures offer their members social support, the sharing of knowledge and the mobilization of collective resources. (Lieberman and Grolnick 1996, p. 41)

It is thus our intention in the chapter to unpick the various aspects of relationships experienced by teachers in our study, exploring how different features of these relationships and their differing qualities help or hinder the achievement of agency.

So how might we understand social structures? They have been defined in various ways by different thinkers. For example, Giddens (1984) views them as rules and resources that govern human behaviour. We dissent from this somewhat deterministic view, taking a position that social structures are primarily relational, concerning the ways in which people are positioned relative to each other. We would partially concur with Porpora (1998, p. 339), who defines structures as the emergent properties of 'systems of human relationships among social positions'. However, this appears to be an incomplete view, and Elder-Vass's (2008) suggestion that social structures comprise the constituent parts, the relations between them, the emergent whole and the emergent properties of the whole seems to offer a more comprehensive and useful definition.

There are a number of points that arise from defining social structures in this manner. First, social structures have emergent properties such as power and trust, which provide relational resources for social actors. Consequently, human agency and human *action* are at least partially shaped or afforded by relational positioning, and in turn, these act back on the system in terms of structural and cultural elaboration (Archer 1995). According to Knoke and Kuklinski (1982, cited by Emirbayer and Goodwin 1994, p. 1418), 'The structure of relations among actors and the location of individual actors in the network have important behavioural, perceptual, and attitudinal consequences both for the individual and the system as a whole.' Second, the causal efficacy of social structures makes the assumption that social networks are real, existing prior to individuals' encounters with them (Emirbayer and Goodwin 1994; Archer 1995). According to Porpora (1998, p. 344), 'The causal effects of structure on individuals are manifested in certain structured interests, resources, powers, constraints and predicaments that are built into each position by the web of relationships.' Such emergent properties, in combination with cultural forms, provide the context by means of which human activity occurs.

Third, relationships provide the medium by which cultural forms percolate around social systems; in this sense, social structures are the means for, or barriers to, cultural diffusion. This manifests itself in different ways: for example in schools, robust external connections may provide the channels by means of which teachers challenge and interrupt prior ways of thinking about their practice; strong dialogical structures in schools may facilitate sense making around new curricular policy (Imants 2002; Ketelaar et al. 2011); or conversely, coercive power structures in schools, or relationships that are predominantly vertical, hierarchical and not reciprocal may prevent the spread of new thinking.

The purpose of this chapter is to illuminate how teacher professional relationships may be significant in enabling them to achieve agency in their professional practice. We address this by first looking at some of the literature relating to teacher professional networks, before drawing upon our empirical findings to illustrate how such relationships might help or hinder in the achievement of agency in different ways, something that, as we will show, to a large extent depends on the particular configurations of the relationships in question, all other factors (such as teacher beliefs, professional discourses, school culture) being similar or equal.

Teacher professional networks

Teacher networks, most notably under the banner of 'Professional Learning Communities' are currently in vogue, and consequently, there has emerged a very large body of literature on this topic. This body of literature is useful in enabling us to foreground some of the key issues relating to how teachers' social and professional relationships impact on their agency but remains limited and problematic in many respects. Foremost among these concerns, and especially pertinent to this chapter, is a lack of attention to teacher agency in this literature. Where agency is utilized as a substantive concept, it tends not to be conceptualized in detail (see, for example, Moll and Arnott-Hopffer 2005; Anderson 2010; Datnow 2012; Riveros, Burgess and Newton 2012). This is not surprising: as we discussed in Chapter 1, agency is often inadequately conceptualized in literature, which purports to be about teacher agency; and if this literature does not adequately conceptualize the term, then literature with a different focus on teacher networks cannot realistically be expected to do so. More often than not, the literature reviewed makes no explicit mention of agency as a theoretical construct. As noted previously, a notable exception is the work of Edwards (2005), who makes the link explicitly between agency and collaborative teacher working and conceptualizes agency in some detail.

Much of the literature does, however, relate to *aspects* of agency, even if only implicitly. Most commonly, this is expressed via the notion of the teacher as an agent of change (Fullan 2003) in externally driven reform and the implementation of policy (see, for example, Lieberman and Grolnick 1996; Stoll et al. 2006; Dooner, Mandzuk and Clifton 2008; Vescio, Ross and Adams 2008; Datnow 2012). Much of the literature overtly focuses on the teacher professional learning community (PLC), a type of network established with the explicit intention of promoting change and teacher learning through collaborative working. There is a high degree of agreement across the literature as to the key features of PCLs: shared values; collective responsibility; reflective professional enquiry, collaboration; and group as well as individual learning (Stoll et al. 2006). The PLC is commonly presented in a rather uncritical manner as an overwhelmingly positive development (Coburn and Russell 2008) and is widely seen as an entity to improve practice, often premised on a view of schools and teachers as being in need of reform.

For some authors, this focus on change is problematic. Little (2003) questions the premise of school improvement underpinning PLCs. Watson (2014) is sceptical about the assumption that PLCs are an axiomatic good, questioning their possibility to facilitate 'change agentry' (Fullan 2003) and suggesting that the emphasis on shared values and community and lack of attention to issues of conflict 'may therefore become a means to produce silence' (Watson 2014, p. 22), imposing 'a rationality and a direction which suppresses possibilities for change' (ibid., pp. 26–7). Literature focusing on the power of conflict (de Lima 2001) and dissonance (Imants 2002), and pointing to the dangers of groupthink (Watson 2014), would appear to be less commonplace than the writing extolling the merits of shared values and compromise.

Vescio, Ross and Adams (2007), in their review of key studies, warn of the danger of the model meeting 'the same dismal fate as other well intentioned reform efforts' (p. 82) if educators uncritically accept the premises of the PLC. A particular problem with the focus on change lies in a parallel tendency to deride agency that emerges from teacher networks and that acts against change, preserving the status quo. Thus, Moolenaar (2012) talks about the 'dark side of social networks' (p. 30), and Bidwell and Yasumoto (1999) point to the 'occupational ethnocentrism' that impedes change efforts.

When viewed through the lens of school improvement, such phenomena might seem to be counterproductive and as teachers stymying worthwhile reform policy; however, viewed differently, such actions might be construed as the exercise of teacher agency, buoyed through resources afforded via social networks and effected to prevent ill-considered reform. Indeed educational literature that focuses on the dominant structures of schooling and teacher engagement with top–down innovation has often characterized such efforts differently. For example, Bowe, Ball and Gold (1992) documented high-capacity, professional departments acting to mitigate the more harmful effects of England's

'National Curriculum'. Osborn et al. (1997) found examples of different forms of mediation of policy – conspiratorial, creative and protective – that seem to suggest teachers achieving agency in their work as resistance to policy and to change; Siskin (1994) researched high school departments where bonds within departments – perhaps 'ethnocentrically' focused – enabled teachers to protect their subjects against the encroachment of interdisciplinary provision. To us, all of these appear to be instances of teacher agency, but to see them clearly as such, one needs to strip away some of the normative assumptions about schools and change, which seem to characterize (and indeed limit) much of the literature on social networks, particularly that focusing on PLCs.

Many benefits have been claimed for teacher networks in general and professional learning communities in particular. We offer a brief summary of these, with the obvious caveat echoing Coburn and Russell (2008) that the literature can tend to be over-positive. As such, benefits would seem to be entirely dependent on the nature and quality of connections between actors (commonly referred to as 'ties' in the literature) and resulting transactions occurring within the network (Lieberman and Grolnick 1996; Coburn and Russell 2008), it is worth labouring this point here. The following features of networks are highlighted in the literature as being instrumental in their success. Stoll et al. (2006) highlight the importance of external agents to interrupt habitual forms of practice (Imants 2002) and 'habits of mind' (Vescio, Ross and Adams 2008, p. 84). This is necessary if teachers are to expand 'horizons of observation' (ibid., p. 89) rather than sharing ignorance (Lieberman and Grolnick 1996).

Various network variables have been identified as significant in determining the quality of interactions within the network. These include frequency of interaction, network density, reciprocity and the centrality of key actors (Daly et al. 2010). According to Daly and his colleagues, density has been shown to correlate closely with an increased focus by teachers on learning and teaching, an enhanced sense of teacher efficacy and teachers coming to seeing value in collaborative working (ibid.).

Another key variable, and an important distinction neglected in some literature, lies in the relative importance of informal ties, as compared with more formal networking structures (Lieberman and Grolnick 19996; Coburn et al. 2012; Daly et al. 2010). Many writers also refer to the pivotal role of school leaders in the smooth functioning of teacher networks. For example, Stoll et al. (2006) discuss how leaders might create the conditions for collegiality. Similarly, Coburn, Choi and Mata (2010) talk about how tie formation is particularly amenable to intervention by school leaders, who can create the necessarily conditions for thriving teacher networks. The style of leadership in schools appears to be an important variable here; for example, over-hierarchical systems of top–down communication have been shown to be detrimental to policy reform (Daly et al. 2010). Conversely, it is important to understand school social structures, changing them as necessary to leverage change, rather than layering reform onto existing structures that may impede reform. Both school and district leaders have a key role to play in this process (ibid.; also see: Datnow 2012).

Within the parameters defined above, it is clear that collaborative working and participation in networks offer considerable benefits for teachers. Yet these benefits are often claimed without being theorized adequately, both in terms of the social dynamics that foster them and the processes that occur as they transpire; however, notwithstanding this, they are common to much of the literature. Many writers point to the capacity of networking to build trust within schools (Moll and Arnot-Hofler 2005; Stoll et al. 2006; Coburn and Russell 2008; Lee, Zhang and Yin 2011). This is perhaps due to the establishment of more frequent connections and denser networking (although we note Dooner, Mandzuk and Clifton's (2008) caveat that conflict resolution strategies are best built into PLCs at an early stage of their evolution). A related benefit lies in the mitigation of risk afforded by networks (Coburn and Russell 2008; Penuel et al. 2009) and a reduction in vulnerability (Stoll et al. 2006), as colleagues offer mutual support. Networks can provide access to expertise – cultural and social resources (Moll and Arnot-Hofler 2005; Stoll et al. 2006; Coburn and Russell 2008); relational resources embedded in networks and accessible via ties (Penuel et al. 2009). This includes access to specialist knowledge (Vescio, Ross and Adams 2008) potentially provided by external partners such as university academics and community stakeholders.

The above features of networks, if realized, have been shown to have considerable personal impact upon the teachers engaging in them. For example, Lieberman and Grolnick (1996) suggest that networks enable teachers to develop professional confidence, as well as building skills in 'communication, negotiation and accommodation' (p. 16). Vescio, Ross and Adams (2008) see their potential to change teachers' 'habits of mind' (p. 84). Networking, through generative dialogue (Imants 2002), facilitates sense making and the generation of more complex ideas about practice (Lieberman and Grolnick 1996; Coburn and Russell 2008), especially valuable when teachers are faced with the unfamiliar, as new policy hits schools. In turn, personal growth has been shown to accompany changed school cultures, the development of more collaborative ways of working and a greater focus on outcomes for students (Vescio, Ross and Adam 2008; Penuel et al. 2009).

The above summary is useful because it illustrates that the research literature on teacher networks, while offering many insights into teacher professional working and the management of educational change, continues to suffer from gaps and other limitations. It also illustrates that agency as a concept, while underused in much of the literature, has considerable resonance with the themes in the literature, particularly in respect of the building of teaching capacity and the importance of the contexts by means of which teachers work. The limitations of the existing body of literature are indeed recognized in many of the research articles, especially those that have recently sought to take a more theory-focused approach to analysing networks (e.g. Coburn and Russell 2008; Penuel et al. 2009; Coburn, Choi and Mata 2010; Daly et al. 2010; Coburn et al. 2011). These and other authors caution that the literature contains significant gaps about teacher networks, perhaps in part due to the aforementioned tendency to extol the virtues of the PLC, and its linkage to change agendas. According to Dooner, Mandzuk and Clifton (2008), 'We know little about how effective professional learning communities develop, how they are sustained, and how teachers learn to work collaboratively throughout the inquiry process' (p. 565). Vescio, Ross and Adams (2008) inform us that

> although current professional development literature is replete with articles that extol the virtues of learning communities as an essential way to organize schools in order to maximize time spent in professional development ..., only recently has the focus of this literature shifted to examining empirically the changes in teachers' practices and students' learning as a result of PLCs. (pp. 80–81)

According to Lee, Zhang and Yin (2011), many western studies have focused on the characteristics and operation of PLCs, but little is known about the relationships between PLCs and other teacher – or school-level – factors such as faculty trust, collective teacher efficacy and teacher commitment (p. 821). Similarly, Coburn, Choi and Mata (2010) state that 'while there is emerging consensus that social networks are important, we know little about how they form or how they change over time' (p. 33). The comparative absence until recently of a serious theoretical base for analysing the workings of teacher networks has arguably impeded the development of significant insights into, for example, the quality of interactions within networks (Daly et al. 2010) and their relations to outcomes in respect of teachers' professional practices. The recent emerging body of literature drawing upon social network (social capital) theory and social network analysis methodologies offers considerable potential to address this lacuna in our knowledge about teacher networks. However, there seems to be considerable work still required. According to Little (2003):

> If we are to theorize about the significance of professional community, or make claims regarding its benefits, we must be able to demonstrate how communities achieve their effects. This will require examining the specific interactions and dynamics by which professional communities constitute a resource for teacher learning and the formation of teaching practice. (p. 917)

This observation still has considerable resonance twelve years on. Our theoretical approach around teacher agency offers an alternative way of developing a more rigorous approach that specifically addresses interactions and dynamics. The next section of this chapter looks at some of the empirical evidence from our research through the theoretical lens presented in Chapter 1.

Relationships and teacher agency

The remainder of this chapter focuses on two of the schools, both secondary, that participated in our project. We present the findings in the following steps. First, we briefly show how our participants shared broadly similar beliefs and values about education. In other words, we show that there are no significant differences between these teachers in terms of the iterational dimension that plays a role in the achievement of agency – that is the experience that these teachers bring with them to particular situations and actions in their working lives. Second, we examine the contexts within which these teachers work. This is done via the development of a vignette for each school, where we focus primarily on the context rather than the individual teachers. We show how differences in context shape their differing responses to the demands posed by new curricular policy. We conclude the chapter by offering some observations about the significance of relationships for teacher agency.

As previously mentioned, the 'Teacher Agency and Curriculum Change' project followed an iterative design, where each successive phase was premised upon the findings of previous phases. Early interviews and observations suggested that relationships were a key factor in the agency achieved by the teachers involved. We were initially puzzled by the wide variance in the agency achieved by the teachers from setting to setting. In one of the secondary schools, we saw high levels of agency, evident primarily through the confidence expressed by teachers as they engaged with the new curriculum, but also through an apparent ability of these teachers to manoeuvre between a wider range of repertoires as they dealt with problematic situations thrown up in implementing the curriculum and addressing other key demands in their work. This contrasted with the primary school and the other secondary school where we saw higher levels of uncertainty and a manifestly lower level of agency in the teachers' working practices. We were especially struck by this contrast in respect of the two secondary schools. Both schools are highly similar in terms of the availability of material resources: both are located within the same local authority, so are subject to the same constraints on budgets, implementing a new curriculum at a time of austerity and staffing cuts; moreover, both schools are located in very similar new buildings, with common spatial characteristics and resourcing. The key difference between the schools lies in how a particular aspect of the structural conditions experienced by the teachers – the nature and extent of their relationships – impacts on how they are able to achieve agency as they engage with a new and unfamiliar curriculum.

On the basis of the early data, we decided to focus on relationships. Initially, the project researcher informally discussed the nature and quality of in and out of school relationships and asked each participant to produce a detailed map of their own personal ties. In each case, the teachers were asked to indicate factors such as the direction (one-directional or reciprocity), strength and frequency of ties. The maps were subsequently analysed by the research team, and follow-up interviews were conducted with each participant to further explore key themes. This included a discussion on how relationships might impact on the teachers' achievement of agency, for example, by affording access to social and cultural resources. The following sections provide an overview and analysis of these findings in relation to the secondary schools; however, we first address the commonalities between the schools.

Commonalities

The purpose of this section is to briefly highlight a number of commonalities among the teachers, illustrating that in many key respects, there was a relatively common baseline for their achievement of agency.

As mentioned earlier, three of the four teachers in the secondary schools had prior experience of working in careers outside of teaching, potentially allowing them to draw on wide experiences in framing their teaching. In each case, we were impressed by the level of commitment to their work. All of the teachers admitted to working in the evenings and sometimes at weekends; preparing lessons, marking and assessing as well as reporting. All of them were highly active participants in the wider civic society of their schools. They each had experience of leading and/or developing initiatives focused on the development of new forms of pedagogy. Each had experience of involvement in whole-school initiatives, for example, working parties to develop aspects of the curriculum. In one case, the teacher had gone beyond this school-level activity, having been regularly involved in national working parties to develop assessment and the curriculum.

Another common strand lay in their strong focus on classroom teaching as a vocation. The four teachers were all enthusiastic about teaching and moreover showed little interest in developing their careers into management positions. One of the teachers had undertaken a temporary role as a faculty leader and experienced discomfort in this role. Another was actively, at the time of the research, resisting pressure from a senior colleague to apply for management positions. All of these teachers were thus characterized by a strong desire to work with students in classrooms.

All of the four teachers articulated a strong commitment to their students and especially to their roles as teachers of the whole child rather than just deliverers of content. These teachers were quite eclectic in their teaching approaches; they all expressed a liking for student-centred, dialogical and active pedagogy, while being equally comfortable with more didactic forms of pedagogy. Student learning was central to their work, and while student attainment was clearly important to them, their teaching was not narrowly focused on this. The teachers clearly cared about their students and highlighted the importance of establishing good relationships with them. One teacher expressed it as follows:

> I'm a firm believer in that so much of teaching is about relationships. You could be the most clued up person in the world about your subject. But if you can't relate to the kids, if you can't engage with them as people, then that's your problem. You are not going to make them enthusiastic. You are not going to make them interested because the relationship isn't there. [Sara]

Such sentiments were common to all four of the teachers, all of whom expressed commitment to strong educational values centred on what they described as 'developing and encouraging the individual pupil's learning.' One teacher planned to come to work even when suffering a debilitating injury, as she thought that her duty lay with teaching students. This teacher exhibited in her work what has been termed 'protective mediation' (Osborn et al. 1997). She mentioned that she sometimes gave tests without telling pupils that they were being tested. When we asked her about this, she stated that she believed that excessive testing placed harmful demands upon students; thus, while she felt obliged by the 'system' that structured the context for her actions to administer tests, she sought to protect students from their worst excesses. The other teachers expressed similar reservations about the culture of attainment within which they worked. We were not surprised to find that all of these teachers were enthusiastic about the opportunities afforded by the new 'Curriculum for Excellence', even where they expressed anxieties about the implementation process. One might expect that what seemed to be a strong projective orientation of these teachers – the clearly thought-out aspirations for their students – would serve to increase their agency as they implemented and enacted the curriculum.

However, despite their focus on their students, it was clear that many of their aspirations and goals were formed and limited by acculturation into their professional environment. Despite the reservations about the pressures wrought by assessment-driven accountability, all of the teachers appeared to subscribe to some extent to the discourses of this culture. More than only a cultural dimension of their contexts for action, it had become part of their orientations and thus also influenced the projective dimensions of their agentic orientations. For example, in both schools, a commonly expressed view was that it would not be right to put students into exams that they are not expected to pass, perhaps echoing Apple's dictum that there has been a 'subtle shift in emphasis ... from student needs to student performance, and from what the school does for the student to what the student does for the school' (Apple 2001, p. 413). Allied to this, we found evidence that much teacher decision-making in these schools was about survival rather than the realization of long-term aspirations.

> Often it is just a survival [laughs] from one day to the next. And not thinking 'this whole exercise has been great'. Stop and think occasionally about what am I actually trying to do as opposed to just get through the day and get on to the next day. [Kate]

Thus, we suggest here that while their focus on students and their conscientious working practices clearly influenced the projective dimensions of their action, the 'force' of these projective orientations was tempered by the culture of accountability and performativity in which they acted (see Chapters 2, 3 and 5 for a more detailed discussion of these issues).

The discussion so far shows how four teachers working in two secondary schools were remarkably similar in many respects. However, as we shall demonstrate in the next sections of this chapter, the achievement of agency played out quite differently. The answer to the question why this might be so must have to do with characteristics of their working environments, which, as we will show, manifest different features in at least one important respect, namely, the qualities of the particular relationships they are engaged in. The following two sections illustrate this difference.

Hillview High School

We noted above the similarities within our group of respondents in terms of their *general* aspirations, with similar strengths and limitations. This projective orientation did, however, work out differently in the two schools that we focus on in this chapter. At Hillview High School, the teachers seemed to be more limited in their aspirations about what was made possible by 'Curriculum for Excellence' and exhibited markedly lower confidence about their abilities to engage with the new curriculum than did their colleagues at the second school, Lakeside High School. In short, there was a reduced *sense* of agency in respect of implementing the new curriculum, in the sense of their judgements of what was actually possible. This thus 'translated' into a more limited *achievement* of agency. The following comments from one of the teachers provide a flavour of this sense of helplessness and lack of progress.

> It will be really difficult for the things that people want to know about. Like the Curriculum for Excellence, I can't think of anybody that's feeling like they are particularly in a position to be an expert and to help people. [Kate]

> Oh my goodness, that is a whole year and I don't know that I am any further forward with feeling confident about implementing Curriculum for Excellence. [Kate]

> A lot of the time it's been reading documents and making sure that we're familiar with the content of what we're supposed to cover. Recording what we've done with pupils. So [name removed] has come up with a system for us recording. There's a template for the level-three Es and Os for first year and/or second year. And just to record what we've covered but for each individual pupil and how well they've done with that. So it's been stuff like that, much more … tasky things. Not discussions about implementation or what it means for us or what I don't know is how other people are doing it. So I'm still no further forward with that than I was when I first spoke to you. I'm just kind of doing my own thing and hoping that it's okay. [Kate]

This is not how things always had been at Hillview High.

But I think we had a clear idea of where we were going with the last head teacher; two head teachers back we were quite far ahead of other schools with our methodologies and initiatives we were bringing in. That all met with the CfE values but I feel some of that has fallen away recently. [Monica]

As at Lakeside High School, the data suggest that senior management at Hillview were approachable and supportive of teachers. Similarly, there is little evidence that these teachers were any more risk averse than were their colleagues at Lakeside, nor that their working environment was inherently more risky. The major difference, we wish to suggest, appears to lie in the nature and scope of relationships in the school. Strong formal connections tended to be vertical; primarily with line managers and within faculties. Formal structures included faculty meetings and weekly meetings of faculty heads with the senior management team. Whole staff meetings were described as information-giving sessions – like 'assemblies' – with limited opportunity for dialogue, other than occasional breakout groups, described as 'not really an ideal forum'.

There appeared to be a paucity of formal horizontal channels for communication in the school. According to one teacher, talking in a focus group interview, 'We do not have a lot of working across faculties.' Principal teachers (PTs)[1] met weekly with senior management, but the outcomes of such meetings were disseminated vertically via faculties. Departmental and faculty meetings tended to focus on routine issues (such as, for example, student behaviour).

It has not been something that we have discussed in faculty. And I don't know if that is just us. I don't think it is. It's everybody. We are all in the same boat. The faculty meeting ends up being taken up with things that are important but not big important things. Like little important things that we need to know about stuff going on in school. So it is giving us information rather than talking at a higher level. [Kate]

Well, we have tried to get going with some curriculum development for S2 and we haven't been able to get on with that because of the other things that need to be discussed at the faculty meetings. It is two or three times I have had these things on the agenda and have had to put them aside. [Monica]

Such formal structures were supplemented by other formal forums for discussion, including peer observation, although increasingly these were noted to be disappearing in response to time and resourcing pressures.

We did have a good system in place where we had an annual review and from the review you could go over your own personal development needs and then from that try to find things appropriate. It is not being done anymore. PTs are finding it more and more difficult to find the time to do that with the staff. It should still be going on. [Kate]

Both teachers were involved in school-wide working initiatives, but it was noted that dialogue was often limited, and dissemination more often than not consisted of briefing, rather than discussion, with some evidence that this did not fully percolate down to mainstream staff. Membership of working groups was decided by senior managers. Opportunities for teachers to engage with colleagues in different faculties (at a level below middle management) were more limited. Other formal horizontal relationships did exist (e.g. guidance issues and increasingly mechanisms for interdisciplinary working, although this was not well developed at the time of the research). However, contact was often instrumental, focused on particular issues – 'I tend not to see people unless it is for something specific' [Monica] – or simply fortuitous.

I had been along in the art department one day. And I just loved the way it was all set out with their glass cases, exhibiting. And I really thought 'I wish we could do something like that in [subject removed]. Why can't we do something like that?' [Monica]

In exploring this case, we were left with a sense of opportunities missed. Both respondents had well-developed educational values and strong aspirations. Both were frustrated by the lack of opportunity to fulfil these aspirations. Our data suggest that the key factor lay in the limitations placed upon agency by the nature and scope of relationships in the school, and a corresponding lack of affordance for generative teacher dialogue – inherently a sense-making process – about the new curriculum.

But then it's now at the point of right so can we do any of these? And it sort of reached a plateau of trying to implement some of these changes because us coming up with the idea is that doesn't mean it's going to happen. It's got to go through a whole process of the senior management team ... and getting the okay from that. So we're at a frustrating stage where we've got lots of things we'd like to do. [Kate]

These teachers' views about the nature and scope of relationships within Hillview are supported to a large extent by the transcript of the interview with a senior manager. A great deal was said about the importance of strong, supportive and visionary leadership, but there was an absence of reference – despite prompting by the interviewer – to the role of managers in developing and sustaining relationships and connections between teachers. We suggest that in this case, teachers struggled to achieve agency in their enactment of the new curriculum, and that their agency was impeded by a lack of available relational resources. Hence, while the iterational and projective dimensions were 'in place', so to speak, acting things out in the concrete here and now – the practical–evaluative dimension of agency – was limited because of the particular character of the relationships within this school.

Lakeside High School

We next turn to Lakeside High School. Here we found a largely contrasting situation. A tangible difference lay in the sense of teachers' confidence and optimism about 'Curriculum for Excellence', something articulated by both teachers and senior managers.

> That's partly why CfE could be a really positive thing because we are constantly looking at what we are doing. And that we also share our ideas across the faculty. Susan]

> That is why I am not scared about the future with 'Curriculum for Excellence' because I made those decisions when it started three, four years ago. And I am feeling fairly secure. But I can totally understand why other people are not. [Susan]

It was thus clear to us that, in contrast to many other schools implementing 'Curriculum for Excellence', these teachers were achieving a higher degree of agency in respect of the implementation of 'Curriculum for Excellence'.

This might be attributed to the *culture* of Lakeside High School. Interviewees talked about a culture where innovation and risk taking is encouraged and supported, as well as a culture of sharing. The following extracts from an interview with a senior manager clearly exemplify this approach to running the school.

> We are quite lucky here in that the staff trust [the Senior Management Team] and they trust that they are doing things for the right reasons. And they are not being Machiavellian and they are not doing things because they are being nasty to people and wanting to score points. [senior manager]

> And if you are encouraging staff to do things that are a wee bit different or to not always follow things in a mainstream way, there is much more chance that they will develop as teachers, as professionals and as members of staff. So when someone comes with a crazy idea and says 'I want to try and do this with the second year class', okay, have a go at that. … If they make a mess of it and it does

not work, well that is okay. 'You tried, it did not work, we will try something different next time'. [senior manager]

Such sentiments were supported by other respondents who pointed to high levels of collegiality and the approachability of managers. One teacher, talking about her line manager, said:

> There is equality because [name removed] has never been 'I am superior to you' or whatever. So it is level on that front. I know that she views herself as a teacher, and I am a teacher and we are totally level. [Sara]

In one case, a team of teachers who were extremely unhappy about an initiative they had been asked to develop felt comfortable about complaining to their link senior manager about the allocated timescales and processes. They were listened to, and their concerns were taken on board to the extent that the timescales were altered.

It would be easy to attribute the tangible sense of teacher agency in this school to this collegial *culture*. However, we note that we found similar sentiments in the other school about approachable senior managers, collegial support and a desire to pull together for the sake of the students. It is in the *social structures of the school* that we found more substantive differences, which might explain differences in achieved teacher agency. There appear to be a number of aspects of this. First, there were strong *informal relationships* at a faculty level; these were characterized by high levels of emergent trust.

> We can all empathise with one another. In this department we can all have our sticky moments but I don't think there are any egos. There isn't anyone who thinks they are more important than anyone else or busier than anyone else. Everybody is aware of everybody else's pressures and I think we do try to have positive relationships. [Sara]

Second, there was a strong push from the senior management of the school to develop strong, reciprocal 'relationships within the school so that staff get on well with staff, staff get on well with pupils and pupils get on with other pupils'. Some of these relationships were clearly vertical; for example, while at least one senior manager was seen as patronizing and unapproachable, the norm was for an open door policy. Others were horizontal. In many cases, as at Hillview, many relationships were informal in nature, growing organically out of short-term needs.

> Because again it comes down to the simple social relationships that you have. And they are all people who understand the pressures of teaching, who get

frustrated by the same things we do, who have the same worries we do. Who very often have similar kids to ourselves as well. So our subjects have made us link. So sometimes the link can be because of individual people or it can be because of your subject. [Sara]

However, unlike the case at Hillview – where our data suggest that formal relationships had been progressively disappearing – at Lakeside, there was a sense that they were burgeoning as a consequence of an active policy of fostering collegial, professional networking both within and across faculties. There are clear parallels here with other studies illustrating the potential for leaders to create the conditions for collaboration (see, for example, Stoll et al. 2006; Penuel et al. 2009; Coburn, Choi and Mata 2010).

> Some have just come about accidentally. But some have come about because of those meetings that we had. [Susan]

A particular focus lay in the need to develop interdisciplinary working, something that was a clearly articulated school priority for 'Curriculum for Excellence'.

> And we share in there what we are doing and good practice and things across these things. So we are all coming together at various points and saying how can we tackle this and what ideas have you got and how should we take this forward and how do you do this in your department. And trying to come up with a common code of skills yeah. Core skills that we can all be promoting across the whole school. [Susan]

We earlier noted the diminishing scope and frequency of peer observation of teaching at Hillview. Conversely, at Lakeside, this was promoted by the senior management as a priority. We note also that this development was not framed in a managerial or hierarchical sense; teachers appeared to be trusted to get on with it, and they appeared to welcome the opportunities it provided for sharing practice.

> We are doing that on a number of levels now. Over the past few years it has developed. It started off as probably about four years ago, five years ago, there was no observation at all in the school. So we started it off at SMT level where we worked out a calendar for the year. And SMT visited every member of staff's class twice in the year. And it was a week in advance saying 'right I am coming to see you teach this higher geography class' or whatever it may be. And then informal feedback was given about how the lesson had gone and so on. And that still happens. But on top of that now we have built a principal teacher observation

as well. ... And also three years ago we started doing, on a voluntary basis, staff matching up with another member of staff. ... And going to visit them in their class and seeing how they teach ... everyone has a matched partner who is not in their faculty. So they are having to go with their art teacher, they are going to science. If they are English they are going to technology or whatever. And they visit each other during the year as many times as they can. And they also talk about collaborative work. They can do that as well. And a new thing we started last year which I described already, we called it follow a pupil day where I took all staff off timetable for a day. And they followed a first or the second year pupil for a whole day. [senior manager]

Another key difference between the schools in terms of relationships concerned the existence of external connections and relationships. At Lakeside High School, one of our respondents reported the benefits of her outside links. In one case, this had involved a formal school role to develop cooperative learning. In another, the formal mechanisms were less tangible, but the benefits evident. In the case of a teacher who had been an active participant in national initiatives – with national agencies to development assessment and curriculum policy – such experience was fed back frequently into school practices and served as a source for new ways of thinking and an interruption to habitual forms of practice.

I think the external links are important. But if you take that I am the only one. In this faculty we are down to nine now are we? I am the only one who is doing the whole 'Curriculum for Excellence', SQA, QDT, LTS,[2] whatever. But what I am bringing back to them, I am not just bringing it just back for [subject removed]. I am bringing it back for the whole faculty. [Susan]

We therefore suggest that, at Lakeside High School, strongly developed relationships acted as a catalyst for the achievement of agency and as such constituted the key difference in context that account for the puzzle as to why teachers with broadly similar experiences, beliefs and values, working in similar schools achieved agency differently and to a different degree.

Conclusions

We started this empirical analysis by asking why there might be significant differences in the agency achieved by teachers, when the teachers involved exhibited similar characteristics – particularly in terms of their values and orientations – and when the professional contexts were ostensibly similar, particularly in terms of school culture and material resources. The case studies demonstrate powerfully that there were significant differences in terms of the quality and scope of relationships experienced by the teachers (the structural dimension of the context in and through which agency in achieved). In turn, this appears to explain the differences in the agency achieved by the teachers.

We suggest here that there are a number of dimensions to the relationships at Lakeside High School, which make them more likely to enable teachers to achieve agency in comparison to their colleagues at Hillview High School. The first relates to the predominant *orientation* of the relationships within the school. At Hillview, these were largely hierarchical or vertical; conversely, at Lakeside, such relationships were supplemented by strong horizontal ties, which appeared to facilitate (or at least be indicative of) a collegial and collaborative culture in the school. Another difference lies in the *symmetry* of the relationships, and linked to this are issues of *reciprocity* (see also Daly et al. 2010). At Hillview, relationships tended to be slightly more asymmetric than that at Lakeside and certainly less reciprocal. Channels of communication were thus more likely to be one way, encouraging a culture of dissemination, rather than one of generative dialogue.

The above factors seem to have the potential to impact on the *formality*, *strength* and *frequency* of relationships (see also Coburn and Russell 2008). Thus at Lakeside, the existence of relatively reciprocal, symmetric relationships seemed to generate a *collaborative culture*, where in turn strong, frequent and informal teacher relationships were able to flourish. Moreover, this appears to be an autocatalytic process, demonstrating the mutually constitutive relationship between schools cultures and structures. Interestingly, there are strong parallels here between our research and a study conducted by Penuel and colleagues (2009), which found similar differences between two schools, both in terms of the nature of the ties experienced by teachers and the apparent outcomes of these interactions.

Our data suggest that even where individual teachers have extensive experience and strong aspirations for their work – thus providing strong iterational and projective orientations to their agency – this can be stymied in situations where collaborative work is limited and difficult. In the case of Lakeside High School, the teachers were able to draw upon powerful relational resources afforded by the strong web of connections within which they worked. This in turn helped to create a strong collaborative culture – which in turn facilitated the further development of relationships, and so on. Conversely, at Hillview High School, a comparative lack of such resources proved to be a disabling factor, which reduced teachers' achievement of agency, inhibiting their capacity to address the complexities encountered in their implementation of a new, national curriculum.

We make the point, also, that the practical–evaluative dimension encountered today becomes the iterational dimension of tomorrow and helps define teachers' future aspirations – the projective dimension of tomorrow. Thus, current contexts that inhibit agency today also hinder the development of the sorts of experience that enhance agency in the future and might lead to a truncated development of future aspirations and expertise. This in turn might seriously limit the potential for today's teachers to achieve agency in future.

We conclude, then, with the suggestion that if teachers are to achieve agency in their professional setting – which is important for meaningful engagement with policy initiatives such as 'Curriculum for Excellence' – then school managers should carefully consider the relational conditions through which teachers achieve agency, bearing in mind that a collaborative culture to strengthen agency is to a large extent dependent upon the nature and scope of relationships within the school.

5

Performativity and Teacher Agency

Introduction

In the foregoing chapters, we have examined several specific issues that impact upon agency: teacher beliefs, teacher discourses and the relational structures that form schools as organizations. These issues primarily relate to internal conditions of schools that impact on the achievement of agency. In this chapter, we turn to an issue that has elicited considerable attention in recent years, namely performativity, understood in its most basic sense as the demand on schools and teachers to 'perform', that is, to generate achievements in a clearly specified range of 'outcomes.' In doing so, we change the focus from the institutional 'logics' of schools to an examination of the potential impact of externally imposed ideological constructs around accountability and value for money, marketization and school autonomy. Such discourses, variously badged as neoliberalism and new public management, are said to be a radical challenge to established practices of schooling. Changes include a shift in the dynamics of power, particularly between schools and external agencies, and the injection of new discourses into schools, via new education policies that often represent a radical shift in the ways in which schooling and education more broadly have come to be construed in public spheres. Such changes to the external environment have been claimed to have exerted similarly radical shifts in the practices of schooling. It is worth repeating here Knoke and Kuklinski's (1982, cited by Emirbayer and Goodwin 1994, p. 1418) suggestion that 'the structure of relations among actors and the location of individual actors in the network have important behavioural, perceptual, and attitudinal consequences both for the individual and the system as a whole'. In particular, such conditions are widely claimed to have engendered cultures of performativity, where professionals must 'perform' in response to externally defined agendas.

Much has been written on the topic of performativity, both in respect of schools and of education more widely, as well as in relation to the public services in general. We do not intend to provide more than a general overview of these oft-repeated arguments in this chapter. Instead, echoing Michael Apple's (2001) concern that 'rather than leading to curriculum responsiveness and diversification, the competitive market has not created much that is different from the traditional models so firmly entrenched in schools today' (p. 413), we focus here on the ways in which performative cultures impact upon teachers' agency as they develop the curriculum in their schools. Performativity can be viewed as primarily a constituent of the practical–evaluative dimension of agency – much of what is demanded from schools and teachers plays out in the here and now – although it also has had a significant impact on the projective dimension, that is, on the definition of what schools are supposed to be for. Performativity is partly structural, at least in its origins, in that it relates to the nature of relations between teachers, school leaders and external agencies. It is cultural on at least two levels. First, school reforms have made teachers subject to new externally introduced discourses that offer challenges to the established ways of doing things. Second, and more pervasive, the reforms have engendered the performative culture mentioned above, which we explore in more detail in due course. Performativity also has material aspects; for example, the development of new technologies has facilitated the proliferation of surveillance and the monitoring of teachers' work. Such factors constitute the social, cultural and material conditions that frame teachers' work.

Nevertheless, performativity is also iterational, as teachers' responses to curriculum policy are shaped to a large extent by the knowledge, skills, attitudes and values shaped by their prior experiences of teaching, which thus sharply delineates their ability to manoeuvre between different repertoires when developing the curriculum. Priestley and Minty (2013) provide an example of this. They examined the practices of primary teachers schooled in curriculum development during the previous '5–14 Curriculum', an outcomes-based curriculum held in place by standardized testing, recording and reporting against curricular outcomes. Their research suggested that these teachers tended to be influenced by these same logics when dealing with the much more flexible 'Curriculum for Excellence'. In short, these teachers saw the enactment of the curriculum as being about developing opportunities to tick off the experiences and outcomes of the new curriculum, as they had been required to do under the auspices of the former curriculum. Performativity is also projective, as teachers' aspirations for their practice and their students can be demarcated, truncated and even distorted by external pressures to perform, whether through cynical strategic compliance with new policy, teaching to the test, subversive mediation of curriculum policy or outright cheating (Osborn et al. 1997; Ball 2003; Sahlberg 2010).

In this chapter, we explore the above issues in more detail. We first provide a brief overview of the concept of performativity, illustrating its origins, forms and effects. This discussion draws out the differences between performativity in England, with its marketized and increasingly decentralized system, and Scotland, with its hierarchical structures and ostensibly softer approach to accountability. Following this contextual discussion, we draw upon the empirical data from our project in order to explore how performativity impacts on teachers' achievement of agency in our case-study schools.

Performativity, professionalism and agency

Michael Apple has argued that school systems have been subject to a 'subtle shift in emphasis ... from student needs to student performance, and from what the school does for the student to what the student does for the school' (Apple 2001, p. 413). This trend is a key dimension of a well-documented culture of performativity, especially visible in schools, but present throughout the education system and more widely across the public services (Banks 2004; Sugrue and Solbrekke 2011; Keddie, Mills and Pendergast 2011). It is a phenomenon that has major implications for teachers and their agency, with enormous potential to shape the everyday lives of teachers in schools, colleges and universities (see, e.g. Gleeson and Shain 1999; Ball 2003; Biesta 2004; James and Biesta 2007; Sahlberg 2010, 2011; Keddie, Mills and Pendergast 2011). Performativity is not simply the demand for teachers to 'perform', but rather a pressure to perform in particular ways, most notably in terms defined and measured by external actors (Shore and Wright 2000). Teachers are therefore obligated to ensure that their students achieve the kind of grades that give their school the desired position in league tables, and the needs of the school thus potentially trump the educational needs of students.

Such requirements are problematic in the current policy context for at least two reasons. First, by positioning the teacher as a curriculum deliverer and producer of performance statistics, rather than as a curriculum developer, a responsible professional and an agent of change, they stand in tension with professional discourses in education (Sahlberg 2011; Biesta 2010). Thus, performativity calls teacher professionalism into question. Second, as noted earlier – and in contradistinction to policies that have apparently increased accountability – the issue of professional agency has been injected with renewed significance in recent years by the widespread development of new rhetorics of professionalism in public policy, which have increasingly emphasized the central position of professional practitioners in the enactment of policy, for example, as agents of change in curriculum making (e.g. Scottish Executive 2006). As we have shown in the introductory chapter, Scotland's 'Curriculum for Excellence', along with other variants of the 'new curriculum' (Priestley and Biesta 2013), explicitly positions teachers in this manner.

This is a significant shift away from teacher-proof curricula (Taylor 2013; Priestley and Biesta 2013), for example, England's 1989 'National Curriculum', framed around strong prescription of content or input regulation (Nieveen and Kuiper 2012; Kuiper and Berkvens 2013; Leat, Livingston and Priestley 2013). This apparent (re)turn to active teacher engagement with curriculum development seems to give explicit permission to teachers to exercise high(er) degrees of professional agency within the contexts in which they work. However, performativity is associated with the more pervasive output regulation (Nieveen and Kuiper 2012; Kuiper and Berkvens 2013; Leat, Livingston and Priestley 2013) or outcomes steering (Biesta 2004), which has arguably eroded teacher autonomy in a more effective way than achieved by input regulation. The important question this raises, therefore, is what happens when a policy imperative for teachers to become agentic 'meets' a culture of performativity within contexts framed by accountability practices.

Performativity has been widely discussed and critiqued in the academic literature, and it is not our intention here to provide a detailed analysis of the phenomenon. Nonetheless, a brief outline is needed to provide the context for the subsequent discussion of how the achievement of agency is influenced by performativity. The following section will provide an overview of the key tenets of performativity in the United Kingdom in the wider context of professionalism, as well as illustrate how Scotland exhibits both features in common with the rest of the United Kingdom, and important differences.

Before tackling performativity, we offer a brief outline of the issues surrounding professionalism, as the way in which this is conceptualized is fundamental to shaping the notion of the agentic teacher. Traditionally, professionalism has been defined as 'the control of work by professional workers themselves, rather than control by consumers in an open market or by the functionaries of a centrally planned and administered firm or state' (Freidson 1994, p. 32). Over time, this definition has been challenged from two sides, particularly in state-funded and state-provided services such as health, education and social work. On the one hand, people who use these services may have gained increased influence, shifting their identity from objects of the service in question to more equal partners in professional action. On the other hand, the role of the state has become more prominent, particularly in the public sector. Modern professionals thus operate in a context in which the interests of four parties need to be balanced: professionals (their expertise and their responsibility); their clients; the state; and their employers (Evetts 2011; see also Biesta 2015). The last fifteen years have witnessed major transformations in the relationships between and identities of these parties (Hupe and Hill 2007). In Scotland, teaching is at the forefront of the Scottish government's latest public service reform programme, which advocates services that are responsive to the needs of individuals and communities, focused on improving outcomes and increasingly mindful of budgetary constraints (Scottish Government 2011). Frontline practitioners such as teachers have a key role in making effective decisions about complex human situations; in other words, their professional agency is vital.

Such policy, including the curricular shift described above, would seem to reposition teachers as autonomous professionals in line with the Anglo-American archetype of the occupational professional (Freidson 1994). However, such constructions are problematic. First, neoliberal forms of governance have introduced a market logic into many professional fields, including teaching. As a result, clients have been redefined as consumers and the state has shifted its role from provider to inspector and quality controller. This has gone hand in hand with the implementation of technical-managerial forms of accountability (Charlton 1999): professionals such as teachers have increasingly found their work regulated externally, for example, through input regulation via prescriptive national curricula and latterly through output regulation such as target setting, external scrutiny through inspections and the development of professional competences, articulated as outcomes (Gewirtz 2002). Evetts (2011) sees this as 'a shift from notions of partnership, collegiality, discretion and trust to increasing levels of managerialism, bureaucracy, standardization, assessment and performance review' (p. 407). Resultant cultures of performativity in professional settings have been linked to diminished professional autonomy (e.g. Gleeson and Husbands 2001).

Wilkins (2011) identifies three main strands of performativity in schools:

1. the audit/target culture, as improvement and quality are measured through statistical data (for example, examinations statistics);
2. interventionist regulatory mechanisms, particularly school inspections. This includes the use of self-evaluation using external defined performance indicators or outcomes steering; and
3. a market environment, where parental choice is facilitated by publicly available data from inspections and attainment statistics.

While to a large extent these strands are part of a wider culture of accountability (see Biesta 2004), what is particular for performativity is the fact that indicators of performance become performance targets in themselves. The means thus become the ends of education. Under a culture of performativity, to put it differently, the performance of the system becomes self-referential. Performativity is accompanied and reinforced by its own rhetoric. Of particular note is the term 'quality' – 'the most empty and abused word of the last decade' (Biesta 2010, p. 69); 'an aerosol word', a deodorant to 'cover up the slightly offensive odour surrounding the decay of the public provision of education' (Smyth and Shacklock 1998, p. 51). Such concepts cease to be defined in substantive terms and become entirely formal; a major component of the strategic ambition of many organizations is to achieve a certain position in a league table and to be further evidenced via kitemarks and public validation through inspection reports.

For two decades, scholars have loudly decried performativity, pointing to a number of serious consequences. Smyth and Shacklock (1998, p. 27) stated that they were 'distressed by the expunging and depletion of educative values and purposes out of schooling by mean spirited politicians and their technocratically minded advisors'. Similar sentiments are clearly evident in the writings of Biesta, who has particularly highlighted how a culture of measurement drives out a concern for what constitutes good education (e.g. see: Biesta 2007, 2010). A particular area of concern has been the development of an increasing encroachment of surveillance, standardization and target-setting technologies into schools. The rhetorics of accountability tend to construe such technologies as rational and neutral – as common-sense practices, against which it would be stupid to argue – but they are founded in values explicitly linked to neoliberal notions of competition, marketization and consumer choice (Apple 2004). Of course, the philosophical roots and motives behind such rhetorics are a matter for debate. However, the effects have been well documented. These include the growth of an 'audit culture' (Strathern 2000), a proliferation of second-order activities associated with comparison and competitiveness (Apple 2004) and teaching to the test (Ball 2006). An emphasis on short-term instrumental goals driven by performativity has been shown to encourage a detachment from big-picture ideas, as teachers distance themselves from their personal values in order to 'play the game' (Gleeson and Gunter 2001; Biesta, Priestley and Robinson 2015). For example, teachers have been shown to be caught between reconciling professional ideals of social equity and student development with institutional performance (Sahlberg 2011). The 'game' can take the form of deliberate fabrication of the school's image – careful impression management and the construction of discourses of excellence (Perryman 2009; Keddie, Mills and Pendergast 2011).

Some writers have gone further in critiquing the destructive nature of performativity. Smyth and Shacklock (1998, p. 8) have suggested that 'reforms that deform' result in what Cowie, Taylor and Croxford (2007) have termed perverse incentives. According to these writers, ethical practices are undermined by performative pressures, as survival strategies readily become tactical, sometimes even becoming cynical compliance with external demands. Emergent practices have been shown to include the concealing of 'dirty laundry' (Cowie, Taylor and Croxford 2007), as well as more serious corruption and cheating (Ball 2003; Sahlberg 2010). The 'game of grades' includes inflation of grades for internally assessed coursework, preventing poorly performing subjects from running examination courses and not entering pupils for examinations (or entering them at a lower level than merited).[1] Further 'collateral damage' (Sahlberg 2010) lies in the effects on teachers. The time spent on 'maintaining and achieving a public image of a good school [means that] less time and energy is spent on pedagogic and curricular substance' (Apple 2001, p. 416). According to Sahlberg (2010), educational quality depends on teachers working within a favourable and collegial social environment; however, the intensification of teachers' work associated with performativity militates against this and may even lead to desocialization (Keddie, Mills and Pendergast 2011), low morale (Troman, Jeffrey and Raggl 2007; van Zanten 2009), stress (Troman 2000) and diminished confidence (Helsby 1999).

Performativity in Scotland

Scotland is extremely similar in many respects to England in terms of the first two dimensions of performativity identified by Wilkins (2011). While macro-level curriculum policy suggests a desire to move away from input regulation, successive guidance and statutory regulation from 1997, known as the 'Quality Improvement Initiative', has established an edifice of control and performativity that has similar effects to its English counterpart (see Boyd and Norris 2006; Cowie, Taylor and Croxford 2007; Reeves 2008). This comprises several mechanisms for external accountability that are characteristic of the first two dimensions of Wilkins's (2011) performativity typology, namely the use of attainment data to evaluate schools and external inspections. With the advent of 'Curriculum for Excellence', there has been some softening of this position and an apparent awareness in government circles of the detrimental effects of standardized testing and the evaluative use of summative assessment data (see below).

A strong attainment agenda has developed in schools, driven by statistical use of data derived from external examination results (primarily the 'gold standard' higher qualification) and national testing (5–14). Until 2013 (and at the time of our research), the former statistics generated what were known as standard tables and charts (STACS), which were used extensively in secondary schools to manage teachers, enabling, for example, subject departments to be compared with each other and the performance of schools and departments to be set against equivalent schools on comparator league tables. League tables do not 'officially' exist in Scotland. National tables are not compiled by the Scottish government, although comparator tables are used within local authorities, and national newspapers compile their own unofficial tables annually. Empirical evidence suggests that these unofficial league tables have been taken seriously in schools, affecting teachers' agency in curriculum making (Priestley et al. 2012; also see the endnotes in this chapter relating to qualification entries). In 2013, the Scottish government introduced a new benchmarking tool, known as Insight, putatively premised on the new principles of 'Curriculum for Excellence' and designed to solve the problems of performativity associated with STACS. At the time of writing, it was not yet possible to determine how this may (or may not) contribute to a culture of performativity in Scottish schools.[2] Primary schools no longer have access to standardized national assessments, as these were phased out following the introduction of 'Curriculum for Excellence'.[3] However, in many local authorities, practices involving comparison of data pertaining to pupils' attainment of the 'Curriculum for Excellence' experiences and outcomes persist; for example, some local authorities have bought into the commercial InCAS attainment tracking programme, which provides baseline and subsequent standardized testing and analysis (see http://www.cem.org/primary).

External inspection forms a second part of this system of output regulation. This falls into two categories. The most high profile are those undertaken by

Her Majesty's Inspectorate of Education (HMIe), now a part of the national agency Education Scotland. Inspections are framed around a set of performance indicators known as 'How good is our school?' (HGIOS) (HMIe 2002). Following the advent of 'Curriculum for Excellence', HGIOS was revamped in 2006–7 (HMIe 2006, 2007), signalling a supposed shift from a hard to a softer managerialism. However, according to Reeves (2008, p. 13), revisions to HGIOS are 'cosmetic, since the basic instruments and methodology remain the same'. The inspection model has been further developed subsequently, placing greater emphasis on self-evaluation. However, given that the aim of inspections is to provide public assurance and accountability, they continue to be high-stakes events for schools and constitute a key component of strong output regulation. A second form of inspection is the quality improvement audit conducted by local authorities. The shift in emphasis after 1997 in many local authorities from a supportive advisory role to a quality improvement role, characterized by audits mirroring the external inspection process, has been documented by several writers (e.g. Cowie, Croxford and Taylor 2007).

The third dimension of the Wilkins typology, the role of markets, is less evident in Scotland, where there is a stronger tradition of comprehensive schooling, albeit with a privately funded school sector of considerable size. Quality improvement mechanisms tend to be kept in place through bureaucracies, notably the local authorities. The effects of such central control were noted in an OECD report (2007), which suggested that centralized control over the curriculum and organizational structures have a detrimental effect on responsiveness and relevance to the needs of many pupils. Nonetheless, there are three features of quality improvement in Scotland that will be familiar to those working in England: compliance; a top–down approach; and a linear approach to change (see Reeves 2008). In particular, 'improvement with pre-specified level descriptors' (MacKinnon 2011, p. 91) requires schools to provide evidence of 'quality', with the attendant dangers of fabrication, as mentioned above.

Performativity and teacher agency

The above-described situation is clearly messy and rife with professional tensions for teachers. 'Curriculum for Excellence' advocates an enhanced professional role for teachers in developing the curriculum, a message reinforced by the influential 2011 Donaldson review of teacher education, which asserted:

> The most successful educating systems invest in developing their teachers as reflective, accomplished and enquiring professionals who are able to teach successfully in relation to current expectations, but who have the capacity to engage fully with the complexities of education and to be key actors in shaping and leading educational change. (Donaldson 2011, p. 14)

These discourses exhibit, however, a number of common professional and pedagogic features that sit uneasily with more performative cultures of schooling – 'a fundamental tension that rests underneath any attempt to apply the logic of schooling to many [new] forms of curriculum and pedagogy' (Ladwig 2010, p. 129). Thus there is, for example, a curricular focus on dialogic pedagogies, active learning, individualization in learning and learner autonomy (or pupils taking responsibility for their own learning), all advocated for their claimed potential in producing modern citizens, well equipped to thrive in a knowledge society and as members of a globalized workforce. While these ideas in themselves are definitely not unproblematic in an intrinsic sense, and while, as mentioned, the language of 'learning' and 'learners' can be said to have contributed to the erosion of a focus on educational purpose (see: Biesta 2007a, 2011), they suggest forms of pedagogy and wider educational practice that are in tension with a top–down culture of schooling driven by the performativity described above. This section of the chapter draws upon our empirical data to explore how these tensions play out in the professional lives of some Scottish teachers. The section comprises two vignettes: the first describing performativity in a primary school; and the second, a description of similar issues in two secondary schools. In both cases, we provide an analysis of the implications in these cases for teachers' achievement of agency as they enact the curriculum.

Performativity in a primary school

An enduring mantra in Scottish education has been the refrain that 'Curriculum for Excellence' has been implemented more effectively – or with greater fidelity (Cuban 1998) – in primary schools. One of the primary teachers participating in our study expressed this belief, and one of the secondary teachers put it thus: 'I think CfE is very much shaped towards the primary sector. Let's face it, primaries have been doing this stuff for years' [Kate]. According to this line of argument, secondary schools are hidebound by subject loyalties and constrained by the needs of getting young people good qualifications in these subjects, whereas primary schools have a more integrated approach, combined with a long tradition of child-centred education. Indeed, it is a popular axiom in Scottish education that primary schools teach children, whereas secondary schools teach subjects. While there is some underlying truth to these notions, they can serve to obscure the realities of curriculum development in both settings. Our data suggest that not only have some Scottish primary schools struggled to enact 'Curriculum for Excellence' – a finding mirrored by other research (Minty and Priestley 2012; Priestley and Minty 2013; Drew and Priestley 2014) – but that these difficulties have their roots to a large extent in the culture of Scottish primary schools, attributable to some extent to an external environment driven by accountability needs and a prior tradition of curriculum development driven by an outcomes-led approach.

The primary school in our study was in many ways an exemplary school. In particular, in a school serving a disadvantaged catchment area, there was considerable evidence in the teacher testimonies of deeply held concerns relating to equity, social justice, tackling deprivation and promoting social mobility and in general a desire to do one's best for the pupils in the school. And yet, the research suggests an environment driven by the need to satisfy the demands of an external accountability agenda, ostensibly to tackle the above issues, but applied to the extent that these demands interfered with the values articulated by teachers and managers and with the educative practices associated with these agendas.

The head teacher, as we have already seen in Chapter 3, was quite frank about the priority given to these practices:

> So we have a quality assurance calendar which [laughs] is usually up here. So these are the different things that we try to do in the course of the year. So in terms of managing my time to make sure I do not just become totally administrative, what I try to do is when I have tracking attainment meetings with the teachers, which I will do termly, if there are issues that come up at these meetings in relation to underperformance, then I prioritise my time, the deputy head teacher's time. [head teacher]

Such surveillance was justified by the need to maintain a relentless focus on raising attainment as a proxy measure for a good education. According to the head teacher and other participants, the source of this was pressure from outside of the school, especially from the local authority. Although, as mentioned, 'Curriculum for Excellence' comes with a discourse of the teacher as an active agent of change, the teachers we interviewed made it clear that, at the level of practice – at least where it concerns questions of audit, targets and the measurement of performance – there has been far less change. The data suggest that this was in part, at least, attributable to the performative culture of the school.

For instance, the head teacher talked about the shame linked to seeing the performance of the school in league tables. She particularly commented on the situation that developed under the former 5–14 curriculum:

> What happened was every year you were expected to do better regardless of the cohort, and that is madness, because you can't possibly, you know, make children Einstein if they haven't got the calibre to do that. I felt under enormous pressure at the end under the scrutiny of 5–14. It wasn't helpful and it had lost what I thought it had been put in place to do. It became too intense and not a tool. It became a whip. [head teacher]

She was concerned about how the introduction of 'Curriculum for Excellence', with a focus on 'active learning' and 'transferable skills', would fit with what she saw as a continued focus on accountability. Recounting a recent head teachers' meeting she explained that

> it was made clear that standardized testing was the way forward. So there is likely to be training for standardized testing of pupils in P3, 5, 7 and S1,[4] I believe. So that is the authority stepping in and doing base lines. So we are not too far away from National Test mark two and Big Brother. [head teacher]

Despite her apparent unease at this situation, this agenda was duly imported back into the school by the senior management in line with local authority priorities.

> And I have got a big folder up there that has got all the experiences and outcomes. So all of the forward plans, everything is being planned in relation to the new experiences and outcomes. But it is still about raising attainment and developing literacy and numeracy. Making sure that that is high on the agenda. [head teacher]

The foregoing quotes indicate the school's approach to curriculum development – a strategic, tick-the-box approach to the coverage of the experiences and outcomes of the curriculum. This approach seems to be common in Scottish primary schools, as we indicated previously, and manifests pressures on the achievement of agency by both the demands of the present context (for example, local authority policy) and prior patterns of curriculum development (as the logics of previous practice are applied to the new context of 'Curriculum for Excellence'). This approach comes, of course, with a strong emphasis on assessment, recording and reporting, as suggested by the head teacher. The school made use of InCAS testing, as discussed earlier in the chapter. This raised concerns for some of the teachers who felt that it constituted an intrusive over-emphasis on second-order activity rather than the core business of learning and teaching.

> Possibly sometimes the amount of things can affect, because there is [sic] these things that you have got to do. But it takes out time. Next term we have got these new tests to do with primary sevens. All on the computers and there is about five of them and they take twenty minutes each. So that is going to take up my ICT time for the majority of next term. Which then, I think, 'well I am not actually teaching them any ICT then'. ... It is a benchmark, so that we can see that in primary five this is what their scores were. But by primary seven it has got better. ... So you can see there has been an improvement. But doing things like that there is [sic] pupil profiles the P7s have got to do. And again that all needs to be typed, I am sure. But then I am going to have to check it all to make sure it is okay, because then that has to go home to parents and that gets sent up to the high school. [Rachael]

These school priorities were accompanied – and enforced – by high degrees of surveillance: internally, involving regular observations of teaching, scrutiny of teachers' planning documentation by senior managers and data recording using spreadsheets; and externally through local authority audits. At the time of the research, the school had not been inspected by HMIe for some years, and these latter inspections were not mentioned by the participating teachers.

The above description forms an impression of a school culture where output regulation is a fact of life for the teachers and managers, thus establishing a culture of low trust. In contrast with the discourses of 'Curriculum for Excellence', teachers seemed to be expected to be technical implementers rather than active developers of the curriculum. This is neatly exemplified by the ways in which a number of 'must-do' techniques or 'best practices' were applied, subsequently monitored and enforced by senior staff and shared at staff development events. These included formative assessment techniques (such as sharing learning intentions), cooperative learning structures and peer observation of teaching. There was an overriding sense that such techniques tended to be put in place to tick boxes rather than being selected to meet specific educational purposes.

This case study raises some interesting questions about how teacher agency emerges when the permissive discourses of 'Curriculum for Excellence' come up against the culture of performativity in Scottish primary schools. Our overall sense was of a group of teachers and a head teacher whose agency was limited by the pressures of an accountability agenda. The following extended extracts from a dialogue between one of the researchers and an experienced teacher (with over 20 years in the classroom) clearly illustrate both the problem and the dilemmas it causes for practitioners.

> The actual Curriculum for Excellence philosophy, if that is the right use of the word, where it is all about the children, it is all about preparing them for all of these things; but then they come up with something that is very airy fairy but they still want the assessment. And it is just … they have gone from one extreme in my opinion, where 5–14 was so prescriptive, and we had to do this, but the assessing was easy within that because it was so prescriptive, to a few things that they want you to do and yet they still want this prescriptive assessment. … The only way you can do that is to make up programs and then by making up programs you have almost slipped back into the 5–14 instead of just going with whatever the children stated. … I think it is now. I don't think initially it did but all of a sudden. … Initially when you started you still had the 5–14 assessing 'where are the children now, where do you want them to be?' And you still used the 5–14 assessments, but you shouldn't do that so all of a sudden I am hearing as well there is [sic] these assessment banks, so you should be using these assessment banks to see where you children are. … I don't know what is right. I really don't know what is right but I am quite sure that we are kind of slipping back into the assessment similar to the 5–14. … In some ways it does restrict you because the council is telling the head teacher that this is what we want and also asking perhaps for levels of attainment or that side of it. So there is this 'well I have got to show that these children are able to do that by then. How are you going to do it?' [Eilidh]

The teacher's frustration and lack of agency are palpable in above transcript, which shows clearly how the present environment in the school – particularly the culture of performativity – is holding in place practices that 'Curriculum for Excellence' was intended to disrupt. In one sense, this shows that this teacher's limited achievement of agency is the result of pressure in the here and now – the practical–evaluative dimension – as a result of which she is unable to utilize her considerable experience to manoeuvre between repertoires because of the demands posed by the current social context. There is also an iterational dimension that plays a role in the (limited) way in which agency is achieved here. She is a teacher who has spent most of her career working within the past context shaped by the 5–14 curriculum and its associated practices. We would argue that this has heavily socialized her into ways of doing that are subsequently limiting the achievement of agency in relation to a more permissive curriculum framework. Nevertheless, this teacher is able to see the potential in 'Curriculum for Excellence' to frame alternative futures, noting especially its flexibility: 'There is some leeway. And I think probably in this school it is getting more leeway than it was because 5–14 was very prescriptive' [Eilidh]. Despite this, she was unable to articulate what those futures might look like.

A less-experienced colleague, acknowledged throughout the school as a trailblazer for 'new' 'Curriculum for Excellence' pedagogies, was even more uncertain about how 'Curriculum for Excellence' (in particular its assessment) might be developed.

> I would not say completely in everything. In the teaching part of it, from what I am doing, I think it is right. But then you think, 'well because it is new, are you missing bits out that possibly you should be doing? Or should we be getting through all this? Or are we just trying to get through it all because it is there?' And because the outcomes are so broad, 'are you covering it in enough detail. … Are you interpreting it in the correct way?' So there is [sic] so many different things, but these just take time. … For some children, they could have been doing level C work and done the test, passed the test and then went on to level D work, but weren't secure enough in level C to progress. But because, well, they have been on that level for 18 months, they really get pushed on because this looks bad on the attainment, so they have to get pushed on. [Rachael]

Again, we see here thinking that is shaped by the discourses of the previous curriculum. We would argue here that there is a serious tension between the developmental, divergent discourses of the new curriculum and the more restrictive and convergent practices associated with performativity, and developed over time within the regime of 5–14. This is probably further exacerbated by mixed messages in 'Curriculum for Excellence' documented in the literature, for example, ambiguities about the place of knowledge (Priestley and Sinemma 2014) and active learning (Drew and Mackie 2011). Such tensions play out in terms of these primary teachers' engagement with the curriculum – characterized by uncertainty, feelings of risk and recourse to tried and tested practices (even where these do not match the new curriculum). The achievement of agency is thus limited as they confront practical difficulties in reconciling the curriculum with other, conflicting demands in their professional working and make cost–benefit judgements about the relative risk of different approaches (both practical and evaluative). Their achievement of agency is further shaped by their experiences of prior contexts (iterational), notably resulting in a view of curriculum development as evidencing outcomes, in enactments, comprising play-safe approaches and strategic compliance and box-ticking, shaped by their prior experiences of curriculum making. Moreover, there is some evidence in these data that these teachers' achievement of agency is further diminished by a lack of capacity to develop a future orientation to their practice, formed around educational thinking and a deep engagement with educational purposes. Instead, their practice has been shaped by – and their agency limited by – the genuine day-to-day difficulties involved in reconciling the old with the new in an environment heavily distorted by the imposition of external imperatives, experienced as output regulation.

Performativity in two secondary schools

If we follow the line of argument that 'Curriculum for Excellence' has been better implemented in primary schools, we might expect to find similar or even higher levels of dysfunctionality in our two secondary case studies. However, as we explored in Chapter 4, this was not the case in one of the secondary schools, where the faculty participating in the research exhibited both achieved agency and purposeful curriculum development in response to the new demands of 'Curriculum for Excellence'. In this case, the strength of relationships in the school appeared to be the decisive factor that differentiated the teachers from the others in the study, resulting in comparatively enhanced levels of achieved agency. This is not to say, however, that there were no issues with performativity; there were, and the strength of relationships acted solely as a set of mitigating factors, which served only to diminish the effects of performativity. In this part of the chapter, we explore how these tensions played out in practice.

As might be expected, attainment plays a major role in the culture of performativity encountered in each school. As we discussed earlier in the chapter, Scottish secondary schools have traditionally tended to have a narrow focus on teaching a limited range of academic subjects. In the senior phase (S3–6), the focus is on the delivery of courses leading to external qualifications. Traditionally, the junior phase (S1–2) courses have tended to reflect what Raffe (2008, p. 30) terms the 'principle of downward incrementalism: that in an education system marked by successive decision or branching points, the later stages influence those before them'. 'Curriculum for Excellence', with its creation of a broad general education phase encompassing the primary years and the secondary years S1–3, was intended to overturn this tendency. However, old habits die hard; in both of our secondary case studies, the provision for the early years remained largely indistinguishable from what had gone before. Indeed in one case, the school had moved to what has been widely termed early presentation, requiring pupils to make their senior subject choices at the end of S1, a year earlier than was traditional. This course of action was justified on the grounds that it raised attainment.

Attainment was clearly the driving factor in both schools, facilitated by the managerial use of STACS to identify and deal with teachers who were seen to be underperforming. As discussed previously, this tool focused on attainment in external qualifications by senior pupils. At both secondary schools, the school year starts typically with a staff meeting where the data from STACs are used as evidence of the school's performance. One teacher said that they 'are very much what the school is measured on'. She explained that the school's performance this year was similar to the previous year. She saw this as

> quite disappointing in some ways, it is quite hard when you are hearing the whole school statistics. It is difficult to relate that to your individual classes. There are things we have learned from. I think we have put people in for exams that we shouldn't have put them in for, which then looks bad on the statistics, and that has certainly happened before. [Kate]

This suggestion that, from the school statistics point of view, it would be better not to put some students in for the exam reflects the aspect of performativity noted by Apple (2001) – that the needs of the school come before the needs of students. This teacher found the school's performance – neither better nor worse than the previous year – to be disheartening.

> if you just saw the results published in the paper it makes the school sound like a not very good school but it doesn't feel like that to me when I come here everyday. I think we are a good school and that the pupils are well behaved and that there is a lot more to it than the exam results. But the exam results are what we are ultimately judged on. [Kate]

Inspections were also mentioned by these teachers. In one case, the school had recently had an inspection and a follow-up inspection.[5] In the other, an inspection was imminent, although no date had yet been set. In such circumstances, a certain degree of anxiety about inspections is natural. As we have mentioned before, in Scottish schools regulatory mechanisms operate at three levels: nationally by HMIe; locally by education officers called quality improvement officers and internally by the school. Within the schools, the inspections were called 'observations' and were carried out by the management teams, head teachers and senior managers. In the secondary schools, an additional level of 'observation' was carried out by the head of faculty.

Several teachers remarked upon their responses to inspections and audits. One teacher commented that preparing for an inspection was 'false' and that 'teachers should always be teaching as if an inspector could walk into your class' [Susan]. Another talked about some teachers 'putting on a show' [Sara]. Inspections, for these teachers, seemed to be part of the environment; the image of teachers teaching behind a closed door was not recognized by them, and they seemed proud of their 'open door' policy. For example:

> I feel you should see a school 'warts and all'. Some people talk about inspections where they appear unannounced and I kind of think, yeah, it is not to put on a show because that is not fair and it is not right. If there are issues they should be aired and if you are doing it right you should be doing that all the time anyway. [Susan]

However, she was critical of the inspections that were carried out at the local level where there had been a shift from support to quality control. These events were termed derogatively as the 'judge in the corner'. She felt frustrated at the lack of either informal or formal feedback following the observation.

> What annoyed me about them that it was conducted by people who were supposed to help and support schools but I never saw these people. They were never a common face in the school or name on your email. What I did feel was that they were people who had not taught in years, coming in and observing and in one case I got feedback and in the other the lady sat at the back and she wrote and she highlighted and said thank you very much and left my room! [Sara]

The advent of 'Curriculum for Excellence', with its overt messages about teacher autonomy, sat uneasily with the culture of performativity, as was the case in the primary school. While these teachers said they welcomed being extended autonomy, they also exhibited some trepidation in the face of it. It is clear that for these secondary school teachers, curriculum development is a balancing act between external criteria and internal ambitions and values. Insecurity about performing 'correctly' was certainly an issue, according to one teacher: 'We ask to be treated like professionals and then, when we are given the chance, some people find that is a bit scary' [Susan]. Another teacher expressed anxiety about autonomy:

> There is still an issue with … not necessarily seeing the big picture as far as the long-term is concerned, with the younger classes anyway. The lessons are

fine with the advanced higher and the third year and fourth year. But with the first and second year, day-to-day it is fine. But I am still feeling it is a problem with lack of direction and where we are trying to go with the Curriculum for Excellence. [Kate]

This quotation exemplifies the basic issue in schools as the culture of performativity meets the permissive features of 'Curriculum for Excellence': the certainty of the senior phase, with the security blanket provided by national qualifications syllabi and their associated and clearly delineated performative demands, contrasts starkly with the uncertainty and vagueness perceived by many to accompany the new curriculum. We note here that our study preceded the introduction of new national qualifications, supposedly aligned with 'Curriculum for Excellence'; these have been subject to high levels of uncertainty and anxiety by teachers, over-assessment and bureaucracy (e.g. see: EIS 2013; Scottish Parliament 2014).

What we see here, therefore, is a dimension of the introduction and implementation of 'Curriculum for Excellence' where old patterns of the culture of performativity seem to continue. While the teachers do note a change in some aspects of the discourse – for example, the idea of 'active learning' – they also note that the changed discourse is not followed by a change in practice where it concerns the apparent need to produce comparative statistical indicators of performance. From our conversations with the teachers, we gained the impression that they mostly accepted this as an inevitable reality – something that is simply happening and being decided elsewhere – and therefore not as something that triggered an agentic response from them, despite their doubts about such systems of performativity. Where we did see agentic responses resulting in action against this culture, they tended to be limited in scope and invariably resulted from a concern for the well-being of students. A good example is provided by the teacher discussed in previous chapters, who sometimes gave tests without telling pupils that they were being tested, to avoid placing what she saw as harmful demands upon students, thus protecting them from the worst excesses of the attainment culture.

This vignette, therefore, not only shows that the discourse of teacher agency that comes with 'Curriculum for Excellence' is in practice limited in secondary schools – which reinforces the point that 'Curriculum for Excellence' is a central policy issued from the top–down and not just a possible option that schools or teachers can decide to adopt. It also demonstrates that, even when secondary teachers have strong professional values, the dynamics of the here and now – the practical–evaluative dimension of agency – to a large extent determines whether such values and the professional habitus through which they are expressed will result in an agentic response or not. Similarly, the ways in which teachers commented on inspection and observation shows that, to a large extent, they seem to accept this as a normal – and even desirable – aspect of their practice, even though they often see the process as unfair or arbitrary. This suggests that the professional values that have informed the habits of these teachers allow them to make a judgement about which aspects they find desirable and which aspects they find troubling. Nevertheless, while they express views about the desirable and undesirable aspects of observation and inspection and attainment-related practices, they do seem to accept the changes, so their professional doubt does not turn into action – at least not within the examples we discussed with the teachers in the interviews. This further suggests that there is a gap between what we might call agentic judgement and agentic action. This gap can perhaps partly be explained by the ways in which the teachers have internalized aspects of the culture of performativity so that they appear to them as either inevitable or as impossible to resist.

Conclusions

All of the above suggests that performativity seriously diminishes teacher agency. Our data illustrate how the intrinsic logics of policy collide in a complex manner with the institutional logics of the contexts within which the policy is supposed to be enacted. This situation is further exacerbated by incoherence within and between policies (Reeves 2008; Priestley and Humes 2010). Policies demanding performativity are a prominent part of this inherent and fundamental tension in teachers' work. Thus, teachers are faced with 'an educational dilemma: how to deal with external productivity demands on the one hand, while simultaneously teaching for the knowledge society with moral purpose' (Sahlberg 2010, p. 48). They are caught between a 'rock and hard place' (Reeves 2008), and as a result their agency is potentially limited.

We note here that some writers have witnessed the ways in which some teachers are able to mediate, mitigate or circumvent some of the more damaging aspects of external demands on their work. For example, Bowe, Ball and Gold (1992) noted the ways in which high-capacity departments were able to work around the national curriculum to maintain what they viewed as their core mission in education. Helsby (1999) suggested that teachers with high confidence in their own capacity and authority were able to act with a high degree of agency in the face of performativity, noting also that collegiality boosted such capacity, but that performativity eroded it. A related theme has emerged in the writings of Osborn and colleagues (1997) and Gleeson and Shain (1999). These authors noted the varied responses of teachers to performative demands; not merely a simple binary of resistance/compliance but more nuanced forms of mediation of policy to reflect differing perspectives and positioning (see also Gewirtz 2002). While our data illustrated the complex demands and affordances that shape teacher agency, we witnessed only limited examples of agency as resistance (Priestley 2011). Instead our participants seemed more likely to go with the flow, even where they were clearly dissatisfied with this. This again raises important questions about whether agency should be construed as a positive aspect of teachers' work. Policy can tend to construe agency as solely a positive capacity – as a factor in 'successful' implementation – whereas one might legitimately take the view that agency could equally well be exercised for 'non-beneficial' purposes, or for decisions and actions that go against the grain of official policy.

There is also the question of the extent to which teachers can actually achieve agency in highly performative cultures, which is a question both about capacity and about resources and opportunities. Here it could well be argued that the combined influence of at least two decades of intrusive input and output regulation may well have to a large extent eroded teachers' capacity for agency and have taken away important resources and opportunities for the achievement of agency from their practice. There are strong iterational and practical–evaluative dimensions to this agency (or lack of), as we have noted throughout the chapter – the consequence of past and present performative cultures in both primary and secondary schools. We also note again the observation made in Chapter 2 – that the teachers in our study struggled to form long-term aspirations based upon consideration of educational (as opposed to shorter-term instrumental) considerations. We would also support recent suggestions (e.g. Education Scotland 2014) that many Scottish teachers are overemphasizing the demands of accountability and quality assurance, which is claimed by those making policy to have been toned down considerably. Whether this claim is the case or not is to some extent irrelevant; we can certainly state with confidence from our data that there are strong perceptions of the reality of these demands, that these are influential in shaping practices, and so the performative culture persists. Associated with these phenomena is widespread anxiety about the perceived autonomy afforded by 'Curriculum for Excellence' (Minty and Priestley 2012; EIS 2013). As Eisner has already suggested long ago, this is not surprising:

> If a bird has been in a cage for a decade and suddenly finds the door open, it
> should not be surprising if the bird does not wish to leave. The familiar is often
> more comfortable than the uncertainty of the unknown. (Eisner 1992, p. 617)

The familiar in this case is the accountability demands – outcomes-driven
curriculum development in the case of the primary school, and exam syllabi
in the case of the secondary school – and the resulting performative cultures
engendered by them. This is a problem because the effects are real; a lack of
agency is associated with a lack of serious engagement with policy, and
consequently the persistence of the status quo, in contradistinction to both the
goals of curriculum policy and the aspirations of those who wish to see a more
purposeful approach to curriculum development.

> Like almost all complex traditional social organizations, schools will
> accommodate in ways that require little or no change. That is not to say that
> accommodation is insincere or deliberately cosmetic, but rather that the strength
> of the status quo – its underlying axioms, its pattern of power relationships, its
> sense of tradition and therefore what seems rights, natural and proper – almost
> always rules out options for change in that status quo. (Sarason 1990, p. 35)

The neoliberal reconstruction of the professional role has thus impacted
radically on the possibilities for agency. It has rendered teachers' repertoires for
manoeuvre in response to problematic situations more limited. It has, at the same
time, undermined professionals' ability to take responsibility for their work, that
is, to act on the basis of informed and negotiated professional judgement. While
standards are important elements of good professional work, they run the risk of
becoming counterproductive when they turn into forms of standardization that
may rule out judgement, for example, in favour of so-called 'evidence-based'
practices (see Biesta 2007b). The same can be said for accountability when the
emphasis on achieving performance targets begins to overshadow the quality of
the work. In those cases, the diminished opportunities for professional agency
lead to forms of action that are increasingly a-responsible and potentially
irresponsible (Sugrue and Solbrekke 2011; Keddie, Mills and Pendergast 2011).
In both situations, it is the users of the services who stand to lose most.

Individual, Cultural and Structural Framings of Agency

Introduction

We started this book by reflecting on a recent policy turn – a trend widely evident in worldwide curriculum policy – towards according teachers greater autonomy in their professional lives. Thus, policies such as Scotland's 'Curriculum for Excellence' highlight the importance of teachers being agents of change and active developers of the curriculum in their own schools. As we have illustrated throughout the book, such a reconceptualization of the role of the teacher is problematic. It is problematic following years of policies that regulate the work of teachers and have greatly eroded teacher autonomy (Biesta 2004); these take the form of *input regulation* in the form of tight prescription of the content (and even the methods) of the curriculum and *output regulation* via external inspections and the evaluative usage of attainment data to judge the performance of schools and teachers (see, also, Kuiper and Berkvens 2013). It is problematic because policy has been invariably focused on the *quality or capacity of the individual teacher*, in line with predominant transnational discourses about school effectiveness, rather than taking into consideration the contexts or conditions by means of which teachers practise.

In the light of the above trends, it is problematic to expect that teachers become agentic, when in their practical contexts they are unable to do so. It is one thing for policy to demand that teachers have agency; it is quite another for this to occur in practice. This is partially recognized within transnational discourses emanating from organizations such as the OECD.

The quality of teaching is determined not just by the 'quality' of the teachers – although that is clearly critical – but also by the environment in which they work. Able teachers are not necessarily going to reach their potential in settings that do not provide appropriate support or sufficient challenge and reward. (OECD 2005, p. 9)

And yet, as we argue in this chapter and throughout the book, such understandings are often underdeveloped and under-theorized and have thus not tended to be adequately reflected in national policies and their resultant practices. Tensions within and between policies, linked to an overemphasis on the individual teacher and lack of systematic approaches to addressing cultural and structural issues, have contributed to creating an environment where teacher agency is difficult to achieve – an environment where teachers are effectively disabled when developing the curriculum as required by policy.

In this chapter, we bring these arguments into a sharper focus, making the case that new policy trends have at least partially changed the conditions – at a macro policy level at least – within which, and by means of which, teachers work. Such policy raises the expectations that teachers will achieve agency while failing to address the cultural and structural conditions that effectively limit or even deny that agency. Thus the changing policy landscape raises new issues and problems, demanding new ways of theorizing the work of teachers and the ways in which schools and teachers operate. At the very least, in a policy landscape that appears to view teachers' agency as a desirable attribute, we need to be able to understand how and why teachers achieve agency and what helps or hinders the achievement of agency.

A more ambitious goal is to avoid the development of policy that 'gives with one hand and takes away with the other' (Leat 2014) and instead to promote the future development of policies and processes that actively encourage and facilitate teacher agency. The chapter thus sets out a detailed rationale for utilizing the ecological understanding of agency, illustrating how a better understanding of teacher agency will in turn foster the future development of more sophisticated policy at both macro and meso levels of the system and facilitate the enactment of policy into practice in schools through more systematic and better-conceived processes for curriculum development. We start the chapter with a summary of the ideas presented so far in the book. Then we discuss the question of what it means to foster agency, looking both at policy and at the individual, the cultural and the structural dimensions, showing how the ecological approach helps us to understand the dynamics of teaching and develop policy and practice through attention to all three levels. Our discussion will be guided by three sets of questions:

1. What is teacher agency? Here we reflect on the features of teacher agency, including a crucial issue: that teacher agency is a normative issue, and that one might consider that there is such a thing as 'good agency'.

2. Where does teacher agency come from? In other words, what are the individual, cultural and structural conditions that facilitate the achievement of agency by teachers? Here, we examine issues such as: (a) the ongoing impact of 'professional habitus (i.e. that you can take the teacher out of old ways of working, but it is not that easy to take the old ways of working out of the teacher); (b) the tension between more open curriculum and ongoing audit culture; and (c) the discursive and relational resources that afford teacher agency.

3. What does teacher agency make possible? Put differently, what advantages are there for schools and for curriculum policy in enabling teachers to achieve agency, and how might better understandings of teacher agency lead to school improvement? It is necessary to address this question if we are to show that the ecological approach to understanding teacher agency is not just yet another educational theory cooked up by ivory-tower academics, but has some practical utility in the framing of policy and practice.

What have we found?

Before we proceed to these substantive questions about teacher agency, we briefly summarize the arguments, findings and conclusions presented in the preceding chapters. In Chapter 1, we set out a comprehensive outline of the ecological approach to agency, showing the lineage of this approach in the context of different thinking about the question of agency. Agency has a long and rich history as a concept and is frequently invoked in writing on educational issues, particularly, as we have noted, in the related fields of educational change and teacher networking and, more recently, in a developing body of literature devoted to teacher agency. Despite this common usage, however, agency remains a rarely defined and poorly conceptualized construct in much of the education literature, often constituting little more than a label, with little appreciation of its problematic nature. It is therefore worth reiterating some of the features of the ecological approach here, especially, as we have emphasized throughout the book, because this approach has distinct differences to the traditional sociological view of agency as a variable in social action (Hollis 1994; Emirbayer and Mische 1998; Biesta and Tedder 2006). The ecological approach has the following features:

- Agency is viewed as an emergent phenomenon, rather than as a capacity of individuals. It is something that people do or achieve, rather than something that people possess (Biesta and Tedder 2006).
- Agency is thus dependent on both the conditions by means of which actors act and the qualities that those actors bring to the situation. Therefore, the 'achievement of agency will always result from the interplay of individual efforts, available resources and contextual and structural factors as they come together in particular and, in a sense, always unique situations' (Biesta and Tedder 2007, p. 137). While high-capacity individuals will invariably experience good possibilities to achieve agency, such agency is also dependent upon the constraints and possibilities afforded by their environment; these include cultural, relational and material resources available to them, as well as their ability to deploy them.
- Agency is temporal as well as relational. Emirbayer and Mische (1998) suggest that agency should be understood as a 'temporally embedded process of social engagement, informed by the past (in its habitual aspect), oriented towards the future (as a capacity to imagine alternative possibilities) and 'acted out' in the present (as a capacity to contextualize past habits and future projects with the contingencies of the moment)' (p. 963). This chordal triad comprises the iterational (past, habit), the projective (future, imagination) and the practical–evaluative (present, judgement) dimensions of agency.

The overview of theory presented in Chapter 1 included discussion of teacher agency. We suggested that it is possible to theorize teacher agency through the application of the chordal triad as follows:

- *The iterational dimension of teacher agency* is formed through teachers' life and professional histories and comprises their professional and personal knowledge and skills, their attitudes, values and beliefs. While the iterational is often concerned with habit (and expectation maintenance), it is also characterized by individuals' ability to choose and manoeuvre between repertoires. This professional habitus is important in framing how teachers might actively respond to dilemmas, problems and opportunities in their work and is an important factor in shaping their practices in response to centrally mandated curriculum reform.
- *The projective dimension of teacher agency* concerns teachers' ability to visualize alternative futures in their practice. Agency is always motivated, and the range of responses (and the degree to which teachers are able to

achieve agency) is at least in part dependent on their ability to develop aspirations around their professional working. Such aspirations can be short-, medium- or long-term and can be expansive or limited in scope. The extent to which teachers can frame aspirations – and imagine alternative futures – will again affect the nature of their responses to curriculum reform policy.

- *The practical–evaluative dimension of teacher agency* relates to the day-to-day navigation of present contexts for action. Agency is achieved in the present and is shaped by the nature of those present-day contexts. Mediating factors are social (cultural and structural) as well as material. Teachers' responses to policy interventions will be both shaped by practical considerations (i.e. what is possible given available resources) and by evaluative considerations (e.g. by judgements of risk), and these are framed by their belief systems.

This framing of agency allowed us to explore the work of teachers, drawing upon the empirical data from our project.

Chapter 2 focused on the issue of teacher beliefs. We noted that the existing literature on beliefs tends to be linked (often uncritically) to agendas of school improvement and educational change, for instance, being premised around a deficit view of schools as being in need of remedial action through policy interventions. It is also not common to see writing that explicitly links beliefs to teacher agency. The chapter first explored the nature of teacher beliefs, which can be seen as a subset of the wider system of beliefs held by individuals, can contradict personal beliefs and are difficult to disentangle from them. They include beliefs about the self, beliefs about others (students, colleagues) and beliefs about practices (pedagogy, content). In the chapter, we differentiate between beliefs and aspirations. The former constitute part of the professional habitus brought to situations by the teachers and are thus a component of the iterational dimension of agency. The latter are projective in nature, concerned with future imaginings, for example, what sorts of practices might be possible in relation to the new curriculum in Scotland. Beliefs and aspirations play out in present-day contexts, providing cognitive and affective resources as teachers deal with situations and enact their practice. A second question relates to where beliefs come from. Many writers note that beliefs are socially and contextually mediated. The literature is clear about the influence of educational experience – teacher education and especially teachers' own schooling – in the formation of teacher beliefs (Eisner 1994). Professional experience – for instance, the strongly formed cultures of performativity in many schools – has been noted to shape teacher beliefs, and dissonance has been linked to belief formation (Pajares 1992).

Our empirical data highlighted many of the above issues and raised some interesting questions about teacher agency. In Chapter 2, we highlighted three broad types of teacher beliefs evident in our data: beliefs about students, beliefs about the role of the teacher and beliefs about the purposes of education. The data painted a picture of teachers, who while skilled, motivated and conscientious, tended to have deficit views of the children they taught. They tended to see their role in quite narrow terms; while they welcomed the developmental language of 'Curriculum for Excellence', this was contradicted by an apparent reluctance to challenge authority and to take the initiative in curriculum development. We also noted the tendency of these teachers to see educational purpose in short term and often narrowly instrumental terms – getting through the day, keeping students interested – rather than in relation to longer-term, educational aspirations. The nature of these teachers' beliefs and the narrow scope of their professional aspirations limited, in our judgement, their possibilities for agency, and this in turn reduced the range of what might be possible under the new curriculum. We also noted the potential of policy discourses to mediate teacher beliefs.

In Chapter 3 we developed this discussion further, moving from the content of teachers' beliefs towards the wider vocabularies and discourses that such beliefs are part of. In terms of agency, we approached such vocabularies and discourses as 'discursive resources' that play an important role in the achievement of agency or lack thereof. Such resources are important because, as we showed through a more detailed reconstruction of parts of the conversations we had with teachers and senior managers in the project, they are the material with and through which teachers think, in the broad sense of the word. The qualities of thought and judgement, which, in turn, will have an impact on the quality of action, crucially depend on the discursive resources teachers have available. In the chapter, we partly tried to show what these resources look like, and here we not only found differences in opinion and belief – that is, at the level of the *content* of the discourses; we also found that some vocabularies and discourses were much more elaborate and nuanced, thus allowing for a more nuanced judgement about the situations in which teachers act. In some cases, this also allowed for a more 'relaxed' attitude towards immediate policy pressures, in part because of the ability to put the 'present' and the 'fashionable' into a wider context.

The latter turned out to have a lot to do with the answer to the questions of where the vocabularies and discourses teachers used came from and which factors had impact on the formation and transformation of them. Here we saw both age and generation effects, that is, both the impact of experience – the length of career was an influential factor here – and the impact of experiences stemming from a different time with different policies, different practices and different 'drivers' of the practice. As part of this, we could also see how policy itself shapes teachers' vocabularies and discourses, particularly in the way in which policy is able to create a 'common sense' about schooling and the work of the teacher. If all a teacher has experienced, both in their teacher education and in their subsequent work, is one 'version' of what schools are supposed to be about, it is not a surprise that this defines the reality for such a teacher. While there was evidence that both less- and more-experienced teachers were enthusiastic about ideas from 'Curriculum for Excellence', and in this regard experienced a 'fit' between their own values, beliefs and understandings and what the new curriculum sought to bring about, it is important to acknowledge that with less-experienced teachers this 'fit' was more the result of the absence of an alternative perspective, whereas for the more-experienced teachers it was the outcome of a more developed judgement about the strengths and weaknesses of 'Curriculum for Excellence' within the context of a wider set of available options and orientations. While at one level, the 'outcome' was the same, we can say that in the second case, there was a more agentic and deliberate engagement with the new curriculum framework than in the former case.

Chapter 3 also made visible how teachers' vocabularies and discourses are influenced by context and location – particularly the location within the educational system. In this regard, we could see that those with a management responsibility in the participating schools were more aware of the outside demands they had to meet, which was partly reflected in the language they spoke as well. Sometimes this was more perceived as a tension between personal and professional ideals and beliefs on the one hand and what 'the system' demands on the other; in other cases – which we might characterize as more agentic – opportunities had been found within the demand of the 'system' to focus on what was considered to be important. The latter also revealed, and we return to this below, that the question of teacher agency is a thoroughly *normative* question, as the ultimate challenge is not simply to achieve agency but to achieve agency that is meaningful in the light of wider questions about the direction and purpose of education.

In Chapter 4, we examined the social networks that contribute to the shaping of agency, with particular attention to the relational resources available to teachers as they develop the curriculum. As we noted in the chapter, teacher networks such as professional learning communities are very much in vogue, and a great deal of literature has been published on the subject. However, as with the teacher beliefs literature, a great deal of the writing is subject to limitations: a tendency to be uncritical, accepting the value of teacher networking as a given; a tendency for the literature to be associated with narrow change agendas and a corresponding deficit view of schools and teachers; and where agency was used as a supporting concept, a lack of an adequate conceptualization of the term, with teachers tended to be framed in a rather limited way as agents of change. This latter tendency is evident in some writing, which is critical of the sorts of agency that might drive, for example, resistance to government policy. This touches, of course, on the issue of what constitutes 'good agency', which we discuss later in this chapter. However, the sorts of discussion in the literature on networks, which we mention here and discuss in detail in Chapter 4, seem to be more narrowly construed than this; they are often less concerned with wider questions of what might constitute agency used for moral purposes and more focused on the 'desirability' of teachers, as a professional body, following instructions and/or implementing predefined, externally mandated policy. Thus the argument here is about the distinction between a restricted professionalism applied to a professional group seen to be in deficit and an extended professionalism, characterized by professional judgement and professional agency and the accordance of trust.

Nevertheless, the literature on networks offers some useful insights as we seek to understand teachers' agency. There is a body of literature, based in sociological analysis, which looks at the nature of networks – their density, span, longevity, etc. (e.g. Coburn, Choi and Mata 2010; Daly et al. 2010). Such literature points to the importance of understanding the ways in which networks are constituted and highlights that reformers should not ignore such issues by simply piling reform on top of existing, unsuitable social structures. These issues are clearly evident in the empirical data discussed in Chapter 4, which was generated in two overtly similar secondary schools, where teachers had similar levels of experience and exhibited similar values and beliefs. In one of the schools, we saw considerable evidence of teacher agency, particularly high levels of confidence expressed by teachers in a faculty developing 'Curriculum for Excellence'. Conversely, in the neighbouring school, we encountered more confusion and a comparative lack of confidence. The question this raises, then, is: 'Why should two such similar schools be so different in relation to teacher agency?'

The data suggested that the substantive difference lay in the nature of professional relationships within the schools. In the former, we saw well-developed relationships – both vertical lines of communication and horizontal, cross-faculty working. Relationships were characterized by trust, reciprocity, comparative symmetry and longevity. Moreover, this situation had been deliberately fostered by school leaders. Conversely, in the latter school, relationships tended to be vertical in nature, with predominantly one-way flow of information and power. As one teacher suggested, staff meetings were like school assemblies. The implications for agency are clear here: teacher networks provide access to relational resources of various kinds, including support, access to new ideas and a protective shield when undertaking innovation. Constructive relationships can mitigate risk and potentially extend the repertoire of ideas and aspirations open to teachers as they develop the curriculum. However, they lose their value if they are simply used to push through predefined and restrictive change agendas, if the collegiality is contrived (Hargreaves 1993) or if they foster groupthink.

Chapters 2, 3 and 4 focused on issues that are largely internal to the schools – teacher beliefs, school cultures and discourses and the social structuring of the school – that have been described as institutional logics (Young 1998). In Chapter 5, we focused on the external pressures formed by accountability practices, which have been shown to be a major influence behind the development of cultures of performativity in schools. In this chapter we also briefly described the features that drive performativity: in Scotland, these are external inspections of schools (by both Her Majesty's Inspectorate and local authorities) and the evaluative use of attainment data to judge the performance of schools. Unlike England, Scotland has not developed market mechanisms involving the public use of league tables, school diversity and parental choice. Nonetheless, accountability and performativity are strong features of the Scottish system, impacting upon agency and affecting practices. As we have noted throughout the book, and especially in Chapter 5, these pressures act in considerable tension with the publicly espoused declarations of teacher autonomy in curriculum policy; the latter presupposes teacher agency, but the former pressures potentially restrict this. In effect, one set of policies is removing [input] regulation, and the other set is re-imposing an alternative form of [output] regulation, which arguably erodes teacher agency more than its predecessor.

The chapter examines a primary school and two secondary schools. Performativity was highly evident in both contexts. In the primary school, we saw performativity as a daily fact of life, through the monitoring of attainment, checklists of 'essential' practices and high levels of surveillance. Such practices, which had developed under the previous 5–14 curriculum, had become the axiomatic routines of the school and were applied to the different intrinsic logics of 'Curriculum for Excellence'. The teachers in the study seemed to conceive of curriculum development primarily as the evidencing of outcomes, and the development of the new curriculum proceeded as a tick-box exercise of identifying, recording and reporting practices against the experiences and outcomes of the curriculum. Agency here is thus limited and is shaped predominantly by the habitus formed by prior practice and the continued emphasis by external bodies on accountability. The secondary schools, while exhibiting similarities, were driven by a different set of logics, albeit also linked to a culture of performativity driven by accountability practices. Here the focus was on fitting existing practices (particularly existing content and resources structured around school subjects) to the new outcomes. A major theme was the pressure of raising attainment in external examinations taken in the senior school; these cast a long shadow down the school, influencing practices in the junior years. While teachers in both contexts expressed dissatisfaction with their situations, they tended to accept it as unchallengeable – a fact of life that had to be negotiated as well as possible. In both contexts, we saw evidence of strategic compliance with policy. In both contexts, there was a sense of agency being limited in a way that negatively impacted upon the possibilities afforded by the new curriculum.

The empirical data discussed in these chapters suggest strongly that teacher agency is shaped by a range of different features of the context of schooling – both cultural and structural – in addition to being formed by the capacity of teachers. They reinforce our core argument that the introduction of radical new curriculum policy – such as Scotland's 'Curriculum for Excellence' – needs to be accompanied by systematic action to address the cultural and structural dimensions of the contexts for professional work and not just focus upon raising individual capacity. We draw out these issues in more detail in the ensuing sections of this chapter.

Fostering teacher agency

As we have argued throughout this book, agency is an emergent phenomenon, dependent on the interplay of both the individual (capacity – skills, knowledge, beliefs, etc.) and conditions (cultural, structural and material resources and constraints). This interplay varies according to the continually shifting nature of the constituent parts of this interrelationship, and so agency is always a unique phenomenon. This view of agency has a number of significant implications in respect of teachers, particularly given the recent policy turn that positions them as 'key actors in shaping and leading educational change' (Donaldson 2010, p. 4). While it is clear that the capacity of teachers, as highly skilled and highly motivated professionals, is important, it is equally clear that attention should be given to understanding and developing the conditions that form such an important part of the interplay. It is worth reiterating here the questions posed earlier in the chapter, to which we shall return in the final section: (1) What is teacher agency – and by implication what sort of teacher agency is desirable? (2) Where does teacher agency come from, or how is it shaped? and (3) What does teacher agency make possible?

The problematic policy focus on the capacity of the individual teacher

Current policy, along with the transnational discourses that influence it, does not adequately address these questions; instead focuses on the qualities of the individual teacher. This focus is evident in influential transnational publications published by bodies such as the OECD (2005, 2011). For example, recent publications stated:

> Improving the efficiency and equity of schooling depends, in large measure, on ensuring that competent people want to work as teachers, that their teaching is of high quality, and that all students have access to high quality teaching. (OECD 2005, p. 7)

> Of those variables potentially open to policy influence, factors to do with teachers and teaching are the most important influences on student learning. In particular, the broad consensus is that 'teacher quality' is the single most important school variable influencing student achievement. (OECD 2011, p. 7)

We acknowledge that these reports mention from time to time the importance of the school environment in facilitating quality teaching (e.g. see the quotation at the head of the chapter). They frequently point to the need for better leadership and support the fostering of collaborative working through teacher learning communities. However, the contextual conditions of schooling do not tend to be spelt out in detail; they are not analysed and developed in the same way as is the emphasis on teacher quality, and there are inadequate methodologies for posing and addressing questions about such issues. Also, the reference to 'student learning' remains either vague or is operationalized in terms of achievement in a small number of (often traditional) curricular subjects (see Biesta 2015).

Instead, the main thrust of such discourses relates to the recruitment and retention of high-quality applicants, getting the 'best' teachers into the 'right' schools, the development of competency frameworks to define a good teacher, lifelong or career-long learning and better professional development to achieve this and processes for dealing with ineffective teachers. The emphasis remains relentlessly on the capacity of the teacher, an individual who has

> strong subject matter knowledge, pedagogical skills, the capacity to work effectively with a wide range of students and colleagues, contribution to the school and the wider profession and capacity to continue developing. (OECD 2011, p. 11)

This focus on individual capacity is perhaps best encapsulated by the axiom commonly [mis]attributed[1] to the McKinsey & Co. (2007) report on worldwide education systems: 'That the quality of an education system cannot exceed the quality of its teachers.'

The singular focus on the teacher in publications such as the McKinsey & Co report has attracted some public criticism. For instance, Chris Husbands (2013) has suggested that the word *teacher* should be replaced by the word *teaching*, shifting the emphasis from the individual to the activity.[2] According to Husbands, this lexical (and conceptual) shift has important ramifications for policy:

> The three letters also have important policy implications. If you pursue the line that the important thing is *teachers*, you focus on people. … If you pursue the line that it is *teaching* that matters (our emph.), you get a different set of policies. It's still important to recruit and train those who can develop as excellent teachers, but you need to work continuously to improve the quality of teaching across schools: every teacher, in every classroom, in every school, getting better at teaching. This involves focusing on what drives really good teaching – committed teachers and high quality instruction, which itself depends on rigorous subject knowledge and knowledge of effective pedagogy, both leavened by imagination.

This analysis takes us part of the way towards addressing the importance of context but continues to focus too narrowly on the qualities of a good teacher and the efficacy of their actions – on individual capacity rather than on the teacher's wider, contextually mediated capability to teach and develop the curriculum. Thus it falls far short of the in-depth analysis offered by the ecological approach to agency. It also continues to forget to pay explicit attention to the question of what schools are *for* (Biesta 2010, 2015), thus contributing to the idea that this question is either not a problem or has already been satisfactorily answered in terms of achievement measured in a rather narrow spectrum of curricular subjects – often limited to literacy and numeracy, or in even more traditional terms, to (first) language, mathematics and science.

In relation to Scotland and its new 'Curriculum for Excellence', we see very similar discourses emerging in official documentation. Two recent, seminal reports are the Donaldson (2010) and McCormac (2011) reports, both of which addressed the issue of teacher professionalism. According to Donaldson, 'Two most important factors which promote excellent education are the quality of the teaching profession and of its leadership' (p. 82). This influential report was commissioned in the light of a perceived need to respond to the changing conditions created by 'Curriculum for Excellence'. As was the case of the OECD reports cited above, it stressed the need for a renewed focus on improving the quality of teachers through a more systematic approach to career-long teacher education. The report made fifty recommendations, including:

> Education policy in Scotland should give the highest priority to further strengthening the quality of its teachers and of its educational leadership (Recommendation 1). (p. 82)

> Education policy should support the creation of a reinvigorated approach to 21st century teacher professionalism. Teacher education should, as an integral part of that endeavour, address the need to build the capacity of teachers, irrespective of career stage, to have high levels of pedagogical expertise, including deep knowledge of what they are teaching; to be self-evaluative; to be able to work in partnership with other professionals; and to engage directly with well-researched innovation (Recommendation 2). (p. 83)

The Donaldson Report did, to be fair, acknowledge the importance of striking an appropriate balance between accountability and autonomy and strongly advocated new leadership, mentoring and partnership arrangements to facilitate quality teaching. Nevertheless, the focus within its multiple recommendations remained sharply on teacher quality, and the report more broadly did not develop in detail any analysis of the conditions that frame teacher working. Moreover, it lacked an appropriate methodology for doing so. Similarly, the McCormac Report (2011) also focused strongly on teacher quality. Interestingly, as suggested by the following extract, there was a strong emphasis in the report on the need to equip teachers to adapt to their [arbitrary] environment, rather than on an appreciation that the environment itself might be disabling to those teachers. In addition, we can see once more vagueness about the question what schools are supposed to be for, for example, in the phrase 'positive learning outcomes' and a reliance on the production metaphor of schooling that oversimplifies the complex dynamics of education.

> The available evidence suggests that well-trained, high-quality teachers working in our classrooms produce positive learning outcomes for young people. Thus our emphasis should be on attracting, developing and retaining individuals as teachers who are highly skilled, have strong personal competence in numeracy and literacy whilst being reflective and committed to professional growth and development. Once in the classroom, these teachers must be able to adapt to an ever-changing environment, reflect on their practice, and develop their skills as their careers develop. An excellent teacher should be open to change and to new ideas, using their experience and research evidence to evaluate and adapt potential innovations to ensure benefit for pupils and for fellow educationalists. (pp. 7–8)

These reports have subsequently driven the development of a number of key policy initiatives in Scotland, including the establishment of a Scottish College for Educational Leadership (SCEL: see http://www.scelscotland.org.uk/), a partnership working between universities and local authorities for the purpose of career-long professional education, and new procedures for professional update and reaccreditation by the General Teaching Council for Scotland (http://www. gtcs.org.uk/professional-update).

This focus on the quality of the teacher is understandable and well intentioned, but ultimately misguided, as – to state one of the main messages from our book one more time – *teacher capacity is a necessary but insufficient condition for the achievement of agency.* As an ecological understanding of teacher agency would suggest, individual capacity is only a particular facet of teacher agency. While we would support the notion that teacher capacity is essential in the achievement of agency and that high-capacity individuals are more likely to achieve agency than their less-skilled and knowledgeable colleagues, it is also likely that such individuals will not achieve agency if the conditions are not propitious for them to do so. Furthermore, the focus on teacher capacity has tended to overemphasize the qualification function of teacher education (Biesta 2010) – skills and knowledge primarily – while neglecting the normative issues and educational questions relating to values and purposes, which should frame good teaching and education. These questions can only be addressed adequately if policy to develop teacher agency addresses the cultural and structural dimensions of teaching *in addition to raising individual capacity.*

Individual, cultural and structural dimensions of teacher agency

Before we address these dimensions, we first turn to the question of what constitutes teacher agency. This is inevitably a normative question and one that, as we have argued in this book, is poorly conceptualized and badly framed in both policy and much of the academic literature. As we have already noted, policy tends to conflate agency with change agentry, and many academic publications offer similar views, seeing agency-as-opposition, for example, as being destructive and unhelpful. These arguments oversimplify teacher agency and merit some comment here.

So what should teacher agency look like? Rather than saying that agency is about the potential to take action – which is part of the definition but not the whole – we would say that teachers achieve agency when they are able to choose between different options in any given situation and are able to judge which option is the most desirable, in the light of the wider purposes of the practice in and through which they act. Agency is restricted if those options are limited. Agency is not present if there are no options for action or if the teacher simply follows routinized patterns of habitual behaviour with no consideration of alternatives.

This relatively simple definition raises difficult questions, not least the issue of where agency comes from, that is, how it is formed. Another implication, already mentioned earlier in this book, lies in an observation by Emirbayer and Mische (1998) that what might pass for agency is not necessarily so. For example, agency may be involved in the reproduction of social patterns through active resistance to change, when to the casual observer what seems to be occurring is habitual behaviour in the context of unproblematic actions by the actors concerned or a lack of agency in the face of insurmountable problems. Priestley (2011) documents the case of a teacher in just such a situation – someone swimming against the tide in a difficult environment, who nevertheless managed to hold true to deeply held principles. This teacher clearly achieved some sort of agency in pursuing his goals, despite the fact that many of his options were closed down by contextual conditions. By contrast, 'Actors who feel creative and deliberative while in the flow of unproblematic trajectories' (Emirbayer and Mische 1998, p. 1008) may not be achieving high levels of agency as they simply go with the flow.

This raises further implications. First, it highlights the important but oft-conflated distinction between *autonomy and agency*. As we have noted elsewhere (Priestley, Biesta and Robinson 2015), many critics of current policy advocate autonomy as a means of freeing up schools and enabling change.

However, autonomy (understood here as a comparative absence of regulation) does not necessarily equate to agency. Teachers granted autonomy may simply fail to achieve agency as they, for example, habitually reproduce past patterns of behaviour or as they lack cognitive and relational resources. Conversely, agency may be shaped and enhanced by externally defined policy that specifies goals and processes, enhancing the capability of teachers to manoeuvre between repertoires, make decisions and frame future actions. An example of this is provided by recent development work conducted in Scotland within a university/ local authority partnership (Drew and Priestley 2014). Here teachers worked with university researchers over the course of a full school year to develop the curriculum, drawing upon a various cognitive resources. These included the goals of 'Curriculum for Excellence' – the capabilities and attributes specified under the headings of the four capacities (Scottish Executive 2004) – as well as a clearly defined process for school-based curriculum development through collaborative professional enquiry, facilitated by university-based researchers (Priestley and Minty 2012; Reeves and Drew 2013).

At the early stages of the project, many participating teachers reported low confidence, confusion about curricular aims, tensions between conflicting messages in their work and a general sense of disempowerment. It is significant that involvement in the project led, in the majority of cases, to the subsequent achievement of agency by these teachers, suggesting how appropriately framed curricular specification might play a powerful role in enabling teacher agency. It is important to note here that these teachers were not simply implementing policy – this was not a case of teachers being manipulated into becoming agents of change. Nor were they being offered carte blanche to do whatever they wished. Instead, the affordances offered by the specification of goals and processes enabled them to become genuinely agentic as they actively developed and adapted the curriculum to meet both curricular goals and local needs. We return to this question, of how macro-level policy and meso-level processes might be framed to enhance agency, in the concluding chapter of the book.

Second, there is the issue of 'good' or constructive agency. Clearly policy makers would not wish to enable or facilitate 'bad' or destructive agency, as this would potentially work against policy intentions to educate young people and improve schools. 'Bad' agency might be said by some – as implied strongly in both academic literature on educational change and in policy discourses – to constitute emergent possibilities where the available choices encourage teachers to act against policy intentions, or act in a way that is unprofessional, destructive to the interests of students and colleagues or that is morally indefensible. In such cases, teachers are not acting as agents of change. Nevertheless, agency is achieved in such situations, for example, in the case of the conspiratorial mediation of policy described by Osborn et al. (1997), where the active intention was to subvert centrally mandated policy. However, to label all such action as being due to 'bad' agency would be to fall into the trap of seeing teacher agency simply as the effective and efficient implementation of policy, which is, of course, what we have been arguing against throughout this book.

Clearly a more nuanced approach is needed to address the question of what constitutes 'good' agency that, while accepting that such judgements are inherently normative, moves the discussion beyond consideration of utilitarian and instrumental conceptions of what should be – that is, the development of orthodoxies or the following of narrow agendas – to more sophisticated and nuanced consideration of educational values and purposes. Thus, for example, using this latter yardstick might lead us to see strategic compliance, driven by the pressures of performative cultures and nominally implementing policy, as 'bad' agency. Conversely, good agency may be exercised to oppose actions and policies that are judged – professionally and reflexively by agentic practitioners – to be damaging to the educational needs of their students.

Key in relation to this is explicit engagement with the question of educational purpose, that is, the question of what education is *for*. While much attention has been paid and is being paid to questions about what education ought to *produce* – particularly notorious in the language of 'learning outcomes' – a specification of what the 'output' of education ought to be is not, in itself, an answer to the question what the purpose or purposes of education should be. (After all, to specify, for example, that children at a particular age should reach a particular standard in a particular subject area still begs the question of what reaching such a standard would be good *for*.) Two things are important here. One is the fact that educational practices necessarily need to engage with the question what the practice is *for*. The practice of education, to put it differently, only exists in what in theoretical terms is called its *telos* (Greek for 'purpose' or 'rationale' – not to be conflated with concrete aims, ends or 'outcomes'). This also reveals what the problem is with using process language such as 'facilitating student learning' as such learning can go in any direction. The second is the fact that education does not function in relation to just one *telos* – or one domain of purpose – but that a case can be made (see Biesta 2010) that there are at least *three domains of purpose* that education needs to take into consideration, as all education has potential 'effects' in relation to these three domains.

One is the domain of *qualification*, which has to do with the transmission and acquisition of knowledge, skills and disposition that allow children and young people to 'do' something – either in the narrow sense of becoming qualified for a job or professional field or in the broad sense as becoming qualified for participation in complex modern societies. The second is the domain of *socialization*, which has to do with the way in which through education children and young people are invited to engage with existing social, political, professional, cultural and normative traditions. Again there is a more narrow sense, such as in the context of vocational and professional education where the ambition is for young people to become part of the ways of doing and being of a particular vocational or professional field, and there is the wider meaning of socialization, which is about finding one's place in existing social practices and traditions. Thirdly, education always functions in relation to the *person* (the domain of 'subjectification' – Biesta 2010) – not with regard to how the individual becomes part of existing traditions but with regard to the question how children and young people can gain independence of thought, (moral) judgement and action. Here the ambition of education is not that of engaging children and young people with existing ways of doing and being, but with emancipation from existing ways of doing and being – and good education always works within the tension between engagement and emancipation.

Questions of purpose clearly highlight the normative dimension of teacher agency. On the one hand, they raise important considerations for the projective dimension of agency, as what should give orientation for teachers' actions is not just a matter of individual preference but ultimately needs to be part of the wider discourse about the purposes of education. On the other hand, they raise important considerations for the practical–evaluative dimension of agency, not least because it is the here and now of the concrete situations in which teachers act, that they constantly need to engage with the question what a meaningful and justifiable balance between the three domains of purpose is – something that highlights the crucial role of judgement in the achievement of agency (see Biesta 2015).

The above discussion leads us back inexorably to the question of where agency comes from. It also confronts us again with the stark message that agency cannot be construed in terms of individual capacity alone, and that policy designed to improve teaching therefore should not simply attend to the raising of such capacity, but should focus carefully on cultural and structural issues. Nevertheless, individual capacity is an important part of agency. We would support the notion posited by the OECD, Donaldson and others that teaching, as an intellectual activity, requires excellent subject and pedagogic knowledge, combined with accomplished levels of skill in enacting these in often complex situations. Moreover, our data support the view that effective teachers require strong professional belief sets derived from consideration of educational issues and questions and the ability to project from these into alternative professional futures, as they choose between different possibilities for action. We would argue that they also require access to a professional vocabulary, distinct from the rhetorical language of policy and derived from educational study, to articulate concepts and to provide the intellectual resources to enact practice critically in response to policy. We can see here that the iterational and projective dimensions of agency are strongly dependent on the nature of the teacher's individual capacity. Such requirements do indeed speak strongly of the need for the sorts of interventions proposed by governments around the world and evident in Scotland to raise capacity: enhanced levels of teacher professional education, a re-engagement by practitioners with the cognitive, discursive and normative resources found in research and scholarship, informed and purposeful teacher learning communities and a corresponding development of dispositions towards career-long learning.

But we keep stressing that while personal capacity is necessary for teacher agency, it is not sufficient. The question remains as to where these skills and this knowledge come from. Professional habitus is formed from the past experiences of teachers and as such is heavily influenced by the cultures and structures of past professional contexts. In the case of our participating teachers, their comparative lack of agency in the face of the new curriculum could be clearly linked to past contextual practices. For example, in the primary school, we witnessed a lack of imagination about what the new curriculum made possible; here curriculum development was framed around the prior practices of evidencing curricular outcomes, even though the new structures of 'Curriculum for Excellence' were less suitable for this approach – something acknowledged by the teachers. At a cultural level, we saw a culture of performativity in the school, which had developed over a considerable number of years. This culture was characterized by low levels of trust, regular surveillance and pressures to perform, most notably manifested through the prevalent approach to curriculum development and a 'fabrication' of a positive school image (for a discussion of this concept, see

Keddie, Mills and Pendergast 2011). At a structural level, we saw management roles and systems predicated around the need to monitor and control practices. These include external structures and relationships, particularly with the local authority, which conducted audits and required the usage of centrally imposed testing and internal structures involving the role of senior managers. This context militated against the development of the curriculum, based around its four capacities, and predicated around the notion of school-based curriculum development by teachers.

Similarly, in the secondary school, the capacity of the teachers to engage in curriculum development was heavily circumscribed by past practices, and the predominant discourses of the cultural milieu of the schools. In these cases, the culture of the schools was driven by performative demands associated with examination results, and the long Scottish secondary tradition of viewing education as the transmission of content framed as subjects. Structurally, these cultures were shaped by long-standing practices such as school timetabling. Logically, one might expect schools responding to the interdisciplinary requirements of 'Curriculum for Excellence' to effect changes to the organization of the school week – for example, longer periods and reconfigured subjects – but this had not happened in either school. Instead, the structure of the school week was a fact of life, which shaped the schools' responses to the curriculum rather than vice versa. As with the primary school, long-term external relationships involving inspections and audit, assessment practices (in this case, national qualifications) and managerial systems within the school were significant in shaping the schools' response to the new curriculum. In the case of one school, Lakeside High School, we saw that a deliberate policy, over time, of fostering collegial working had actively increased the agency of the teachers.

In both cases, we see that the iterational and projective dimensions of teacher agency – ostensibly a matter of teacher capacity – have their roots in past cultures and structures, which have played a role on the socialization of teachers and which shape the agency of teachers as they engage with present-day contexts. We would argue that the historical cultures and structures of Scottish schools have limited the possibilities for teachers to fully realize the potential of the new curriculum and especially reduced their capacity to exercise judgement in their professional working. In particular, teacher socialization into practices associated with performativity plays a role in shaping teachers' present beliefs and knowledge and limiting educational discourses in a way that has precluded a full engagement with the curriculum and limited their sense of what might be possible to develop from it. A further point here is to note that the present structures and cultures of Scottish schooling will exert a similarly powerful effect on future teacher agency, suggesting an urgent need to explicitly address the cultural and structural issues that inhibit such agency.

What does teacher agency make possible? Or why teacher agency is needed!

The issue that has been implicit throughout this book but nonetheless is the main motiving force behind it is the idea that teacher agency – or, to be more precise, *good* teacher agency – is desirable for the simple reason that if it works well it contributes significantly to the overall quality of education. What we do not mean by stating this claim is that high levels of teacher agency will result in high test scores or a higher overall measured performance of the educational system. This is not only a very narrow interpretation of what makes education good, but, more importantly, is not what we mean when we say that teacher agency contributes significantly to the overall quality of education. Using a concept from John Dewey (see Biesta and Burbules 2003), the main thing that good teacher agency contributes is that it makes the overall operation of the system more *intelligent*.

If we look at major education policy trends in many countries around the world over the past decades, we can see that many of the solutions for the alleged problems and flaws in the education system are solutions at a systemic level. They are solutions at the level of the education system, trying to change the ways the system operates, including how the system is monitored, measured and managed. Input steering through central definition of the content of education, process steering through central definition of the forms of education, outcome steering through central definition of the outputs of education, combined with systems of bureaucratic accountability, invasive and often oppressive regimes of inspection and control, performance-related pay, standard setting, league tables, naming and shaming, and so on, are all examples of ways to improve education that intervene at the *system level* and that introduce *systemic solutions* for alleged problems.

What is vividly expressed in the idea of teacher-proof curricula is the fact that systemic solutions seek to create systems in which the actions of individual actors do not really matter so that, in the extreme case, individuals become interchangeable units. Systemic solutions not only start from the assumption that the individuals in the system *should not really matter* – that is why the ambition is to create fool-proof systems; by moving forward in this way, they also send out the strong message that the individuals in the system *do not really matter*. It is no surprise, therefore, that many teachers feel dissatisfied with these developments, not just because it has constrained and in some cases completely destroyed their space for agency but also because it sends out the message that as individual professionals they do not really matter as long as they do what the system requires from them. Intelligent engagement with the complexities of the here and now is not required and, in extreme cases, is actually seen as a liability. Systemic approaches to the improvement of education ultimately make the operations of teachers, the key actors in the system, increasingly *less* intelligent.

The defenders of systemic approaches to educational improvement may argue that this is the price we should be willing to pay for the overall and ongoing improvement of education, which is one reason why so much is invested in measuring the outcomes of education, trying to make the case that an unintelligent system is able to deliver 'the goods' – where part of the whole defence of systemic approaches is also that 'the goods' are being defined in a way that is often quite convenient for the argument. There are two critical questions here. The first question, which is partly empirical but also crucially relies on how education quality is defined, is whether systemic approaches to educational improvement are indeed better at delivering what education ought to deliver. The second question – which in our view is more fundamental and ultimately may trump the answer to the first question – is whether systemic approaches to educational improvement are desirable.

There are three reasons why we think that a systemic approach is ultimately not desirable – which are three reasons in favour of good teacher agency. One important reason is that unintelligent systems are indeed what they are; they are unintelligent, which means that they are unable to respond in a meaningful way to new and unique situations. Unintelligent systems have protocols and rules – and technology can of course make the protocols more refined and the application of rules quicker – but unintelligent systems are not capable of judgement in the here and now, and in this regard, we can say that unintelligent systems lack the flexibility that is needed in such complex domains as education. A second important reason in favour of good teacher agency is that many of the systems that have been put in place over the last decades to control education only work because of the intelligence of the teachers who have to implement them (on this see also James and Biesta 2007). We could say that it is precisely because there is still so much good teacher agency in the system, including in the empirical case we have presented in this book, that attempts to control the system from the top–down have not yet resulted in a total meltdown of education. Many teachers have become very skilful in 'managing the managerialism', so to speak (see particularly Gewirtz 2002), always for the benefit of the children and young people entrusted to them. Thirdly, teacher agency is important for what we might call teachers' 'job satisfaction' – although the term sounds a bit too lazy. Teacher agency, in other words, contributes to making teaching a meaningful profession rather than just 'a job', that is, a means to earn a living. This is an important argument in itself – we should take teachers' job satisfaction seriously, as we should take everyone's job satisfaction seriously. But particularly in an 'enterprise' such as education the weight of the 'enterprise' lies for a very large extent on the shoulders of teachers. That is why their satisfaction and their motivation matters, and a sense of being able to achieve agency, of course within the wider picture of what schools in a democratic society are for, is crucial.

Teacher agency, if it works well, thus has the capacity to make the operation of the educational system, both at the systemic level and at the individual and collective level of teacher practice, more intelligent and, therefore, more able to engage with the complexities and the uniqueness of the here and now in meaningful and purposeful ways. Teacher agency approaches the question of good education from the bottom–up, seeking to enhance the intelligence of the overall operation of the system at all levels and thus offers an alternative that is radically different from the way in which much thinking and policy about educational improvement has been conceived over the past decades. To put teacher agency at the heart of what it means to make education good does of course put a significant responsibility with teachers, both individually and collectively. In this regard, we may say that a focus on teacher agency is not the easiest way forward. It requires more from teachers rather than less, just as it requires more from those who have responsibility for shaping the conditions of teachers' agency: the material conditions, the cultural conditions, the structural and relational conditions and the discursive and normative conditions. But we do believe that in the longer term, enhancing teacher agency – at individual, cultural and structural level – is the only sustainable way towards the maintenance of everything that is good in education and the improvement of that which needs improvement.

Conclusions: Fostering Teacher Agency

Introduction

In this book, we have made a case for the importance of teacher agency. As should be clear from the previous chapters, this term needs to be accompanied by a number of strong caveats. First, we advocate an ecological understanding of agency – one that pays attention to the conditions by means of which agency is achieved, as much as it does to the capacity of individual teachers. Second, we do not advocate a position of complete teacher autonomy, characterized by a lack of regulation. Instead, we would emphasize the importance of regulation so long as it is of the right sort; that is, the sort that recognizes the professionalism of teachers and enables them to achieve agency in their work. Such regulation might be better described as guidance to facilitate teacher engagement with core principles of education, including those enshrined in the curriculum.

The above two points reinforce the importance of understanding that curricular practices at various levels of the system – in other words, curricular policies, the processes and procedures in government agencies and local authorities that operationalize them and the internal processes, structures and cultures in schools that frame teachers' day-to-day working practices – play an important role in the ecology of teacher agency. This role can be negative, as we have seen in much of the empirical analysis in this book. Thus, for example, we have seen the negative impact of narrow discourses about education and cultures of performativity on teachers' agency as they develop the curriculum. Conversely, we have witnessed how carefully thought-out school structures can provide relational resources and how the aspirations of 'Curriculum for Excellence' can inspire teachers. One thing is clear: the situation is complex, and messages are often contradictory. The result can be, as powerfully suggested by Eisner's (1992) birdcage metaphor, to deny teachers agency, encouraging them to play safe, to play the performative game and avoid risky innovation.

> If a bird has been in a cage for a decade and suddenly finds the door open, it should not be surprising if the bird does not wish to leave. (p. 617)

There is an important point here, which we wish to develop in this final chapter. If teacher agency is a good thing – and we believe that it is, and government curricular policy in many countries including Scotland is beginning to reflect the same view – then we owe it to teachers to take a considered look at what makes it possible for them to achieve agency. As we have already pointed out, it is one thing to *expect* teachers to be agentic in developing the curriculum, but it is quite another thing for it to happen in practice. This is where the ecological approach to understanding teacher agency is useful, providing a practical means of developing policy and practice. In this concluding chapter, we offer a number of practical suggestions for achieving this. The suggested strategies are framed in the context of Scottish policy and practices, but the general conclusions can be extrapolated easily to other contexts. We offer an analysis on three levels of practice.

- *The macro level of policy formation.* This is the field of contextualization, to use Bernstein's (1996) terminology, where global discourses and more local imperatives merge to produce statements of policy, through what has been termed process of glocalization (Green 1999; see Priestley 2002, for a discussion of how globalization shapes curriculum policy). Policy produced at this level can take the form of input regulation – strong, as in the case of England's prescriptive 1988 'National Curriculum', or comparatively weaker as in the case in 'Curriculum for Excellence'. Alternatively, it can set the parameters for output regulation, for example the establishment of regulatory bodies for inspection or procedures for using and gathering data and setting targets. As we have seen, both forms of macro-level policy potentially impact on curriculum practices at other levels of the system because they help constitute the conditions within which and by means of which the curriculum is enacted.
- *The meso level of policy interpretation.* In this field, high-level policy statements are re-contextualized, often according to quite different logics to those driving the macro-level contextualization. At this level, we see activity by national bodies such as Education Scotland and district bodies such as local government authorities. Re-contextualization involves the selective reproduction and interpretation of government policy. In some cases, it can take the form of the successive and repeated reinterpretation of policy – a form of the childhood game commonly known as Chinese whispers – which can result in emergent practices that are antithetical to the original policy intentions. Meso-level practice also involves activities – for

example, inspection – associated with output regulation, which can have a powerfully shaping effect on the curriculum.

- *The micro level of policy enactment.* This is the field in which teachers further re-contextualize the curriculum, developing whole-school and classroom practices to enact the curriculum. We have primarily focused in this book on this level, looking outward from the testimonies and perspectives of the teachers in our study to the conditions that shape their work. At this level, we can see how curriculum making is influenced and shaped by the beliefs and knowledge of teachers, the cultures and structures of schools, as well as by external pressures such as accountability demands.

In discussing how interventions at each level might affect teacher agency, we consider how these can contribute to changes in structure, culture and capacity across the system.

Macro-level policy

In order to address how activity at this level shapes teacher agency, it is first necessary to ask 'what is the function of high-level curriculum policy?' Is it, as has been attempted in many cases, for instance, England's National Curriculum, a tight prescription of aims, content and even method? This is, of course, a valid approach to framing national curriculum policy. However, it is an approach that seems antithetical to the notion of teacher agency, one that has even been termed a teacher-proof curriculum. This is an approach that seeks to restrict teacher agency, to control, rather than guide or facilitate. Thus, we would argue strongly that if a goal of curriculum policy is to enable and enhance teacher agency, this input regulation model is simply not appropriate if we have any sort of view of teachers as thinking, reflexive professionals, able to use their professional judgement to develop educational practice in a wise, considered and intelligent way. What is instead required is a *guiding framework*, something that provides the parameters for school-based curriculum development. This has, indeed, been recognized by policy makers around the world, as is evidenced by the proliferation of the 'new curriculum' (Priestley and Biesta 2013); curricula such as Scotland's 'Curriculum for Excellence' and the 'New Zealand Curriculum Framework' explicitly acknowledge, as we have seen, the importance of the teacher as an agent of change and an active participant in the process of curriculum development.

However, as we have argued throughout this book, it is not sufficient to simply state that this should be the case; curricular policy forms part of the ecology that shapes teachers' agency, and the above-mentioned curricula have certain structural features that can inhibit agency. It is not just the degree of prescription that is significant; the ways in which the curriculum is framed around purposes and the starting points it sets up for curriculum development are also important. A key issue at the macro level is a trend to frame the curriculum as learning outcomes. This is significant for two reasons. First, it is associated with the accountability practices of output regulation and contributes to the development of these practices at the meso and micro levels of curriculum enactment. It is argued by proponents of this model that it offers autonomy to teachers, and yet as we have argued in this book and elsewhere (Biesta and Priestley 2013), this approach is associated with performativity and perverse incentives, which in fact erode teacher agency. Second, and linked to this, such a focus creates a set of expectations about how education should be construed and enacted; it contributes to the development of particular curriculum development practices, for example, as we have seen in the primary school in our study, based around evidencing outcomes.

Learning outcomes have become ubiquitous within worldwide curriculum policy in recent years (Young 2009). This move is claimed to bring many potential benefits, as it shifts the focus from providers to users of education, and it introduces a common language, addressing issues of progression, transparency and equity (CEDEFOP 2009). To a large extent, outcomes continue a long tradition of framing curriculum as aims and objectives. One can trace the genesis of the current fashion for defining learning as outcomes in the objectives movement in the United States (c.f. Bobbitt, Tyler, Bloom etc.), with its roots in Taylorist scientific management, and which became extremely popular in the 1960s.

There are also clear lines of descent from the development of competency-based vocational education and training in the United Kingdom from the 1980s onwards through the worldwide extension of this model to national academic qualifications (for example, the Scottish, New Zealand and South African qualifications frameworks) in the 1990s (for a fuller account of this, see: Kelly 2004; Biesta and Priestley 2013). These developments manifest a desire to provide preset definitions of what an educated person might know or do as a result of being educated. For example, according to CEDEFOP (2009), 'Learning outcomes can best be defined as statements of what a learner knows, understands and is able to do after completion of learning' (p. 9). This definition clearly illustrates a distinction between outcomes and their predecessors: the shift towards framing education in terms of learners and their development, rather than in terms of what is to be taught. This is not a new distinction, as discussed by Biesta and Priestley (2013). However, it is one that has been given a renewed force by recent developments such as the publication of competency frameworks by organizations such as the OECD and the European Union.

The move to defining education through learning outcomes has not been uncontroversial. Issues and questions have been raised in a number of areas. These include:

- *philosophical questions* relating, for example, to whether it is ethical in a democracy to predefine what people should learn, and how they should be;
- *conceptual/definitional* issues relating to how outcomes should be framed and in what level of detail, and how they might relate to other curriculum components; and
- *enactment/implementation* issues relating to how teachers make sense of educational policy, and how they enact practice on the basis of this.

The first set of questions are important, raising questions as to whether we should even be seeking to define education in this way. Nevertheless, as they do not relate directly to our analysis of teacher agency, we do not address them in detail here. Readers interested in more detailed discussion of them should refer to Kelly (2004), Biesta (2010) and Biesta and Priestley (2013). The second and third set of questions are highly relevant to the discussion in this chapter; they clearly relate to teacher agency, have been comprehensively mapped out in this book and have a particular resonance for policy making, policy development and school practices. We therefore offer several further observations.

A particular issue lies in the specificity of outcomes. According to CEDEFOP (2009):

> It is worth bearing in mind that detailed targets can become so narrow and specific that the original aims for learning or reform can get lost in the implementation of the detail ('losing sight of the wood for the trees') (CEDEFOP 2009, p. 28). ... In contrast, a more holistic approach to learning outcomes can, in the right circumstances, empower stakeholders to reach new solutions. (CEDEFOP 2009, p. 42)

Many writers (e.g. Wolf 1995) have noted the tendency for outcomes to become increasingly specific and linked to assessment practices as they are operationalized. This has been evident in 'Curriculum for Excellence' in its early-stage macro-level policy, through the translation of the generic four capacities into the more detailed grid of learning outcomes (the E's and O's), which have subsequently come to be used as assessment standards. There are at least two problems here that impact upon teacher agency. First, we have seen a drift from a stated desire to avoid the curriculum becoming driven by assessment against outcomes, to a situation where the E's and O's of the curriculum are now described as assessment standards (Education Scotland 2011). This, as we have demonstrated throughout the book, has been associated with performativity, bureaucratic approaches to recording assessment and strategic, attainment-driven approaches to curriculum development. We come back to this issue in the next section of the chapter. A second issue lies in the contradictions between the competing curriculum development models inherent in 'Curriculum for Excellence', which offers both a generic set of competencies (the four capacities) and a detailed set of learning outcomes (the E's and O's). This constitutes a lack of clarity and mixed messages in the curriculum design, by offering alternative starting points for curriculum development (for an extended discussion of this issue, see Priestley and Humes 2010). Outcomes, whether detailed and specific or of the more generic variety are premised on the notion that it does not matter *how* the outcome is achieved, so long as it *is* achieved. In theory, they offer scope for teacher agency, even if only a procedural autonomy. In practice, and as we have seen in the empirical data presented in this book, they are often associated with strategic compliance with policy – evidencing of outcomes and box-ticking, rather than genuine engagement with curriculum principles. As an antidote to this, we suggest that curricula such as 'Curriculum for Excellence' would be better framed in terms of generic outcomes or goals of education, enshrining clear educational principles and purposes, combined with indicative (but not too specific) statements of content and guidance on pedagogy, which are clearly identified as being fit-for-purpose. Such policy guidance would supply the direction and the framing for meaningful school-based curriculum development, without being over-prescriptive and, importantly, without losing sight of nationally agreed goals of education. Significantly, it would provide more potent cognitive and cultural resources to support teachers' agency.

In addition, there are the questions of what education is supposed to be for, and whether it should be formulated in the language of 'outcomes' in the first place. There are two issues here. The first is that the language of 'outcomes' belongs to a production–conception of education, which ultimately leads to the suggestion that the task of students is to produce something – learning outcomes – and where it is the task of teachers to facilitate such production and monitor the quality of what has been produced. Stated in these terms, we can easily see the underlying factory- or assembly-line metaphor: a metaphor that actually has little to do with the dynamics of education where the 'task' of students is not to make things but to become educated – which is not a product at all. The second issue is that any specification of desired outcomes or goals always needs to be justified in relation to the wider purposes of education. Purposes should not be conflated with ends or goals – which are precise statements of what to aim for or seek to achieve – but have to do with the wider rationale for education. As we have suggested in the previous chapter, what is particular about education is that there are actually at least three domains of purpose that need to be taken into consideration when engaging in discussions about what education should be for. One of the key challenges is to keep these three domains in a meaningful balance (see also Biesta 2015), rather than that the educational effort becomes dominated by only one of them – current education policy in many countries seems to be out of balance by putting too much emphasis on the domain of qualification only.

Meso-level curriculum development

While it is important to appropriately frame policy at a macro level, we should not forget the potential for meso-level processes and artefacts to shape agency. Broadly, these fall into two areas: input regulation that takes the form of additional guidance to practitioners as they enact the curriculum; and output regulation, in the form of inspection and audit activity, and the evaluative use of attainment data to support these. In Scotland, the main meso-level actors are Education Scotland (the national agency that develops curriculum materials and conducts inspections[1]), the SQA and the thirty-two local authorities, who have a statutory duty to run schools. Scotland's education system has been traditionally hierarchical, with long chains of command from government through local authorities, and the influence of these agencies on school-level practices is therefore significant (see Boyd and Norris 2006; Priestley 2014).

Because of this, meso-level curriculum guidance has tended to emerge as additional material. 'Curriculum for Excellence' has not been short of guidance, both online and in the form of very large ring-binders, full of paper and issued to each teacher in Scotland. And yet the nature of this guidance is open to question in terms of its potential to increase the agency of teachers as they develop the curriculum. We would make the case here for guidance that actively increases the potential for teachers to achieve agency. This might include the provision of cognitive, theoretical and normative resources, for example, clear explication of the principles and purposes of the curriculum that is not already provided in the macro-level documents. It might also include detailed guidance on curriculum development processes that are known, from previous experience and research to be effective in enabling schools to develop curriculum practice from the basis of centrally mandated policy.

In our view, the primary purpose of meso-level guidance is to facilitate teacher sense making of the core principles and purposes of the curriculum – the big ideas – in a way that maximizes the potential for teachers' agency as they develop good educational practice. We note here that this is something to be undertaken by teachers, in a guided manner with clear processes. Knowledgeable meso-level actors presumably have a role in this process at a school level (for example, as coaches and mentors), but the primary meso-level function here must surely be to define, resource and support such processes. It should not be wholesale interpretation of policy on the behalf of teachers, as this potentially derogates teacher professionalism, erodes their capacity to make professional judgements and ultimately denies them agency.

We would argue that this unsatisfactory approach has largely been the case with 'Curriculum for Excellence'. Guidance has tended to focus on interpreting the curriculum for teachers. Publications subsequent to the development of the original policy documents (including the experiences and outcomes) have included the *Building the Curriculum* series, a set of extremely detailed publications that fleshed out the macro-level documents. These were subject to criticism by many stakeholders, so subsequently, a series of short summaries was produced. More recently, a series of briefings has been published on a range of topics as diverse as religious observance, political literacy and curriculum design.[2] It is fair to say that such guidance has proliferated, and that the terrain has proven to be difficult for many teachers who see the guidance as confusing, vague and often contradictory (see Priestley and Minty 2012; Minty and Priestley 2012). Much of the guidance seems to have been socially mediated by the particular and time-limited agendas of the authors, and a significant trend is in evidence. This is the successive re-contextualization or reinterpretation of policy by these meso-level actors, leading to often subtle, and sometimes marked changes in emphasis to the curriculum. In some cases, these changes represent practices that are at odds with the original aims of 'Curriculum for Excellence'.

A notable example, which we have mentioned already, is the shift towards an assessment-driven curriculum. Early policy documentation (e.g. Scottish Executive 2004a,b, 2006) recognized the dangers of assessment dominating learning and teaching and called for assessment systems that would support learning. The cover paper for the draft 'Experiences and Outcomes' (Learning and Teaching Scotland 2007) stated that the outcomes 'are not designed as assessment criteria in their own right'. And yet by 2011, *Building the Curriculum* 5 (BTC5: Education Scotland 2011) described these as standards for assessment, stating that 'in Curriculum for Excellence, the standards expected for progression are indicated within the experiences and outcomes at each level' (p. 13) and 'assessment tasks and activities provide learners with fair and valid opportunities to meet the standards' (p. 36). BTC5 defines a standard as 'something against which we measure performance' (p. 11). When taken in combination with intrusive inspection practices and the evaluative use of data derived from such assessment, it is not surprising that 'Curriculum for Excellence' has become known in some schools as the Curriculum for Audit, or that a prominent head teacher, speaking at a national conference, in June 2014 could describe it as an attainment-driven curriculum.[3] And as we have shown throughout this book, such conditions do not promote the achievement of agency by teachers but instead contribute to the development of performative cultures in schools, strategic compliance with curricular policy and an impoverished approach to curriculum development.

The above discussion illustrates that the nature and scope of input regulation – curriculum development guidance – at the meso level is a significant factor shaping teacher agency. The other aspect of this – *output regulation* – also merits some further discussion here. As we discussed in some detail in Chapter 5, Scotland has well-developed systems for accountability, including external inspections by Education Scotland, local authority audits and the evaluative use of attainment data, via tools such as STACs and its recent replacement Insight. We do not intend to revisit this discussion here, except to make some observations about how an alternative approach might enhance teacher agency.

Since the turn of the millennium, there has been a progressive softening of the language associated with accountability, perhaps indicative of a realization in policy circles of its detrimental and performative effects on schools. Thus, Scotland has resisted the publication of league tables, increasingly emphasized the value of self-evaluation by schools and sought to broaden the scope of attainment tracking tools such as Insight. Nevertheless, the basic methodology has remained the same (Reeves 2008). The emphasis is still on performance and its measurement. Inspections continue to be one-off snapshot events conducted by external 'experts' with little contextual knowledge of the schools they are inspecting. Student attainment in external qualifications and the evidencing of achievement of outcomes continue to provide the main foci for judging the effectiveness of schools. Consequently, these remain as high-stakes issues for schools – we continue to value what we can measure, rather than measuring what we value (Biesta 2010).

A number of cumulatively applied initiatives at this level would contribute to lessening this emphasis on performance and re-establishing a focus on *good* education as an explicitly normative question, rather than on effective education (which only says something about the effectiveness of processes but not what those processes are supposed to result in) or excellent education (which immediately introduces a competitive mindset into the discussion) (see Biesta 2010). One would be a reversion of the local authority's role to one of support (through, for example subject advisors) rather than their present focus on quality and their mirroring of inspection processes (Biesta 2010). Another worthy initiative would be a reconfiguring of inspection teams to incorporate local teachers – peer and self-evaluators – who have some knowledge of the context being evaluated. This would potentially transform the inspection process into an ongoing and long-term supportive improvement process, rather than a one-off performance for outsiders. We suggest that the focus of these activities should be on the enhancement of the agency of teachers, equipping them to engage more constructively with curriculum development.

There is a clear role for meso-level actors to work with colleagues in schools to develop the curriculum. Part of this role lies in the provision of resources. We noted in Chapters 2 and 3 that many teachers lack a professional language to critically engage with education policies and issues and that their belief sets are often narrowly circumscribed by prosaic rather than professional issues. Engagement with research is one means of addressing this problem because of its potential to broaden and deepen educational perspectives. An enduring complaint about teachers is that they do not tend to engage with research into their professional field. Part of the problem is accessibility, and it is pleasing to see that this has been addressed in Scotland, where teachers registered with the General Teaching Council now have access to scholarly journals.[4] Of course, access is only part of the equation; if teachers are not making use of the access accorded to them, then their perspectives will remain limited.

This is where the role of meso-level actors could be more significant, than at present, in facilitating processes such as collaborative professional enquiry, which engages practitioners with curriculum development in an informed, purposeful and research-informed manner (see Reeves and Drew 2013; Drew and Priestley 2014; Butler, Schnellert and MacNeil 2015). This in turn raises questions about the agency of meso-level actors as they take such roles. This is partly a question of personal capacity: to what extent do such actors personally engage with research themselves; and what proportions of them have higher degrees in education, in a field where practice tends to be privileged over theory? But it is also fundamentally an issue of culture, in a system characterized by anti-intellectualism (Humes 2013), with a relentless focus on quality assurance and outcomes and a corresponding neglect of consideration of purpose and process. We would argue here that a change to the culture of the meso-level organizations that support schools in developing the curriculum is needed to support the further achievement of teacher agency. What is also important in this regard is that research is not taken in a narrow sense, for example, only to include empirical studies or, even more narrowly, only empirical studies that claim to provide evidence about 'what works'. What is needed is engagement with a broad range of forms of educational enquiry, both empirical and theoretical (see Biesta, Allan and Edwards 2014). The latter, the theory dimension, is particularly important in order to broaden and deepen teachers' discourses and vocabularies: the resources that play a crucial role in seeing, thinking, judging and acting.

The above discussion suggests that meso-level activities play a major role in shaping the cultures of schools. The ecological approach to understanding teacher agency provides insights into the processes that occur as curriculum is re-contextualized in different settings. It allows us to analyse how particular practices at the meso level might influence and shape practices at the micro level. An understanding of how existing practices and processes – both input and output regulation of school curriculum-making practices – shape the cultures of schools will in turn allow us to develop new practices that are fitter-for-purpose, especially where that purpose is explicitly defined as enhancing teacher agency to improve education. As we have illustrated in this and the previous section, the ways in which practice is constructed at both the macro and meso levels of the system impact on practices at the micro level. In the next section, we briefly focus on this latter level, showing how an ecological understanding of agency might allow us to maximize teacher agency via school-based interventions.

Micro-level curriculum enactment

The quotation by Elliott Eisner on the first page of this chapter suggested that it is difficult to entice teachers out of a cage constructed by years of prescriptive regulation of their work. We witnessed such difficulties in our research – a 'just tell us what to do' attitude is fairly common among teachers who are subject to performative external demands, intensification of their work and a general lack of trust.[5] As we discussed in Chapter 6, the typical policy response is to focus on raising the quality of teachers. It is argued that high-capacity teachers will have the skills and knowledge to break free from the cage. However, as we have also argued, this is not simply a matter of capacity; recent curriculum policy has opened the cage door, providing the permission for teachers to escape. And yet, such policy, as we have discussed in this chapter, has tended to fail to address the conditions outside the cage, which make it unsafe to venture out. A simple conclusion here is that we can raise capacity all we like, but if it remains dangerous to venture out, we cannot blame teachers for not wanting to leave the security of the cage, that frustrating and often peculiar environment that is at least safe in its familiarity. We have discussed the issues that might be addressed at the macro and meso levels of the system in order to enable teachers to achieve agency. Here we look briefly at a range of strategies that can be formulated at the micro level of the school.

As we discussed in Chapter 4, the importance of fostering appropriate professional relationships should not be underestimated. Teaching has traditionally been an isolated profession, conducted behind closed doors. This, as we demonstrated in Chapter 4, has been acknowledged in a great deal of literature on teacher learning communities; such writings illustrate the value of spaces for generative dialogue (Imants 2002) and collegial professional working. However, as we also illustrated, the literature tends to focus rather narrowly on preset change agendas and, with a few notable exceptions, tends to neglect the underlying structures and social dynamics of learning communities, often assuming unproblematically that teacher collegial working is a good thing *per se*. We would support the institution of collegial working as an essential prerequisite for enhancing teacher agency. Teacher agency depends on the relational resources afforded by networks and social connections, as well as on the cognitive dissonance stimulated by the flows of alternative cultural ideas, which promotes new professional learning.

There are several implications here for practice. First, purposeful (and protective) leadership is essential. What are professional networks being established for? What are their short- and long-term goals? Are teachers trusted to work towards these goals? Second, they need to be established with a clear view of the structures and cultures that enable and hinder professional working? What are the key roles and who should fill them? How does power flow through the networks? Are there asymmetrical and/or non-reciprocal relationships, and does this matter? Are relationships horizontal or vertical, and how does this accord with the purposes of the network in question? What resources are available to ensure the networks run smoothly? The key issue here is the establishment of structures and cultures that are propitious to collegial professional working. While such factors can never be controlled completely, an efficient and effective network can certainly be fostered by paying attention to the above issues. Third, the networks need to have a clear focus on purpose *and* process. The collaborative professional enquiry approaches discussed here and in Chapter 4 provide a useful means for operating purposeful teacher collegial practices. We would argue that getting these conditions and processes right increases the chances of the constructive development of teacher belief systems, professional discourses and professional knowledge that will in turn contribute to the future achievement of a more expansive form of teacher agency.

Unfortunately, school cultures and structures often militate against such activity. Time is always an issue in poorly resourced public education systems. In Scotland, and arguably more widely, schools are hierarchical organizations nested in a hierarchical system, where dissenting voices are not generally welcomed. Many schools, particularly in the secondary sector, are fragmented organizations, with professionals organized into silos, differentiated by school subject (Siskin 1994). Moreover, secondary schools are subject to rigid temporal stratification as well as rigid organizational differentiation. The school timetable is a major barrier to innovation, considered in many schools to be sacrosanct. Consequently, we see the tendency to fit innovation to the existing systems and structures, as noted by many writers over the years (e.g. Sarason 1990; Cuban 1998). These structural and cultural features of schools are, as we have illustrated throughout this book, a major constraint on teacher agency.

The final point to make is that the question of teacher agency can of course not be resolved by putting the responsibility 'one level up.' Although senior managers, local authorities and even policy makers can make significant contributions with regard to the shaping of the conditions that foster and promote teacher agency, they themselves also work under specific ecological conditions that may support or limit their agency as well. In this regard, promotion of good and meaningful agency across all levels of the education system remains a challenge of the utmost importance.

Conclusions

We have come to the final paragraph of this book. In the preceding chapters, we have tried to deepen our understanding of what teacher agency is, why it is important for meaningful educational practice, and what might help and what might hinder good teacher agency. We have done this along three lines: through engagement with existing research and policy, through theoretical development and reflection, and through the presentation of empirical research that looked at concrete cases where teachers sought to achieve agency within the context of a large-scale educational reform. We hope to have shown that agency is a more complex concept than is often represented in the literature. We hope to have provided an approach that is not just theoretically meaningful but that also provides guidance for practice. And we hope to have made the case for why teacher agency matters and why the promotion of teacher agency – at individual, cultural and structural level – may contribute to countering many top–down developments that, over the past decades, have tried to control the educational system rather than promote its intelligent operation.

Notes

Introduction

1 The research was funded by the UK Economic and Social Research Council. Reference: RES-000-22-420.
2 There is a common discourse in Scottish education that older teachers are a barrier to 'Curriculum for Excellence', accompanied by a notion that younger teachers are more innovative. In fact, research has suggested that, conversely, older teachers have both a great deal of experience to offer, and also often support the new curriculum as a return to practices they remember from days of less intrusive government regulation of their teaching. See Priestley and Minty (2012), Minty and Priestley (2012).

Chapter 2

1 E's and O's is the common abbreviation used to refer to documentation produced by Education Scotland, which provides a very detailed 'translation' of the broad curriculum framework of 'Curriculum for Excellence'. While this documentation has no legal status with regard to the implementation of 'Curriculum for Excellence', it nonetheless plays an interesting and to some degree influential role in the translation of the framework into practice and thus affects teacher agency. For the documentation, see: http://www.educationscotland.gov.uk/thecurriculum/howisthecurriculumorganised/experiencesandoutcomes/index.asp.
2 See Chapter 5 for further discussion of the mechanisms (or lack of) for sense making to occur in schools.

Chapter 3

1 Assistant Principal Teacher.
2 *A Teaching Profession for the 21st Century*, commonly known as the McCrone Agreement (2001) related to teachers' pay and conditions of working. See http://www.scotland.gov.uk/Resource/Doc/158413/0042924.pdf.

3 National Assessment Bank tests, used for Higher courses to assess mastery of course content.
4 Preliminary examinations – a dress rehearsal for the real exam to be taken later in the year.

Chapter 4

1 Principal Teachers have management responsibility for a subject, or equivalent.
2 Scottish Qualifications Authority; [local authority] Quality Development Team; Learning and Teaching Scotland (curriculum development agency).

Chapter 5

1 Statistical evidence supplied by the Scottish Qualifications Authority for examinations held in 2009 showed that 14,035 pupils were entered for level 5 Intermediate 2 examinations when they had previously achieved passes in the equivalent Standard Grade Credit course for the same subject. This practice was widespread in Scotland, preventing so-called 'high-risk pupils' (i.e. those deemed to be at risk of failing) from taking level 6 higher qualifications and affecting the school's placing on comparator league tables (although schools often justify the practice as being in the pupil's best interests). Numbers were especially high in English (5,756, representing nearly one quarter of the total cohort).
2 While Insight claims to allow schools to move away from a narrow focus on attainment to a broader reflection on wider achievement, its supporting material continues to reflect a preoccupation with performance, measurement and comparison. The website states 'Insight allows schools to benchmark against schools in their local authority, nationally and against their "virtual comparator".' There is emerging evidence of at least one performative trend in relation to Insight. Private correspondence between the authors and teachers suggests that some schools are deliberately downgrading borderline students from level 5 to level 4 of the Scottish Credit and Qualifications Framework, following comparison with results achieved at other schools. Further details about Insight may be found at http://www.scotland. gov.uk/Topics/Education/Schools/curriculum/seniorphasebenchmarking.
3 The use of such tests was said to be 'voluntary' under Scotland's former 5–14 curriculum, but in practice, schools were 'encouraged' by local authorities to use a national bank of assessments rather than teacher-designed assessments. These data were routinely collected and used for quality improvement purposes, including comparing schools and identifying poor performers.

4 Scottish schools refer to cohorts using the categories primary 1–7, and secondary 1–6, instead of the more widely utilized years 1–13.

5 It is usual for schools with a negative inspection report to have a follow-up inspection within a year or two of the original event – to ensure that appropriate actions have been taken to address concerns raised in the original report.

Chapter 6

1 According to Chris Husbands, this quotation was in fact a statement by a South Korean education official, but has come to be widely quoted as a conclusion of McKinsey & Co. and has assumed the status of a law of education. See https://ioelondonblog.wordpress.com/2013/10/10/great-teachers-or-great-teaching-why-mckinsey-got-it-wrong/.

2 Interestingly, Husbands attributes these conclusions to an insight in a response by US academics to the 2005 OECD publication (see Schwartz, Wurtzel and Olson 2007). This insight is based on an apparent misquote of Schwartz et al., whom Husbands quotes as saying: 'What is the most important school-related factor in student learning? The answer is *teaching*'. In fact, the piece in question does not say this, but instead echoes the OECD language and supports its overall message, stating: 'What is the most important school-related factor in student learning? The answer is *teachers*' (our emph.). See http://www.oecdobserver.org/news/archivestory.php/aid/2235/Attracting_and_retaining_teachers.html.

Conclusions: Fostering Teacher Agency

1 Following the 2011 merger of Her Majesty's Inspectorate of Education and the curriculum quango, Learning and Teaching Scotland – see https://www.tes.co.uk/article.aspx?storycode=6060861.

2 See http://www.educationscotland.gov.uk/thecurriculum/whatiscurriculumforexcellence/keydocs/index.asp.

3 See http://www.scotlandpolicyconferences.co.uk/forums/showpublications.php?pid=810.

4 See http://www.gtcs.org.uk/research-engagement/research.aspx.

5 This latter point was brought home starkly to one of the authors in a conversation with a senior Scottish policy maker shortly after the release of the 2004 *A Curriculum for Excellence* document. The civil servant in question was quite frank in expressing a view that the major barrier to the successful implementation of the curriculum was teachers, who could not be 'trusted' to develop it properly.

References

Anderson, L. (2010), 'Embedded, emboldened, and (net)working for change: Support seeking and teacher agency in urban, high-needs schools', *Harvard Educational Review*, 80: 541–72.

Apple, M. W. (2001), 'Comparing neo-liberal projects and inequality in education', *Comparative Education*, 37: 409–23.

Apple, M. W. (2004), 'Creating difference: Neo-liberalism, neo-conservatism and the politics of educational reform', *Educational Policy*, 18: 12–44.

Archer, M. (1988), *Culture and Agency: The Place of Culture in Social Theory*, Cambridge: Cambridge University Press.

Archer, M. (1995), *Realist Social Theory: The Morphogenetic Approach*, Cambridge: Cambridge University Press.

Archer, M. (2000), *Being Human: The Problem of Agency*, Cambridge: Cambridge University Press.

Avalos, B. (2011), 'Teacher professional development in Teaching and Teacher Education over ten years', *Teaching and Teacher Education*, 27: 10–20.

Banks, S. (2004), *Ethics, Accountability and the Social Professions*, Basingstoke: Palgrave Macmillan.

Ball, S. J. (2003), 'The teacher's soul and the terrors of performativity', *Journal of Education Policy*, 18: 215–28.

Ball, S. J. (2006), *Education Policy and Social Class*, London: Routledge.

Baumfield, V., Hulme, M., Livingston, K. and Menter, I. (2010), 'Consultation and engagement? The reshaping of teacher professionalism through curriculum reform in 21st Century Scotland', *Scottish Educational Review*, 42: 57–73.

Beane, J. A. (1997), *Curriculum Integration: Designing the Core of a Democratic Education*, New York: Teachers College Press.

Belo, N. A. H., van Driel, J. H., van Veen, K. and Verloop, N. (2014), 'Beyond the dichotomy of teacher- versus student-focused education: A survey study on physics teachers' beliefs about the goals and pedagogy of physics education', *Teaching and Teacher Education*, 39: 89–101.

Ben-Peretz, M. (2011), 'Teacher knowledge. What is it? How do we uncover it? What are its implications for schooling?', *Teaching and Teacher Education*, 27: 3–9.

Bernstein, B. (1996), *Pedagogy, Symbolic Control and Identity*, London: Taylor & Francis.

Bidwell, C. E. and Yasumoto, J. Y. (1999), 'The collegial focus: Teaching fields, collegial relationships, and instructional practice in American high schools', *Sociology of Education*, 72: 234–56.

Biesta, G. J. J. (1998), 'Mead, intersubjectivity, and education: The early writings', *Studies in Philosophy and Education*, 17: 73–99.

Biesta, G. J. J. (2004), 'Education, accountability and the ethical demand. Can the democratic potential of accountability be regained?', *Educational Theory*, 54: 233–50.

Biesta, G. J. J. (2007a), *Beyond Learning: Democratic Education for a Human Future*, London: Paradigm Publishers.

Biesta, G. J. J. (2007b), 'Why "what works" won't work. Evidence-based practice and the democratic deficit of educational research', *Educational Theory*, 57: 1–22.

Biesta, G. J. J. (2008), 'What kind of citizen? What kind of democracy? Citizenship education and the Scottish Curriculum for Excellence', *Scottish Educational Review*, 40: 38–52.

Biesta, G. J. J. (2010), *Good Education in an Age of Measurement: Ethics, Politics, Democracy*, Boulder, CO: Paradigm Publishers.

Biesta, G. J. J. (2011), 'From learning cultures to educational cultures. Values and judgements in educational research and educational improvement', *International Journal of Early Childhood*, 43: 199–210.

Biesta, G. J. J. (2013a), 'Responsible citizens: Citizenship education between social inclusion and democratic politics', in M. Priestley and G. J. J. Biesta (eds), *Reinventing the Curriculum: New Trends in Curriculum Policy and Practice*, 99–116, London: Bloomsbury.

Biesta, G. J. J. (2013b), 'Knowledge, judgement and the curriculum: On the past, present and future of the idea of the practical', *Journal of Curriculum Studies*, 45: 684–96.

Biesta, G. J. J. (2015a), 'What is education for? On good education, teacher judgement, and educational professionalism', *European Journal of Education*, 50: 75–87.

Biesta, G. J. J. (2015b), 'On the two cultures of educational research and how we might move ahead: Reconsidering the ontology axiology and praxeology of education', *European Educational Research Journal*, 14: 11–22.

Biesta, G. J. J. (2015c), 'How does a competent teacher become a good teacher? On judgement, wisdom and virtuosity in teaching and teacher education', in R. Heilbronn and L. Foreman-Peck (eds), *Philosophical Perspectives on the Future of Teacher Education*, 3–22, Oxford: Wiley Blackwell.

Biesta, G. J. J. and Burbules, N. (2003), *Pragmatism and Educational Research*, Lanham, MD: Rowman and Littlefield.

Biesta, G. J. J. and Tedder, M. (2006), *How is Agency Possible? Towards an Ecological Understanding of Agency-as-achievement. Working Paper 5*, Exeter: The Learning Lives project.

Biesta, G. J. J. and Tedder, M. (2007), 'Agency and learning in the lifecourse: Towards an ecological perspective', *Studies in the Education of Adults*, 39: 132–49.

Biesta, G. J. J. and Priestley, M. (2013), 'Capacities and the curriculum', in M. Priestley and G. J. J. Biesta (eds), *Reinventing the Curriculum: New Trends in Curriculum Policy and Practice*, 35–50, London: Bloomsbury.

Biesta, G. J. J., Allan, J. and Edwards, R. G., eds (2014), *Making a Difference in Theory: The Theory Question in Education and the Education Question in Theory*, London and New York: Routledge.

Biesta, G. J. J., Biesta, M. and Robinson, S. (2015), 'The role of beliefs in teacher agency', *Teachers and Teaching: Theory and Practice*.

Blumer, H. (1969), *Symbolic Interactionism: Perspective and Method*, Englewood Cliffs, NJ: Prentice-Hall.

Borg, S. (2003), 'Teacher cognition in language learning: A review of research on what language teachers think, know, believe, and do', *Language Teaching*, 36: 81–109.

Borg, S. (2011), 'The impact of in-service teacher education on language teachers' beliefs', *System*, 39: 370–80.

Bourdieu, P. (1977), *Outline of a Theory of Practice*, Cambridge: Cambridge University Press.

Bowe, R., Ball, S. and Gold, A. (1992), *Reforming Education and Changing Schools: Case Studies in Policy Sociology*, London: Routledge.

Boyd, B. and Norris, F. (2006), 'From development to improvement – a step too far? The evolving contribution of Quality Improvement Officers to the school improvement agenda in Scottish local authorities', *Scottish Educational Review*, 38: 213–24.

Brown, S. and McIntyre, D. (1993), *Making Sense of Teaching*, Buckingham: Open University Press.

Brown, G. T. L., Harris, L. R. and Harnett, J. (2012), 'Teacher beliefs about feedback within an assessment for learning environment: Endorsement of improved learning over student well-being', *Teaching and Teacher Education*, 28: 968–78.

Bunzell, D. (2008), 'Agency-structure debate', in S. Clegg and J. R. Bailey (eds), *International Encyclopedia of Organization Studies*, 47–50, London: Sage.

Butler, D., Schnellert, L. and MacNeil, K. (2015), 'Collaborative inquiry and distributed agency in educational change: A case study of a multi-level community of inquiry', *Journal of Educational Change*, 16: 1–26.

CEDEFOP (2009), *The Shift to Learning Outcomes: Policies and Practices in Europe*, Luxembourg: Office for Official Publications of the European Communities.

Charlton, B. G. (1999), 'The ideology of "accountability"', *Journal of the Royal College of Physicians of London*, 33: 33–5.

Coburn, C. E. and Russell, J. L. (2008), 'District policy and teachers' social networks', *Educational Evaluation and Policy Analysis*, 30: 203–35.

Coburn, C. E., Choi, L. and Mata, W. (2010), '"I would go to her because her mind is math": Network formation in the context of mathematics reform', in A. J. Daly (ed.), *Social Network Theory and Educational Change*, 33–50, Cambridge, MA: Harvard Educational Press.

Coburn, C. E., Russell, J. L., Kaufman, J. and Stein, M. K. (2012), 'Supporting sustainability: Teachers' advice networks and ambitious instructional reform', *American Journal of Education*, 119: 7–39.

Connelly, F. M. and Clandinin, D. J. (1988), *Teachers as Curriculum Planners: Narratives of Experience*, New York: Teachers College Press.

Cowie, M., Taylor, D. and Croxford, L. (2007), '"Tough, intelligent accountability" in Scottish secondary schools and the role of Standard Tables and Charts (STACS): A critical appraisal', *Scottish Educational Review*, 39: 29–50.

Cuban, L. (1998), 'How schools change reforms: Redefining reform success and failure', *Teachers College Record*, 99: 453–77.

Daly, A. J., Moolenaar, N. M., Bolivar, J. M. and Burke, P. (2010), 'Relationships in reform: The role of teachers' social networks', *Journal of Educational Administration*, 48: 359–91.

Datnow, A. (2012), 'Teacher agency in educational reform: Lessons from social networks research', *American Journal of Education*, 119: 193–201.

Davies, B. (2006), 'Subjectification: The relevance of Butler's analysis for education', *British Journal of Sociology of Education*, 27: 425–38.

de Lima, J. Á. (2001), 'Forgetting about friendship: Using conflict in teacher communities as a catalyst for school change', *Journal of Educational Change*, 2: 97–122.

Dépelteau, F. (2008), 'Relational thinking: A critique of co-deterministic theories of structure and agency', *Sociological Theory*, 26: 51–73.

Devine, D., Fahie, D. and McGillicuddy, D. (2013), 'What is "good" teaching? Teacher beliefs and practices about their teaching', *Irish Educational Studies*, 32: 83–108.

Donaldson, G. (2010), *Teaching Scotland's Future: Report of a Review of Teacher Education in Scotland*, Edinburgh: Scottish Government.

Dooner, A. M., Mandzuk, D. and Clifton, R. A. (2008), 'Stages of collaboration and the realities of professional learning communities', *Teaching and Teacher Education*, 24: 564–74.

Drew, V. and Mackie, L. (2011), 'Extending the constructs of active learning: Implications for teachers' pedagogy and practice', *Curriculum Journal*, 22: 451–67.

Drew, V. and Priestley, M. (2014), *School-based Curriculum Development through Collaborative Professional Enquiry*, A paper presented at the European Conference for Educational Research, 3 September 2014, Porto.

Education Scotland (2011), *Building the Curriculum 5: A Framework for Assessment*, Edinburgh: Scottish Government.

Education Scotland (2012), *Curriculum for Excellence Briefing 4: Interdisciplinary Learning*, http://www.educationscotland.gov.uk/resources/c/genericresource_ tcm4732286.asp (accessed 21 January 2013).

Education Scotland (2014), *Tackling bureaucracy*, http://www.educationscotland.gov.uk/ resources/t/tacklingbureaucracy/intro.asp (accessed 3 January 2015).

Edwards, A. (2005), 'Relational agency: Learning to be a resourceful practitioner', *International Journal of Educational Research*, 43: 168–82.

EIS (2013), *Final Results of National CfE Survey Confirm Teachers' Concerns*, http:// www.eis.org.uk/public.asp?id=2195 (accessed 3 January 2015).

Eisner, E. W. (1992), 'Educational reform and the ecology of schooling', *Teachers College Record*, 93: 610–26.

Eisner, E. W. (1994), *Cognition and Curriculum Reconsidered*, New York: Teachers College Press.

Elder-Vass, D. (2008), 'Integrating institutional, relational, and embodied structure: An emergentist perspective', *British Journal of Sociology*, 59: 281–99.

Emirbayer, M. and Goodwin, J. (1994), 'Network analysis, culture and the problem of agency', *The American Journal of Sociology*, 99: 1411–54.

Emirbayer, M. and Mische, A. (1998), 'What is agency?', *The American Journal of Sociology*, 103: 962–1023.

Eraut, M. (1994), *Developing Professional Practice and Competence*, London: Falmer Press.

Ertmer, P. A. and Ottenbreit-Leftwich, A. T. (2010), 'Teacher technology change: How knowledge, confidence, beliefs, and culture intersect', *Journal of Research on Technology in Education*, 42: 255–84.

Eteläpelto, A., Vähäsantanen, K., Hökkä, P. and Paloniemi, S. (2013), 'What is agency? Conceptualizing professional agency at work', *Educational Research Review*, 10: 45–65.

European Council (2006), *Recommendation 2006/962/EC of the European Parliament and of the Council of 18 December 2006 on Key Competences for Lifelong Learning [Official Journal L 394 of 30.12.2006]*.

Evers, J. and Kneyber, R., eds (2015), *Flip the System: Changing Education from the Bottom Up*. London: Routledge.

Evetts, J. (2011), 'A new professionalism? Challenges and opportunities', *Current Sociology*, 59: 406–22.

Fang, Z. (1996), 'A review of research on teacher beliefs and practices', *Educational Research*, 38: 47–65.

Fenstermacher, G. (1994), 'The knower and the known: The nature of knowledge in research on teaching', in L. Darling-Hammond (ed.), *Review of Research in Education*, vol. 20, 3–56, Washington: AERA.

Ford, C. (2011), 'The trouble and truth about Curriculum for Excellence', *Times Educational Supplement Scotland*, 19 December 2011.

Freidson, E. (1994), *Professionalism Reborn: Theory, Prophecy and Policy*, Cambridge: Polity Press, in association with Blackwell Publishers.

Fuchs, S. (2001), 'Beyond agency', *Sociological Theory*, 19: 24–40.

Fullan, M. (2003), *Change Forces with a Vengeance*, London: Routledge Falmer.

Gewirtz, S. (2002), *The Managerial School: Post-welfarism and Social Justice in Education*, London: Routledge.

Giddens, A. (1984), *The Constitution of Society: Outline of the Theory of Structuration*, Cambridge: Polity.

Gill, S. and Thomson, G. (2012), *Rethinking Secondary Education: A Human-centred Approach*, Harlow: Pearson.

Gillies, D. (2006), 'A Curriculum for Excellence: A question of values', *Scottish Educational Review*, 38: 25–36.

Gleeson, D. and Shain, F. (1999), 'Managing ambiguity: Between markets and managerialism: A case study of "middle" managers in further education', *The Sociological Review*, 47: 461–90.

Gleeson, D. and Gunter, H. (2001), 'The performing school and the modernisation of teachers', in D. Gleeson and C. Husbands (eds), *The Performing School: Managing, Teaching and Learning in a Performance Culture*, 139–58, London: Routledge Falmer.

Gleeson, D. and Husbands, C., eds (2001), *The Performing School: Managing, Teaching and Learning in a Performance Culture*, London: Routledge Falmer.

Goodson, I. F. (2003), *Professional Knowledge, Professional Lives*, Maidenhead: Open University Press.

Goodson, I. F., Biesta, G. J. J., Tedder, M. and Adair, N. (2010), *Narrative Learning*, London and New York: Routledge.

Green, A. (1999), 'Education and globalization in Europe and East Asia: Convergent and divergent trends', *Journal of Education Policy*, 14: 55–71.

Hargreaves, A. (1993), *Changing Teachers, Changing Times*. London: Cassell.

Hargreaves, A. (1998), 'The emotional politics of teaching and teacher development: With implications for educational leadership', *International Journal of Leadership in Education*, 1: 315–36.

Hay McBer (2000), *Research into Teacher Effectiveness: A Model of Teacher Effectiveness, Report by Hay McBer to the Department for Education & Employment, June 2000*. London: DfEE.

Hayward, L., Priestley, M. and Young, M. (2004), 'Ruffling the calm of the ocean floor: Merging practice, policy and research in assessment in Scotland', *Oxford Review of Education*, 30: 397–415.

Heilbronn, R. (2008), *Teacher Education and the Development of Practical Judgement*, London: Continuum.

Helsby, G. (1999), *Changing Teachers' Work*, Buckingham: Open University Press.

HMIe (2002), *How Good Is Our School? Self-evaluation Using Quality Indicators*, Edinburgh: HMIe.

HMIe (2006), *The Journey to Excellence, Parts 1 & 2*, Edinburgh: HMIe.

HMIe (2007), *How Good Is Our School? The Journey to Excellence, Part 3*, Edinburgh: HMIe.

Hoban, G. F. (2002), *Teacher Learning for Educational Change*, Buckingham: Open University Press.

Hollis, M. (1994), *The Philosophy of Social Science: An Introduction*, Cambridge: Cambridge University Press.

Humes, W. (2013), 'The origins and development of Curriculum for Excellence: Discourse, politics and control', in M. Priestley and G. Biesta (eds), *Reinventing the Curriculum: New Trends in Curriculum Policy and Practice*, 13–34, London: Bloomsbury.

Hupe, P. and Hill, M. (2007), 'Street-level bureaucracy and public accountability', *Public Administration*, 85: 279–99.

Husbands, C. (2013), *Great Teachers or Great Teaching? Why McKinsey Got It Wrong*, https://ioelondonblog.wordpress.com/2013/10/10/great-teachers-or-great-teaching-why-mckinsey-got-it-wrong/ (accessed 16 January 2015).

Hutchinson, C. and Hayward, L. (2005), 'The journey so far: Assessment for learning in Scotland', *Curriculum Journal*, 16: 225–48.

Imants, J. (2002), 'Restructuring schools as a context for teacher learning', *International Journal of Educational Research*, 37: 715–32.

James, D. and Biesta, G. J. J. (2007), *Improving Learning Cultures in Further Education*, London: Routledge.

Keddie, A., Mills, M. and Pendergast, D. (2011), 'Fabricating an identity in neo-liberal times: Performing schooling as "number one"', *Oxford Review of Education*, 37: 75–92.

Kelly, A. V. (2004), *The Curriculum: Theory and Practice*, 5th edn, London: Sage.

Ketelaar, E., Beijaard, D., Boshuizen, H. P. A. and Den Brok, P. J. (2012), 'Teachers' positioning towards an educational innovation in the light of ownership, sense-making and agency', *Teaching and Teacher Education*, 28: 273–82.

Keys, C. W. and Bryan, L. A. (2001), 'Co-constructing inquiry-based science with teachers: Essential research for lasting reform', *Journal of Research in Science Teaching*, 38: 631–45.

Kuiper, W. and Berkvens, J., eds (2013), *Balancing Curriculum Regulation and Freedom Across Europe. CIDREE Yearbook 2013*, Enschede, The Netherlands: SLO.

Ladwig, J. (2010), 'Beyond academic outcomes', *Review of Research in Education*, 34: 113–41.

Lasky, S. (2005), 'A sociocultural approach to understanding teacher identity, agency and professional vulnerability in a context of secondary school reform', *Teaching and Teacher Education*, 21: 899–916.

Leander, K. M. and Osborne, M. D. (2008), 'Complex positioning: Teachers as agents of curricular and pedagogical reform', *Journal of Curriculum Studies*, 40: 23–46.

Learning and Teaching Scotland (2007), *Introduction to Draft Experiences and Outcomes*, Glasgow: Learning and Teaching Scotland.

Leat, D. (2014), 'Curriculum regulation in England: Giving with one hand and taking away with the other', *European Journal of Curriculum Studies*, 1: 69–74.

Leat, D., Livingston, K. and Priestley, M. (2013), 'Curriculum deregulation in England and Scotland: Different directions of travel?', in W. Kuiper and J. Berkvens (eds), *Balancing Curriculum Regulation and Freedom across Europe, CIDREE Yearbook 2013*, 229–48, Enschede, The Netherlands: SLO.

Lee, J. C., Zhang, Z. and Yin, H. (2011), 'A multilevel analysis of the impact of a professional learning community, faculty trust in colleagues and collective efficacy on teacher commitment to student', *Teaching and Teacher Education*, 27: 820–30.

Lieberman, A. and Grolnick, M. (1996), 'Networks and reform in American education', *Teachers College Record*, 98: 7–46.

Lipponen, L. and Kumpulainen, K. (2011), 'Acting as accountable authors: Creating interactional spaces for agency work in teacher education', *Teaching and Teacher Education*, 27: 811–968.

Little, J. W. (2003), 'Inside teacher community: Representations of classroom practice', *Teachers College Record*, 105: 913–45.

Lukacs, K. S. (2009), 'Quantifying "the ripple in the pond": The development and initial validation of the Teacher Change Agent Scale', *The International Journal of Educational and Psychological Assessment*, 3: 25–37.

McCormac, G. (2011), *Advancing Professionalism in Teaching: The Report of the Review of Teacher Employment in Scotland*, http://www.scotland.gov.uk/Resource/Doc/920/0120759.PDF (accessed 10 January 2015).

MacKinnon, N. (2011), 'The urgent need for new approaches in school evaluation to enable Scotland's Curriculum for Excellence', *Educational Assessment, Evaluation and Accountability*, 23: 89–106.

McKinsey & Co. (2007), *McKinsey Report: How the World's Best Performing School Systems Come Out On Top*, http://mckinseyonsociety.com/downloads/reports/Education/Worlds_School_Systems_Final.pdf (accessed 7 January 2015).

Meirink, J. A., Meijer, P., Verloop, N. and Bergen, T. C. M. (2009), 'Understanding teacher learning in secondary education: The relations of teacher activities to changed beliefs and teaching and learning', *Teaching and Teacher Education*, 25: 89–100.

Milner, A. R., Sondergeld, T. A., Demir, A., Johnson, C. C. and Czerniak, C. M. (2012), Elementary teachers' beliefs about teaching science and classroom practice: An examination of pre/post NCLB testing in science', *Journal of Science Teacher Education*, 23: 111–32.

Minty, S. and Priestley, M. (2012), *Developing Curriculum for Excellence in Highland Schools: A report on the Qualitative Findings for the Highland Council and the Scottish Government*, Stirling: University of Stirling.

Moll, L. C. and Arnott-Hopffer, E. (2005), 'Sociocultural competence in teacher education', *Journal of Teacher Education*, 56: 242–7.

Moolenaar, N. M. (2012), 'A social network perspective on teacher collaboration in schools: Theory, methodology, and applications', *American Journal of Education*, 119: 7–39.

Murphy, J. (2005), *Connecting Leadership and School Improvement*, Thousands Oaks, CA: Corwin Press.

Nespor, J. (1987), 'The role of beliefs in the practice of teaching', *Journal of Curriculum Studies*, 19: 317–28.

Nichols, N. and Griffith, A. I. (2009), 'Talk, texts, and educational action: An institutional ethnography of policy in practice', *Cambridge Journal of Education*, 39: 241–55.

Nieveen, N. and Kuiper, W. (2012), 'Balancing curriculum freedom and regulation in the Netherlands', *European Educational Research Journal*, 11: 357–68.

Nishino, T. (2012), 'Modeling teacher beliefs and practices in context: A multi-methods approach', *The Modern Language Journal*, 96: 380–99.

OECD (2005), *Teachers Matter: Attracting, Developing and Retaining Effective Teachers*, Paris: OECD.

OECD (2007), *Quality and Equity of Schooling in Scotland*, Paris: OECD.

OECD (2011), *Teachers Matter: Attracting, Developing and Retaining Effective Teachers. Pointers for Policy Development*, Paris: OECD.

Osborn, M., Croll, P., Broadfoot, P., Pollard, A., McNess, E. and Triggs, P. (1997), 'Policy into practice and practice into policy: Creative mediation in the primary classroom', in G. Helsby and G. McCulloch (eds), *Teachers and the National Curriculum*, 52–65, London: Cassell.

Pajares, M. F. (1992), 'Teachers' beliefs and educational research: Cleaning up a messy construct', *Review of Educational Research*, 62: 307–32.

Penuel, W., Riel, M., Krauses, A. and Frank, K. (2009), 'Analyzing teachers' professional interactions in a school as social capital: A social network approach', *Teachers College Record*, 111: 124–63.

Perryman, J. (2009), 'Inspection and the fabrication of professional and performative processes', *Journal of Education Policy*, 24: 611–31.

Porpora, D. V. (1998), 'Four concepts of social structure', in M. Archer, R. Bhaskar, A. Collier, T. Lawson and A. Norrie (eds), *Critical Realism: Essential Readings*, 339–55, London: Routledge.

Priestley, M. (2002), 'Global discourses and national reconstruction: The impact of globalization on curriculum policy', *The Curriculum Journal*, 13: 87–104.

Priestley, M. (2010), 'Curriculum for Excellence: Transformational change or business as usual?', *Scottish Educational Review*, 42: 22–35.

Priestley, M. (2011), 'Schools, teachers and curriculum change: A balancing act?', *Journal of Educational Change*, 12: 1–23.

Priestley, M. (2014), 'Curriculum regulation in Scotland: A wolf in sheep's clothing is still a wolf', *European Journal of Curriculum Studies*, 1: 61–8.

Priestley, M. and Humes, W. (2010), 'The development of Scotland's Curriculum for Excellence: Amnesia and déjà vu', *Oxford Review of Education*, 36: 345–61.

Priestley, M. and Minty, S. (2012), *Developing Curriculum for Excellence: Summary of Findings from Research Undertaken in a Scottish Local Authority*, Stirling: University of Stirling.

Priestley, M. and Minty, S. (2013), 'Curriculum for Excellence: "A brilliant idea, but …"', *Scottish Educational Review*, 45: 39–52.

Priestley, M. and Biesta, G. J. J., eds (2013), *Reinventing the Curriculum: New Trends in Curriculum Policy and Practice*, London: Bloomsbury Academic.

Priestley, M. and Sinnema, C. (2014), 'Downgraded curriculum? An analysis of knowledge in new curricula in Scotland and New Zealand', *Curriculum Journal*, Special Edition: Creating Curricula: Aims, Knowledge, and Control, 25: 50–75.

Priestley, M., Robinson, S. and Biesta, G. J. J. (2012), 'Teacher agency, performativity and curriculum change: Reinventing the teacher in the Scottish Curriculum for Excellence?', in B. Jeffrey and G. Troman (eds), *Performativity Across UK*

    Education: Ethnographic Cases of its Effects, Agency and Reconstructions, 87–108, Painswick: EandE Publishing.

Priestley, M., Biesta, G. J. J. and Robinson, S. (2013), 'Teachers as agents of change: Teacher agency and emerging models of curriculum', in M. Priestley and G. J. J. Biesta (eds), *Reinventing the Curriculum: New Trends in Curriculum Policy and Practice*, 187–206, London: Bloomsbury.

Priestley, M., Minty, S. and Eager, M. (2014), 'School-based curriculum development in Scotland: Curriculum policy and enactment', *Pedagogy, Culture and Society*, 22: 189–211.

Priestley, M., Biesta, G. J. J. and Robinson S. (2015), 'Teacher agency: What is it and why does it matter?', in J. Evers and R. Kneyber (eds), *Flip the System: Changing Education from the Bottom Up*. London: Routledge.

Priestley, M., Edwards, R., Priestley, A. and Miller, K. (2012), 'Teacher agency in curriculum making: Agents of change and spaces for manoeuvre', *Curriculum Inquiry*, 43: 191–214.

Pyhältö, K., Soini, T. and Pietarinen, J. (2012), 'Comprehensive school teachers' professional agency in large-scale educational change', *Journal of Educational Change*, 13: 95–116.

Pyhältö, K., Pietarinen, J. and Soini, T. (2014), 'Comprehensive school teachers' professional agency in large-scale educational change', *Journal of Educational Change*, 15: 303–25.

Raffe, D. (2008), 'As others see us: A commentary on the OECD review of the quality and equity of schooling in Scotland', *Scottish Educational Review*, 40: 22–36.

Rata, E. (2012), *The Politics of Knowledge in Education*, London: Routledge.

Reeves, J. (2008), 'Between a rock and a hard place? Curriculum for Excellence and the Quality Initiative in Scottish schools', *Scottish Educational Review*, 40: 6–16.

Reeves, J. (2013), 'The successful learner: A progressive or an oppressive concept?', in M. Priestley and G. J. J. Biesta (eds), *Reinventing the Curriculum: New Trends in Curriculum Policy and Practice*, 51–74, London: Bloomsbury.

Reeves, J. and Drew, V. (2013), 'A productive relationship? Testing the connections between professional learning and practitioner research', *Scottish Educational Review*, 45: 36–49.

Riveros, A., Newton, P. and Burgess, D. (2012), 'A situated account of teacher agency and learning: Critical reflections on professional learning communities', *Canadian Journal of Education*, 35: 202–16.

Rubie-Davies, C. M., Flint, A. and McDonald, L. G. (2012), 'Teacher beliefs, teacher characteristics, and school contextual factors: What are the relationships?', *British Journal of Educational Psychology*, 82: 270–88.

Sachs, J. (2003), *The Activist Teaching Profession*, Buckingham: Open University Press.

Sahlberg, P. (2010), 'Rethinking accountability in a knowledge society', *Journal of Educational Change*, 11: 45–61.

Sahlberg, P. (2011), *Finnish Lessons: What Can the World Learn from Educational Change in Finland?*, New York: Teachers College Press.

Salomon, G. (1992), 'The changing role of the teacher: From information transmitter to orchestrator of teaching', in F. K. Oser, A. Dick, J-L. Patry (eds), *Effective and Responsible Teaching: The New Synthesis*, 37–49, San Francisco: Jossey-Bass.

Sammons, P. and Bakkum, L. (2012), 'Effective schools, equity and teacher effectiveness: A review of the literature', *Profesorado Revista de Curriculum y Formación del Profesorado*, 15: 9–26.

Sannino, A. (2010), 'Teachers' talk of experiencing: Conflict, resistance and agency', *Teaching and Teacher Education*, 26: 838–44.

Sarason, S. B. (1990), *The Predictable Failure of Educational Reform*, Oxford: Jossey-Bass Publishers.

Schön, D. A. (1983), *The Reflective Practitioner: How Professionals Think in Action*, New York: Basic Books.

Schön, D. A. (1987), *Educating the Reflective Practitioner*, San Francisco: Jossey-Bass.

Schwab, J. (2013 [1970]), 'The practical: A language for curriculum', *Journal of Curriculum Studies*, 45: 591–621.

Schwartz, R. B., Wurtzel, J. and Olson, L. (2007), *Attracting and Retaining Teachers*, http://www.oecdobserver.org/news/archivestory.php/aid/2235/Attracting_and_retaining_teachers.html (accessed 20 January 2015).

Scottish Executive (2004a), *A Curriculum for Excellence: The Curriculum Review Group*, Edinburgh: Scottish Executive.

Scottish Executive (2004b), *A Curriculum for Excellence: Ministerial Response*, Edinburgh: Scottish Executive.

Scottish Executive (2006), *A Curriculum for Excellence: Progress and Proposals*, Edinburgh: Scottish Executive.

Scottish Government (2008), *Building the Curriculum 3: A Framework for Learning and Teaching*, Edinburgh: Scottish Government.

Scottish Government (2011), *Commission on the Future Delivery of Public Services*, Edinburgh: Scottish Government.

Scottish Parliament (2014), *Minutes of the Education and Culture Committee*, 22nd Meeting, 2014 (Session 4), Tuesday, 30 September 2014, http://www.scottish.parliament.uk/S4_EducationandCultureCommittee/Meeting%20Papers/EC_Committee_papers_20140930.pdf (accessed 03 January 2015).

Shore, C. and Wright, S. (2000), 'Coercive accountability: The rise of audit culture in Higher Education', in M. Strathern (ed.), *Audit Culture: Anthropological Studies in Accountability, Ethics and the Academy*, 57–89, London: Routledge.

Shulman, L. S. (1986), 'Those who understand: Knowledge growth in teaching', *Educational Research*, 15: 4–14.

Siskin, L. S. (1994), *Realms of Knowledge: Academic Departments in Secondary Schools*, London: The Falmer Press.

Smyth, J. and Shacklock, G. (1998), *Re-making Teaching: Ideology, Policy and Practice*, London: Routledge.

Song, Y. and Looi, C-K. (2012), 'Linking teacher beliefs, practices and student inquiry-based learning in a CSCL environment: A tale of two teachers', *International Journal of Computer-Supported Collaborative Learning*, 7: 129–59.

Stéger, C. (2014), 'Review and analysis of the EU teacher-related policies and activities', *European Journal of Education*, 49: 332–47.

Stoll, L., Bolam, R., McMahon, A., Wallace, M. and Thomas, S. (2006), 'Professional learning communities: A review of the literature', *Journal of Educational Change*, 7: 221–58.

Strathern, M., ed. (2000), *Audit Culture: Anthropological Studies in Accountability, Ethics and the Academy*, London: Routledge.

Strauss, V. (2013), *What if Finland's Great Teachers Taught in U.S. Schools?* Washington Post, 15 May 2013, http://www.washingtonpost.com/blogs/answer-sheet/wp/2013/05/15/what-if-finlands-great-teachers-taught-in-u-s-schools-not-what-you-think (accessed 10 January 2015).

Sugrue, C. and Dyrdal-Solbrekke, T., eds (2011), *Professional Responsibility: New Horizons of Praxis*, London: Routledge.

Taylor, M. W. (2013), 'Replacing the "teacher-proof" curriculum with the "curriculum-proof" teacher: Toward more effective interactions with mathematics textbooks', *Journal of Curriculum Studies*, 45: 295–321.

Troman, G. (2000), 'Teacher stress in the low-trust society', *British Journal of Sociology of Education*, 21: 331–53.

Troman, G., Jeffrey, B. and Raggl, A. (2007), 'Creativity and performativity policies in primary school cultures', *Journal of Education Policy*, 22: 549–72.

van der Schaaf, M. F., Stokking, K. M. and Verloop, N. (2008), 'Teacher beliefs and teacher behaviour in portfolio assessment', *Teaching and Teacher Education*, 24: 1691–704.

van Driel, J. H., Beijard, D. and Verloop, N. (2001), 'Professional development and reform in science education: The role of teachers' practical knowledge', *Journal of Research in Science Teaching*, 38: 137–58.

Vaughn, M. (2013), 'Examining teacher agency: Why did Les leave the building?', *New Educator*, 9: 119–34.

Verloop, N., van Driel, J. and Meijer, P. (2001), 'Teacher knowledge and the knowledge base of teaching', *International Journal of Educational Research*, 35: 441–61.

Vescio, V., Ross, D. and Adams, A. (2008), 'A review of research on the impact of professional learning communities on teaching practice and student learning', *Teaching and Teacher Education*, 24: 80–91.

Vongalis-Macrow, A. (2007), 'I, teacher: Re territorialisation of teachers' multi-faceted agency in globalised education', *British Journal of Sociology of Education*, 28: 425–39.

Wallace, C. S. and Kang, N-H. (2004), 'An investigation of experienced secondary science teachers' beliefs about inquiry: An examination of competing belief sets', *Journal of Research in Science Teaching*, 41: 936–60.

Wallace, C. S. and Priestley M. (2011), 'Teacher beliefs and the mediation of curriculum innovation in Scotland: A socio-cultural perspective on professional development and change', *Journal of Curriculum Studies*, 43: 357–81.

Watson, C. (2010), 'Educational policy in Scotland: Inclusion and the control society', *Discourse: Studies in the Cultural Politics of Education*, 31: 93–104.

Watson, C. (2014), 'Effective professional learning communities? The possibilities for teachers as agents of change in schools', *British Educational Research Journal*, 40: 18–29.

Westheimer, J. and Kahne, J. (2004), 'Educating the "good" citizen: Political choices and pedagogical goals', *Political Science and Politics*, 37: 241–7.

Whitty, G. (2010), 'Revisiting school knowledge: Some sociological perspectives on new school curricula', *European Journal of Education*, 45: 28–44.

Wilkins, C. (2011), 'Professionalism and the post-performative teacher: New teachers reflect on autonomy and accountability in the English school system', *Professional Development in Education*, 37: 389–409.

Wolf, A. (1995), *Competence-Based Assessment (Assessing Assessment)*, Buckingham: Open University Press.

Yates, L. and Collins, C. (2010), 'The absence of knowledge in Australian curriculum reforms', *European Journal of Education*, 45: 89–101.

Yerrick, R., Parke, H. and Nugent, J. (1997), 'Struggling to promote deeply rooted change: The "filtering effect" of teachers' beliefs on understanding transformational views of teaching science', *Science Education*, 81: 137–57.

Young, M. (1998), *The Curriculum of the Future: From the New Sociology of Education to a Critical Theory of Learning*, London: The Falmer Press.

Young, M. (2009), 'Alternative educational futures for a knowledge society', *Socialism and Education*, http://socialismandeducation.wordpress.com/2009/12/06/ alternative-educational-futures-for-a-knowledge-society (accessed on 1 January 2010).

Young, M. and Muller, J. (2010), 'Three educational scenarios for the future: Lessons from the sociology of knowledge', *European Journal of Education*, 45: 11–27.

Index